ATLANTIC AMERICAN SOCIETIES

REWRITING HISTORIES
Series editor: Jack R. Censer

THE INDUSTRIAL REVOLUTION AND WORK IN
NINETEENTH-CENTURY
EUROPE
Edited by Lenard R. Berlanstein

SOCIETY AND CULTURE IN THE SLAVE SOUTH
Edited by J. William Harris

GENDER AND AMERICAN HISTORY SINCE 1890
Edited by Barbara Melosh

NAZISM AND GERMAN SOCIETY 1933–1945
Edited by David Crew

DIVERSITY AND UNITY IN EARLY NORTH AMERICA
Edited by P. Morgan

ATLANTIC AMERICAN SOCIETIES

From Columbus through abolition
1492–1888

Edited by
Alan L. Karras and J. R. McNeill

London and New York

First published in 1992 by
Routledge
11 New Fetter Lane, London EC4P 4EE

Simultaneously published in the USA and Canada
by Routledge
a division of Routledge, Chapman and Hall, Inc.
29 West 35th Street, New York, NY 10001

Editorial contributions © 1992 Alan L. Karras and J. R. McNeill
© Individual contributions

Set in 10/12pt Palatino by Intype, London
Printed and bound in Great Britain by
Clays Ltd, St Ives plc

British Library Cataloguing-in-Publication Data
A CIP catalogue record for this book is available
from the British Library

Library of Congress Cataloging-in-Publication Data

Atlantic American societies : from Columbus through abolition, 1492
to 1888 / edited by Alan L. Karras and J. R. McNeill.
p.   cm.
Includes bibliographical references.
1. America—Social conditions. 2. America—Civilization—
European influences. 3. America—Civilization—African
influences.
4. America—History—To 1810. 5. America—History—1810–
I. Karras, Alan L.   II. McNeill, John Robert.
HN50.A87   1992
970—dc20   92–11919

ISBN 0–415–08072–X
0–415–08073–8 (pbk)

CONTENTS

Editor's preface   vii
Acknowledgments   xi

1 THE ATLANTIC WORLD AS A UNIT OF STUDY   1
  Alan L. Karras

Part I Implantation, 1492–c.1650

2 ILLS   19
  Alfred W. Crosby

3 TRAGEDY AND SACRIFICE IN THE HISTORY OF
  SLAVERY   40
  Patrick Manning

4 THE LABOR PROBLEM AT JAMESTOWN   73
  Edmund Morgan

Part II Maturity c.1650–c.1770

5 THE COSMIC ORDER IN CRISIS   99
  Nancy M. Farriss

6 SLAVE RESISTANCE IN COLONIAL SOUTH
  CAROLINA   144
  Peter Wood

7 PORTS OF COLONIAL BRAZIL   174
  A. J. R. Russell-Wood

8 THE FUR TRADE AND EIGHTEENTH-CENTURY
  IMPERIALISM   212
  W. J. Eccles

CONTENTS

Part III Transitions *c.*1770–1888

9 THE END OF THE OLD ATLANTIC WORLD:
AMERICA, AFRICA, EUROPE, 1770–1888   245
J. R. McNeill

Glossary   269
Select bibliography   270

EDITOR'S PREFACE

Rewriting history, or revisionism, has always followed closely in the tow of history writing. In their efforts to re-evaluate the past, professional as well as amateur scholars have followed many approaches, most commonly as empiricists, uncovering new information to challenge earlier accounts. Historians have also revised previous versions by adopting new perspectives, usually fortified by new research, which overturn received views.

Even though rewriting is constantly taking place, historians' attitudes towards using new interpretations have been anything but settled. For most, the validity of revisionism lies in providing a stronger, more convincing account that better captures the objective truth of the matter. Although such historians might agree that we never finally arrive at the "truth", they believe it exists and over time may be better and better approximated. At the other extreme stand scholars who believe that each generation or even each cultural group or subgroup necessarily regards the past differently, each creating for itself a more usuable history. Although these latter scholars do not reject the possibility of demonstrating empirically that some contentions are better than others, they focus upon generating new views based upon different life experience. Different truths exist for different groups. Surely such an understanding, by emphasizing subjectivity, further encourages rewriting history. Between these two groups are those historians who wish to borrow from both sides. This third group, while accepting that every congerie of individuals sees matters differently, still wishes somewhat contradictorily to fashion a broader history that incorporates both of these particular visions. Revisionists who stress empiricism fall into the first of the three camps, while others spread out across the board.

Today the rewriting of history seems to have accelerated to a blinding speed, as a consequence of the evolution of revisionism. A variety of approaches has emerged. A major factor in this process has been the enormous increase in the number of researchers. This explosion has reinforced and enabled the retesting of many assertions. Significant ideological shifts have also played a major part in the growth of revisionism. First, the crisis of Marxism, culminating in the events in eastern Europe in 1989, has given rise to doubts about explicitly Marxist accounts. Such doubts have spilled over into the entire field of social history which has been a dominant subfield of the discipline for several decades. Focusing on society and its class divisions implies that these are the most important elements in historical analysis. Because Marxism was built on the same claim, the whole basis of social history has been questioned, despite the very many studies that had little directly to do with Marxism. Disillusionment with social history simultaneously opened the door to cultural and linguistic approaches largely developed in anthropology and literature. Multiculturalism and feminism further generated revisionism. By claiming that scholars had, wittingly or not, operated from a white European/American male point of view, newer researchers argued other approaches had been neglected or misunderstood. Not surprisingly, these last historians are the most likely to envision each subgroup rewriting its own usable history, while other scholars incline towards revisionism as part of the search for some stable truth.

Rewriting Histories will make these new approaches available to the student population. Often new scholarly debates take place in the scattered issues of journals which are sometimes difficult to find. Furthermore, in these first interactions, historians tend to address one another, leaving out the evidence that would make their arguments more accessible to the uninitiated. This series of books will collect in one place a strong group of the major articles in selected fields, adding notes and introductions conducive to improved understanding. Editors will select articles containing substantial historical data, so that students – at the least those who approach the subject as an objective phenomenon – can advance, not only their comprehension of debated points, but also their grasp of substantive aspects of the subject.

This volume by Alan Karras and John McNeill not only chronicles the revisionism of others but itself adds to the process. The authors seek to define an Atlantic world with its own historical rhythms. Although others have worked within this concept, the editors considerably advance this notion, in particular by demonstrating that, for their period, bodies of water linked rather than separated peoples. But in advocating this view, they have not been immune from general trends sweeping history. In particular, the interest in multiculturalism has contributed to this wider view of the Atlantic region by placing Amerindians and Africans as actors alongside Europeans. In addition, selections in this volume benefit from environmentalism, another concern stimulating revisionism. A product both of broader developments and of innovations specific to this field, this volume greatly furthers the goals of the series.

Jack R. Censer

ACKNOWLEDGMENTS

We would like to thank the following of our students and colleagues who read various parts of the manuscript and provided us with useful comments and criticisms: Ed Baptist, Georgette Dorn, Tom Dodd, Richard Duncan, Nancy Farley, David Johnson, and Aviel Roshwald.

Jack Censer's encouragement, suggestions, and guidance helped us produce this volume with minimal pain. We would also like to thank Claire L'Enfant, at Routledge, for her support and willingness to accommodate us whenever possible. Finally, we would like to thank all of our contributing authors for allowing us to reprint their essays.

1

THE ATLANTIC WORLD AS A UNIT OF STUDY

Alan L. Karras

I

Christopher Columbus first crossed the Atlantic Ocean in 1492. When he died in 1506, four transatlantic voyages later, he still had not realized that his mission had failed. Columbus had sailed westward from Spain, hoping to find a faster route to southern and eastern Asia. Despite his steadfast belief to the contrary, he never approached those destinations. Instead, Columbus and his crew happened upon a vast land mass which we now call the Americas. Although a great sailor, when in the Americas Cristobal Colon never knew exactly where he was; he could never have fathomed the historical significance of his "discovery."[1] Columbus' voyages profoundly affected both the region's populations and its physical environments for centuries to come; they ended a prolonged period of geographic isolation.

Columbus' first voyage, in 1492, serves as an historical reference point. From this moment in time forward, the histories of Europe, America, and Africa became inextricably linked. Peoples and cultures began to interact regularly. Such contact effectively forced all of the societies which border the Atlantic Ocean (including those in Europe) to confront new – and interrelated – problems.[2]

Winners and losers quickly emerged. The Europeans fared best of all – especially if we judge them according to their own ambitions. They seized control of vast areas of land which local populations had previously held. They appropriated colossal amounts of bullion, the existence of which they could scarcely have imagined before 1492. Moreover, they did not have to

1

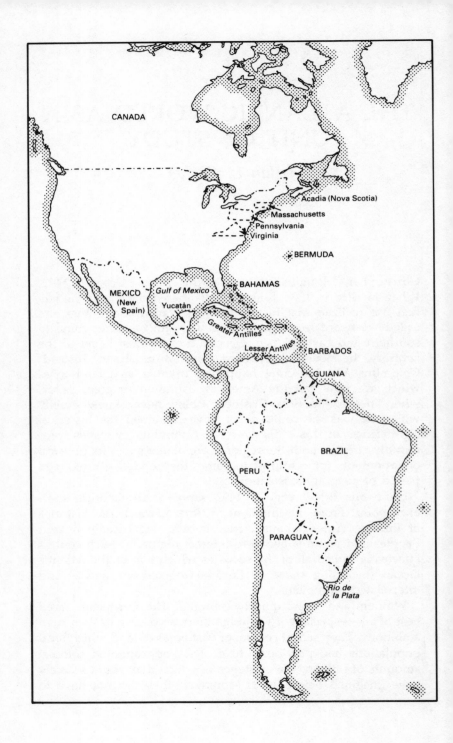

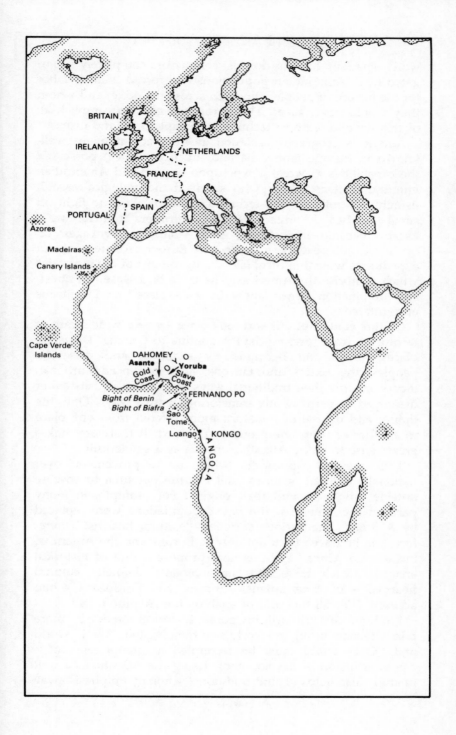

work especially hard to do this; conquerors completely subjugated huge Amerindian populations and forced them to labor for the benefit of people who lived across the ocean and whom they would never meet. The Europeans could accomplish all of this for two reasons: technological superiority and disease.

America's geographic isolation meant that pathogens well-known in Europe (and Asia and much of Africa) possessed the capabilities to wreak havoc upon unprepared Amerindian immune systems. Those who survived the biological assault usually did not have the technological capabilities to fight off small, but heavily armed, bands of intruders from far-away. Escape became impossible. After Columbus' voyages on Spain's behalf, each major Western European state sent out expeditions which, in turn, laid claims to most of the territories which comprise the Americas. The cycle of disease, conquest, and domination began anew in each place the Europeans encountered.

Culture contact of this sort took place across a wide swath of territory – from (present-day) Argentina to Canada. Disparate places, Brazil and Bermuda for example, and dissimilar peoples, the Aztecs and Hurons, all experienced European incursions into their traditional ways of life. These visits either destroyed or permanently transformed native ways. Only the timing and degree of transformation differed from one place to another or from one group to the next. It therefore makes great sense to study Atlantic America as a single unit.

This regional approach, while an improvement over nationally defined histories, still has the potential to obscure outside influences and their origins. For example, in many parts of the Americas, the native populations were replaced by Africans. The various societies' "cultural hearths," therefore, can be traced back not only to Europe and the Americas, but also to Africa.[3] We therefore propose a unit of historical analysis which takes the three broadly defined "cultural hearths" – of Amerindians, Africans, and Europeans – into account. We call this unit of analysis the Atlantic world.

We hope that this will invigorate historical inquiry by more nearly reconstituting the world as it then existed. "New" world and "Old" world must be recoupled as components of a common historical development. Using the Atlantic as a unit of study also helps to shift traditional scholarly emphasis away from terrestrial national and imperial borders and towards an ocean where national characteristics easily broke down. By the same token, religious and racial distinctions maintained their integrity from one side of the Atlantic to the other.

Conceptualizing the colonial period in Atlantic terms may seem obvious to students in 1992. Most scholars, however, have traditionally approached colonization from the perspective either of an individual colony or of the empire to which it belonged. Historians of Latin America, for example, have generally explored the connections between Spain or Portugal and their American possessions.[4] British historians have similarly investigated the British colonies in the Americas (and, in fact, principally those colonies which would later become the United States).[5] This approach has provided us with a deep understanding of the metropole (or parent society). It has also generated a great deal of information about life in particular colonies at any given moment. In some cases, it has led to studies of the connections between metropole and colony.[6]

Nonetheless, we believe that this work addresses only one part of a much broader problem. Few scholars have yet begun to explore the interactions between the residents of colonies in different European empires – Portuguese Brazil and French Saint-Domingue for example. There is an obvious need, as well, for African contributions to colonial social and cultural development to be more effectively integrated into historical consciousness. Seeing the Atlantic as a unit allows us to do all of this more effectively; it brings us closer to recreating an important part of the world as it operated in the decades and centuries after 1492.[7]

One need only look at the body of historical scholarship about one of the Americas' biggest countries – the United States – to observe the advantage of using the Atlantic as a unit of analysis. The idea that the United States of America developed along a unique trajectory, a doctrine known as American exceptionalism, held a great deal of currency until relatively recently.[8] This concept influenced (subtly in many cases) the questions which historians asked and, thus, the answers they obtained. Some scholars of colonial North America, within the last decade or so, have "discovered" that Atlantic history can be a powerful analytical concept.[9] This has certainly helped to diminish parochial nationalistic tendencies.

Nevertheless, most of these revisionists consider the Atlantic world to have been an English (or, by the eighteenth century, a British) phenomenon. Students in colonial American history courses, as a result, have increasingly learned about the existence and development of other British colonies, such as those in the West Indies. But they are not often instructed about interimperial connections. Nor are many of them encouraged to explore historical patterns and developments which took place beyond the boundaries of a particular empire. Students fortunate enough to encounter interimperial studies, moreover, will generally find that they are concerned largely with economic, political, or perhaps military, questions.[10] But the colonies of the Atlantic world also shared the same developmental rhythms. These have largely gone unnoticed.

Our understanding about the Atlantic world thus remains incomplete on two accounts. First, intersocietal and interimperial interactions warrant more of our historical attention and imagination; scholarship needs to break beyond rigid national or imperial boundaries. Second, the nature of our inquiries should not remain cloistered by politics and economics. Indeed, much can be revealed by probing social and cultural characteristics and interactions in places with demonstrably different populations.

Though we would welcome it, our call to study the Atlantic as a single unit is not merely a plea for more comparative history. Indeed, many questions upon which comparative history rests ultimately derive from the historiography of one or the other of the places being compared. What we need is a new set of questions. They would take full account of the shifting *connections* among peoples, cultures, politics, economics, and environments. In other words, we want to explore the history of a *system* rather than comparing the histories of its component parts. It is our expectation that modifying the unit of analysis in this way will result in fertile fields for further study, a more precise idea of the colonial era, and a new intellectual excitement from students who are approaching the subject for the first time.

II

If Atlantic history has a clear starting-point (1492), identifying its conclusion is a more challenging task. In the present volume, we have chosen the 1880s for what we believe is a compelling reason. Cuba and Brazil, the last two American societies to rely upon enslaved African labor, abolished the institution in (respectively) 1886 and 1888. This marked the disappearance of slavery from the Atlantic's western shores. A shift away from one socioeconomic system and toward another had clearly and definitively taken place.

We have divided the years from 1492 to 1888 (and thus our book) into three unequal parts. Each section is organized around a particular theme which, we believe, describes the processes which occurred throughout the Atlantic region as a whole. The first of these sections, "Implantation," begins chronologically with Columbus' expedition in 1492. It concludes during the middle of the seventeenth century.

During this first phase of Atlantic colonialism, the Europeans began their explorations, conquered territories which they encountered, subjugated native populations, and initiated colonial settlements.[11] By the end of the period, the basic elements of the geopolitical and institutional frameworks of overseas empires – Spanish, Portuguese, British, French, and Dutch – were all in place.[12]

The most fundamental characteristic of the implantation process was the destruction of the Amerindian populations and their replacement by Africans and Europeans. Native populations shrank steadily until the mid-seventeenth century, after which they began to recover everywhere but in the region's temperate zones (what eventually became the United States, Canada, and Argentina) and where they had been completely exterminated (in most Caribbean islands).

The pace of destruction and recovery, however, was far from uniform. Spain, for example, penetrated the West Indies in 1492 and conquered Mexico in 1522. At the end of this process most of the native American societies which they encountered soon lay in ruins – victims of warfare and disease. By the middle of the sixteenth century, much of Spain's territorial acquisitions had begun to resemble mature colonies in government and organization. The Portuguese began colonizing Brazil

7

in the 1530s. They introduced sugar production – and its companion, African slavery – by the middle of the sixteenth century. European-style governmental institutions, nonetheless, required another fifty years or so before they appeared. By contrast, the English only established a true colonial presence in 1607 with Virginia. The colony's first Africans arrived soon afterwards, in 1619. But the idea of permanent African slavery was not codified until the 1660s.[13] Only then did African importations dramatically accelerate. So too did demonstrably European institutions proliferate.

The French and Dutch experiences during this period were of a lesser order of magnitude. By 1608, the French had established a small settlement at Quebec. Its residents had one of two purposes: most were traders, who wanted to acquire furs from the Amerindians; the rest were Christian missionaries, who wanted to save the Amerindians' souls. In the 1620s and 1630s, the French established colonies in a few Caribbean islands: St Christopher (now known as St Kitt's), Martinique, and Guadeloupe.[14] By the 1640s, Dutch refugees from Brazil had introduced sugar to these places. That they did so is indicative of the nature of Dutch imperial expansion. The Dutch generally preferred trading and raiding to planting, especially when they set their sights on Spanish galleons. As a result, they concentrated their colonial efforts on establishing bases from which they could fulfill their mission. Manhattan Island, the Hudson River Valley, Curação, and Pernambuco in Brazil (among others) all came under Dutch control for at least part of this phase of colonialism.[15]

The Protestant Dutch, while often acting from religious conviction in their dealings with Amerindians, Africans, and Iberian Catholics, had a proverb which expressed their views: "Jesus Christ is good, but trade is better."[16] No higher motive than capital accumulation motivated European monarchs to authorize colonization. With the possible exception of Puritans in New England and missionary enterprises, such as Paraguay, all of the Atlantic's colonies were designed to profit their European proprietors – whether monarch, aristocrat, or *bourgeois gentilhomme*. In some cases, Mexico for example, this meant stripping as much of the area's natural resources as possible. In places like Brazil, Barbados, or Virginia, colonists quickly implemented plantation agriculture. There was nothing new in this: Europeans had long profited from far-flung agricultural production.

English aristocrats had colonized Ireland and its Gaelic residents, beginning in the middle of the sixteenth century. Subduing the native Irish (without exterminating them), English nobles quickly established plantations in the 'Emerald Isle' which were designed to bring their owners wealth, power, and prestige. This experience served as the proximate model for English plantation colonies in the Americas.[17] The Iberian model derived largely from Genoese and Venetian practice. In the twelfth century, demand for sugar had led to the creation of plantation agriculture in the eastern Mediterranean. As the European sweet tooth developed, sugar cultivation – partnered with coerced labor – moved westward to some of the Atlantic islands: Cape Verde, the Canaries, São Tomé, and Fernando Po.[18]

The presence of land in the Americas which was suitable for wide-scale production of staple crops allowed supply to grow. Demand increased correspondingly. Expansion into Atlantic America allowed some Europeans an opportunity to seek their fortunes by producing crops in demand by 1650, notably sugar and tobacco. They did so at the expense of Amerindians, Africans, and indentured European laborers. Furthermore, heavy plantation agriculture generally destroyed the very environmental conditions which allowed it to thrive in the first place.

The Caribbean region played host to European powers which, during the implantation phase, conspicuously competed for territory and dominance. The British, French, and Dutch intermittently raided treasure fleets bound for Spain. The various European nationals soon discovered that contraband trade provided a much steadier source of income than piracy. Their efforts to establish trading entrepots led them to establish settlements on depopulated Caribbean islands, particularly those of the Lesser Antilles. As these colonial enterprises matured, they spread to the larger islands of Jamaica and Hispaniola.[19]

The book's second part, which we call "Maturity," describes a period which began around 1650 and lasted just over a century – until about 1770. Compared to the implantation phase, which was marked by sudden and dramatic transformations, the mature colonial society appeared to operate in its own broad equilibrium. All of the European colonies which had earlier been implanted, along with their respective empires, continued to grow conspicuously in population, production, and trade. Amerindian demographics had now stabilized, permitting mines and plantations – especially in Spanish America – to function more predictably and profitably. Slave traders and their customers forced millions of Africans to cross the Atlantic as permanent bondsmen. The attitudes, laws, and institutions which governed relations between Amerindians and Europeans, and between Africans and Europeans, rigidified and began to shape the societies which would emerge after colonial rule ended. Finally, interimperial relations crystallized into enduring patterns of mercantilist competition, featuring commercial rivalry, privateering, and sporadic warfare.

Mature colonies had recognizably European governmental institutions in place. These organizations ranged from those at the local level (the New England town meeting, the *Senado da Camara* in Brazil, and the *cabildo* in Spanish America) to those on the colonial level (the Virginia House of Burgesses, the Jamaica Assembly, and the *Conseil Souverain* of Saint-Domingue). Such institutions increasingly balanced the demands of the metropole with the needs of local residents.

The economic system operated as the metropolis intended. European goods entered the colony and, in general, raw materials left on the return voyage. As time went on, however, local markets began to spring up. Surrounded by a productive hinterland, the urban area provided a new center for local economic activity. The rise to prominence of the port city is an example of this. Those in Spanish America developed first – in the sixteenth and seventeenth centuries. Cities in British North America – Philadelphia and New York for example – rose to prominence in the late seventeenth and early eighteenth centuries.

Increasingly, social orders on the Atlantic's western shores began to resemble those in Europe, with one important distinction – slavery and miscegenation. In most if not all societies, African slaves were at the bottom, and Indians were only slightly higher. The development of social classes which were based fundamentally upon racial distinctions took place in the years from 1660 to 1770. A mature colonial society was one in which those of European descent stood at the top, resting firmly on the backs of non-Europeans.[20]

Though migration from Europe continued, European segments of the population were successfully reproducing themselves in 1770. Moreover, the Creole population developed a sense of its own communal history as members of a particular colonial society.[21] At the same time, patterns of landscape usage had become distinctly European. In Atlantic America, forest clearance was well advanced in 1770. European agriculture, including the Mediterranean plantation variant, had imposed its familiar patterns on unfamiliar areas.

Our final phase, which we will call "Transition," lasted from roughly 1770 through Brazilian slavery's abolition in 1888. This period can be defined by a general shift in focus away from the Atlantic. It can also be characterized by a rise in the Creole elite's self-consciousness and power throughout the Americas. Beginning with the American Revolution in 1776, questions about the nature of colonial authority and the meaning of ideas like independence and liberty captivated various segments of the colonial populations. They were carried to new heights with the Haitian Revolution from 1791 to 1804; this insurrection resulted not only in the colony's political independence from France but also in the first enduring abolition of slavery anywhere in the plantation complex. Elites in the Americas were terrified that Haiti would export its radicalism; they correctly believed that the Haitians' ideas of freedom fundamentally challenged social orders based upon racial distinctions.[22]

It is not a little ironic, then, to learn that France was one of the last Atlantic countries to end slavery and the slave trade. Moreover, it did so only under pressure from its principal European rival, the United Kingdom.[23] Britain abolished its Atlantic slave trade in 1807; slave emancipation in the British colonies followed in 1834. The Westminster government, of course, compensated slaveowners for the loss of their "property." But by the time British planters had lost their slaves in 1834, the Spanish had lost most of their Atlantic empire.

In the Spanish colonies, nationalist movements overthrew colonial rule during the first part of the nineteenth century: in Argentina in 1816, in Venezuela and Mexico in 1821, and in Central America in 1823. In places where slavery had not already disappeared, political independence secured its

11

abolition. With the exception of Haiti, the Caribbean island colonies remained part of their imperial systems throughout this period.[24] The importance of their exports, however, decreased as Europe industrialized and found new sources in other parts of the world.

We attempt, in this book, to move beyond the tendency of previous historians to describe the economic, political, and military interactions which connected the Atlantic region. We will do so by focusing principally upon social and cultural history and the interdependence of European, African, and Amerindian peoples and cultures. Each essay will address one of four principal themes: (1) Amerindian contact/interaction; (2) slavery and the slave trade; (3) European migration and settlement; and (4) interimperial interaction and rivalry. In keeping with the purpose of this series, our selections are all drawn from relatively recent scholarship. Two contributions are about twenty years old; the rest have all appeared since 1983. Our essays all employ the kinds of intersocietal questions which derive from the broad historical conceptualization which we have been urging.

Nevertheless, some of our essays are concerned with only one geographic area. In such instances, they are best taken as case studies. We anticipate that each author's method and argument will suggest new ways of examining the issues in other settings. Finally, we have made a conscious effort to include as many of the societies, from Argentina to Canada, as possible. It is our aim to provide students with a mechanism for viewing this historical epoch from the Atlantic perspective: the one which best reveals the realities of the age.

NOTES

1 The Americas were so named after Amerigo Vespucci, who believed that he encountered a New World on his second voyage to the South American mainland in 1501–2. Use of the term "America" to describe the entire land mass spread slowly throughout the sixteenth century.

2 For a useful categorization of these problems, see Franklin Knight, "Afro-American Perspectives of the Christopher Columbus Quincentenary," *The New World* (Spring/Summer 1991): 8. Knight posits the importance of questions in five areas: (1) culture contact and social diversification; (2) encounter and exchange; (3) national and

regional identity; (4) ethnocentricity and racism; and (5) America in a changing world system.

3 We have borrowed the notion of the cultural hearth from D. W. Meinig, *Atlantic America, 1492–1800* (New Haven, Conn., 1986), 51–2. Meinig, however, applied this cultural hearth idea only to differentiate among Europeans. The idea is equally applicable, if not more so, in differentiating among Europeans, Africans, and Amerindians.

4 For examples, see Charles Gibson, *Spain in America* (New York, 1966); James Lockhart, *Spanish Peru, 1532–1560* (Madison, Wis., 1968); C. R. Boxer, *The Portuguese Seaborne Empire, 1415–1825* (London, 1969); Stuart Schwartz, *Sovereignty and Society in Colonial Brazil: The High Court of Bahia and its Judges, 1609–1751* (Berkeley, Calif., 1973); and Kenneth R. Andrews, *The Spanish Caribbean: Trade and Plunder, 1530–1630* (New Haven, Conn., 1978).

5 Perhaps the best starting points for historiographical overviews here are Jack P. Greene and J. R. Pole, *Colonial British America* (Baltimore, Md, 1984), and John McCusker and Russell Menard, *The Economy of British America, 1607–1789* (Chapel Hill, NC, 1985).

6 Migratory and cultural relationships between Europe and British America are discussed in Bernard Bailyn, *Voyagers to the West: A Passage in the Peopling of the Americas on the Eve of the Revolution* (New York, 1986); Ned Landsman, *Scotland and its First American Colony, 1683–1765* (Princeton, NJ, 1985); and David Hackett Fischer, *Albion's Seed: Four British Folkways in America* (New York, 1989). For an example of environmental interactions, see William Cronon, *Changes in the Land: Indians, Colonists, and the Ecology of New England* (New York, 1983).

7 Useful histories which use the Atlantic as a unit of analysis include Alfred W. Crosby, *The Columbian Exchange: Biological and Cultural Consequences of 1492* (Westport, Conn., 1972); Marcus Rediker, *Between the Devil and the Deep Blue Sea: Merchant Seamen, Pirates, and the Anglo-American Maritime World, 1700–1750* (New York, 1987); Sidney Mintz, *Sweetness and Power* (New York, 1985); and Robin Blackburn, *The Overthrow of Colonial Slavery* (London, 1988). Richard Dunn's excellent article, "The English Sugar Islands and the Founding of South Carolina," *Shaping Southern Society*, ed. T. H. Breen (New York, 1976), 48–58, provides an example of the sorts of connection which still remain shadowy.

8 In some cases, we believe that it still does. See the forum between Ian Tyrrell, "American Exceptionalism in an Age of International History," 1031–55 and Michael McGerr, "The Price of the New Transnational History," 1056–72, in the *American Historical Review* 96, no. 4 (October, 1991).

9 See, for example, Ian Steele, *The English Atlantic, 1675–1740: An Exploration of Communication and Community* (New York, 1986) and Meinig, *Atlantic America*.

10 Students interested in interimperial economic histories should begin with Jacob Price, *France and the Chesapeake* (Ann Arbor,

Mich., 1974), and Ralph Davis, *The Rise of the Atlantic Economies* (Ithaca, NY, 1973). For an attempt to move out of the economic frameworks, see Nicholas Canny and Anthony Pagden, eds, *Colonial Identity in the Atlantic World 1500–1800* (Princeton, NJ, 1987).

11 We also have modified Meinig's idea of implantation, which derives principally from the experiences of British North America (Meinig, *Atlantic America*, p. 66).

12 While the Swedes and Danes also participated in this period of European expansion, neither of them fared particularly well.

13 For details about the British colonial codification of slavery and its impact upon the existing population of African descent, see Winthrop Jordan, *White Over Black* (New York, 1968); T. H. Breen and Stephen Innes, *Myne Owne Ground* (New York, 1980); and Edmund Morgan, *American Slavery, American Freedom* (New York, 1974). For Brazil, see Katia de Quieros Mattoso, *To Be A Slave in Brazil* (New Brunswick, NJ, 1986). For Mexico, see Colin Palmer, *Slaves of the White God* (Chapel Hill, NC, 1975). Barbara Solow, *Slavery and the Rise of the Atlantic System* (New York, 1991) has several useful essays in it.

14 It is important to note here that Saint-Domingue, France's most important sugar colony, only came under French control in 1697.

15 We are a bit uncertain about including the Dutch here. They were successful at achieving their aims of trade and plunder. Nonetheless, they never succeeded in implanting Dutch societies in the New World.

16 Cited in David Watts, *The West Indies: Patterns of Development, Culture, and Environmental Change since 1492* (Cambridge, 1987), 128.

17 See Nicholas Canny, "The Ideology of English Colonization: From Ireland to America," *William and Mary Quarterly* 30 (1973): 575–98.

18 See Philip Curtin, *The Rise and Fall of the Plantation Complex* (New York, 1990), 3–25.

19 See David Watts, *The West Indies: Patterns of Development, Culture, and Environmental Change since 1492* (Cambridge, 1987); Cornelis Goslinga, *The Dutch in the Caribbean and the Guianas 1680–1791* (Dover, NH, 1985); Kenneth R. Andrews, *The Spanish Caribbean*; Richard S. Dunn, *Sugar and Slaves; The Rise of the Planter Class in the West Indies, 1624–1713* (New York, 1972); and Bonham Richardson's forthcoming historical geography of the Caribbean.

20 For an argument of this type, see Edmund Morgan, "Slavery and Freedom: The American Paradox," *Journal of American History* 59 (1972–3): 5–29. Morgan argues that freedom for all Whites could only be guaranteed by slavery's existence for all Blacks. His argument could be applied to all Atlantic American slave societies. The presence of mixed-race racial distinctions and socio-economic hierarchies based upon them demonstrates how Europeans defined freedom. In places outside of the United States, the degree of one's European ancestry dictated the degree of one's freedoms.

21 For an example of this, see Jack P. Greene, "Changing Identity in

the British Caribbean: Barbados as a Case Study," *Colonial Identity*, ed. Canny and Pagden, 213–66.

22 The classic work on Haiti's slave revolt is C. L. R. James, *The Black Jacobins* (New York, 1963). For a good synopsis of the events, see David Geggus, "The Haitian Revolution," in *The Modern Caribbean*, ed. Franklin W. Knight and Colin Palmer (Chapel Hill, NC, 1989). David Geggus, *Slavery, War, and Revolution: The British Occupation of St Domingue, 1793–1798* (Oxford, 1982), speaks directly to the question of European fears. Also see David Brion Davis, *The Problem of Slavery in the Age of Revolution, 1770–1823* (Ithaca, NY, 1975).

23 For a discussion of the few French attempts to end slavery and the slave trade, see Dale Tomich, *Slavery in the Circuit of Sugar: Martinique and the World Economy, 1830–1848* (Baltimore, Md, 1990), 53–61.

24 See John Lynch, *The Spanish American Revolutions, 1808–1826* (New York, 1973).

Part I

IMPLANTATION
1492–*c*.1650

2

ILLS

Alfred W. Crosby

In his Ecological Imperialism *(1986), Alfred W. Crosby argues that one of the key reasons behind the success of European colonization was the unconscious teamwork among plants, animals, diseases, and humans carried across the oceans. In the decades and centuries after 1492, this teamwork, and European imperialism, had the strongest effect in lands which by virtue of climate were hospitable to the various species of Europe. Those lands in which the European biota largely supplanted indigenous ones he calls Neo-Europes, a category which includes Australia, New Zealand, Siberia, as well as temperate North and South America. In this selection (from which we have excised the sections pertaining to Australasia) Crosby explains how various infectious diseases, notably smallpox, wrought the greatest known demographic catastrophe in the history of the world. The unwitting carriers were the sailors of early modern Europe (Crosby uses the Portuguese term* marinheiros*); the victims were the Amerindians from one end of the Americas to the other.*

The demographic disaster that followed upon Columbus' visits to the Americas paved the way for the implantation of European colonies. The specific characters of those colonies depended in part on the severity of the disaster: in some places the new societies had no Amerindian component at all; in others, particularly highland zones, where the Old World diseases had lesser impacts, Amerindians survived in numbers sufficient to form majorities. In the tropical lowland Atlantic regions, disease had its strongest effect. There the near-complete destruction of the Amerindians foiled European hopes of using an indigenous labor force, and opened the way first for white servitude and then for African slavery. In more temperate latitudes, stronger streams of European settlement displaced those Amerindians whom the new diseases did not kill.

* * *

19

> The colony of a civilized nation which takes possession, either of waste country, or of one so thinly inhabited, that the natives easily give place to the new settlers, advances more rapidly to wealth and greatness than any other human society.
>
> Adam Smith, *An Inquiry into the Nature and Causes of the Wealth of Nations* (1776)

Old World germs were entities having size, weight, and mass, just like Sweet Betsy, her Ike, and their animals; germs required transportation across the oceans, which the *marinheiros* unintentionally supplied. Once ashore and lodged in the bodies of new victims in new lands, their rate of reproduction (as often as every twenty minutes) enabled them to outperform all larger immigrants in rapidity of increase and speed of geographical expansion. Pathogens are among the "weediest" of organisms. We must examine the colonial histories of Old World pathogens, because their success provides the most spectacular example of the power of the biogeographical realities that underlay the success of European imperialists overseas. It was their germs, not these imperialists themselves, for all their brutality and callousness, that were chiefly responsible for sweeping aside the indigenes and opening the Neo-Europes to demographic takeover.

Until recently, the chroniclers of human history had no knowledge of germs, and most believed epidemic disease to be supernatural in origin, something to be piously endured but rarely chronicled in detail. Therefore, the epidemiological history of the European colonies beyond the seams of Pangaea* is like a jigsaw puzzle of 10,000 pieces, of which we have only half – enough to give us an idea of how large the original was and of its major features, but not enough for a neat reassembly. We bemoan the spottiness of our information; yet so great is its quantity and so neatly does it parallel accounts of the modern experience of what happens to isolated peoples when they are dragooned into the world community that we cannot doubt its general validity. Before we approach the history of Old World pathogens in the Americas, let us take a look at a few

---

* By "beyond the seams of Pangaea" Crosby means across the Atlantic or Pacific Ocean. Pangaea is the name of the single continent from which the Americas, Africa, and Eurasia were formed in geological movements more than 250 million years ago.

recent examples of what science calls virgin soil epidemics (rapid spread of pathogens among people whom they have never infected before), in order to accustom ourselves to the possibilities of epidemiological catastrophe. When in 1943 the advance of the Alaska Highway exposed the Amerindians of Teslin Lake to fuller contact with the outside world than they had ever had before, they underwent in one year epidemics of measles, German measles, dysentery, catarrhal jaundice, whooping cough, mumps, tonsillitis, and meningococcal meningitis. When in 1952 the Amerindians and Eskimos of Ungava Bay, in northern Quebec, had an epidemic of measles, 99 per cent became sick, and about 7 per cent died, even though some had the benefit of modern medicine. In 1954, an epidemic of the same "minor" infection broke out among the people of Brazil's remote Xingu National Park. The death rate was 9.6 per cent among those of the afflicted who had modern medical treatment, and 26.8 per cent among those who did not. In 1968, when the Yanomamas of the Brazilian–Venezuelan borderland were struck by measles, 8 or 9 per cent died despite the availability of some modern medicines and treatment. The Kreen-Akorores of the Amazon basin, contacted for the first time a few years later, lost at least 15 per cent of their people in a single brush with common influenza.[1] The evidence is that when isolation ceases, decimation begins; hence the reasonable belief of the Yanomamas that "white men cause illness; if the whites had never existed, disease would never have existed either."[2]

The isolation of the indigenes of the Americas from Old World germs prior to the last few hundred years was nearly absolute. Not only did very few people of any origin cross the great oceans, but those who did must have been healthy or they would have died on the way, taking their pathogens with them. The indigenes were not without their own infections, of course. The Amerindians had at least pinta, yaws, venereal syphilis, hepatitis, encephalitis, polio, some varieties of tuberculosis (not those usually associated with pulmonary disease), and intestinal parasites, but they seem to have been without any experience of such Old World maladies as smallpox, measles, diphtheria, trachoma, whooping cough, chicken pox, bubonic plague, malaria, typhoid fever, cholera, yellow

21

fever, dengue fever, scarlet fever, amebic dysentery, influenza, and a number of helminthic infestations.[3]

Indications of the susceptibility of Amerindians to Old World infections appear almost immediately after the intrusion of the Whites. In 1492, Columbus kidnapped a number of West Indians to train as interpreters and to show to King Ferdinand and Queen Isabella. Several of them seem to have died on the stormy voyage to Europe, and so Columbus had only seven to display in Spain, along with some gold trinkets, Arawack finery, and a few parrots. When, less than a year later, he returned to American waters, only two of the seven were still alive.[4] In 1495, Columbus, searching for a West Indian commodity that would sell in Europe, sent 550 Amerindian slaves, twelve to thirty-five years of age, more or less, off across the Atlantic. Two hundred died on the difficult voyage; 350 survived to be put to work in Spain. The majority of these soon were also dead "because the land did not suit them."[5]

What killed the Arawacks in 1493 and 1495? Maltreatment? Cold? Hunger? Overwork? Yes, and no doubt about it, but could this be the entire answer? Columbus certainly did not want to kill his interpreters, and slavers and slaveholders have no interest whatever in the outright slaughter of their property. All or almost all of these victims seem to have been young adults, usually the most resilient members of our species – except in the case of unfamiliar infections. The hale and hearty immune system of one's prime years of life, when challenged by unprecedented invaders, can overreact and smother normal body functions with inflammation and edema.[6] The most likely candidates for the role of exterminator of the first Amerindians in Europe were those that killed so many other Arawacks in the decades immediately following: Old World pathogens.[7]

We shall turn now to the colonies, but obviously we cannot include within the limits of this chapter even a cursory epidemiological history of all of Europe's overseas colonies or even of the Neo-Europes alone. Let us restrict ourselves to the peregrinations of one Old World pathogen in the colonies, the most spectacular one, the virus of smallpox. Smallpox, an infection that usually spreads from victim to victim by breath, was one of the most communicable of all diseases and one of the very deadliest.[8] It was an old human infection in the Old World, but it was rarely of crucial importance in Europe until it flared up in the sixteenth century. For the next 250–300 years – until the advent of vaccination – it was just that, of crucial importance, reaching its apogee in the 1700s, when it accounted for 10–15 per cent of all deaths in some of the Western European nations early in the century. Characteristically, 80 per cent of its victims were under ten years of age, and 70 per cent under two years of age. In Europe, it was the worst of the childhood diseases. Most adults, especially in the cities and ports, had had it and were immune. In the colonies, it struck indigenes young and old and was the worst of all diseases.[9]

Smallpox first crossed the seams of Pangaea – specifically to the island of Española* – at the end of 1518 or the beginning of 1519, and for the next four centuries it played as essential a role in the advance of white imperialism overseas as gunpowder – perhaps a more important role, because the indigenes did turn the musket and then the rifle against the intruders, but smallpox very rarely fought on the side of the indigenes. The intruders were usually immune to it, as they were to other Old World childhood diseases, most of which were new beyond the oceans. The malady quickly exterminated one-third or one-half of the Arawacks on Española, and almost immediately leaped the straits to Puerto Rico and the other Greater Antilles, accomplishing the same devastation there. It crossed from Cuba to Mexico and joined Cortés's forces in the person of a sick black soldier, one of the few of the invaders not immune to the infection. The disease exterminated a large fraction of the Aztecs and cleared a path for the aliens to the heart of Tenochtitlán and to the founding of New Spain. Racing ahead of the *conquistadores*, it soon appeared in Peru, killing a large proportion of the subjects of the Inca, killing the Inca himself and the successor he had chosen. Civil war and chaos followed, and then Francisco Pizarro arrived. The miraculous triumphs of that *conquistador*, and of Cortés, whom he so successfully emulated, are in large part the triumphs of the virus of smallpox.[10]

This first recorded pandemic in the New World may have reached as far as the American Neo-Europes. The Amerindian population was denser than it was to be again for centuries,

* Hispaniola.

and utterly susceptible to smallpox. Canoeists of the Calusa tribe often crossed from Florida to Cuba to trade in the early sixteenth century, and certainly could have carried smallpox home to the continent with them; and peoples in at least sporadic contact with each other ringed the Gulf of Mexico from areas where the disease was rife all the way around to the thickly populated regions of what is now the southeastern part of the United States. The Mississippi, with villages rarely so much as a day's journey apart along its banks, at least as far north as the Ohio, would have given the disease access to the entire interior of the continent. As for the pampa, the pandemic certainly spread through the Incan Empire to present-day Bolivia, and from there settlements with easy access to each other were sprinkled across Paraguay and down along the Río de la Plata and its tributaries to the pampa. Smallpox may have ranged from the Great Lakes to the pampa in the 1520s and 1530s.[11]

Smallpox is a disease with seven-league boots. Its effects are terrifying: the fever and pain; the swift appearance of pustules that sometimes destroy the skin and transform the victim into a gory horror; the astounding death rates, up to one-fourth, one-half, or more with the worst strains. The healthy flee, leaving the ill behind to face certain death, and often taking the disease along with them. The incubation period for smallpox is ten to fourteen days, long enough for the ephemerally healthy carrier to flee for long distances on foot, by canoe, or, later, on horseback to people who know nothing of the threat he represents, and there to infect them and inspire others newly charged with the virus to flee to infect new innocents. To give one example (a precise rather than sensational example), most of the Abipones with whom the missionary Martin Dobrizhoffer was living in mid-eighteenth-century Paraguay fled when smallpox appeared among them, some as far as 80 kilometers. In some instances this quarantine-by-flight worked, but often it simply served to spread the disease.[12]

The first *recorded* epidemic of smallpox in British or French North America erupted among the Algonquians of Massachusetts in the early 1630s: "Whole towns of them were swept away, in some not so much as one soul escaping Destruction."[13] William Bradford of Plymouth Plantation, a few miles south, provided a few more details on just how hard the Algonquians nearby were hit, and how the death rates could soar to such heights in these epidemics. Some of the victims, he wrote,

> fell down so generally of this disease as they were in the end not able to help one another, no not to make a fire nor fetch a little water to drink, nor any to bury the dead. But would strive as long as they could, and when they could procure no other means to make fire, they would burn the wooden trays and dishes they ate their meat from, and their very bows and arrows. And some would crawl out on all fours to get a little water, and sometimes die by the way and not be able to get in again.[14]

The disease raged through New England, on west into the St Lawrence–Great Lakes region, and from there no one knows how much farther. Smallpox whipsawed back and forth through New York and surrounding areas in the 1630s and 1640s, reducing the populations of the Huron and Iroquois confederations by an estimated 50 per cent.[15]

After that, smallpox never seemed to stay away for more than two or three decades at a time.[16] The missionaries, Jesuit and Mennonite, the traders from Montreal and Charleston – they all had the same appalling story to tell about smallpox and the indigenes. In 1738 it destroyed one-half of the Cherokee, in 1759 nearly one-half of the Catawbas, in the first years of the nineteenth century two-thirds of the Omahas and perhaps half the entire population between the Missouri River and New Mexico, in 1837–8 nearly every last one of the Mandans and perhaps one-half of the people of the high plains.[17] Every European people to establish major settlements in North America – the English, French, Dutch, Spanish, and Russian – recorded, sometimes in gloom, sometimes in exultation, the horrors of smallpox running loose among Americans who had never known it before.

Smallpox may have reached the pampa as early as the 1520s or 1530s, as suggested above. In 1558 or 1560, smallpox appeared again (or for the first time) in the grasslands of the Río de la Plata and killed, says a hearsay account, "more than 100,000 Indians."[18] We have only one source for this, but the explosion of smallpox in Chile and Paraguay at about the same time and in Brazil from 1562 to 1565, killing masses of indigenes, provides strong support for this report of the disease afflicting the people of the lower reaches of the Río de la Plata.[19]

From the last decades of the sixteenth century and into the second half of the nineteenth century, smallpox swept the southern steppes and adjacent areas again and again, seemingly arising whenever enough susceptibles had been born since the last epidemic to support a new one. The seventeenth century opened with the government at Buenos Aires asking the Spanish crown for permission to import more black slaves, because smallpox had struck down so many of the Amerindians. That city alone had at least four epidemics of smallpox in less than a hundred years (in 1627, 1638, 1687, and 1700), and many others followed in the next two centuries. The first solid reference to the disease in Rio Grande do Sul did not appear until 1695, but this firestorm of a disease must have swept that province, contiguous to both Portuguese and Spanish areas where epidemics blazed up again and again, long before the end of the seventeenth century.[20]

The death rates could be very high. In 1729, two churchmen, Miguel Ximénez and a priest named Cattaneo, started out from Buenos Aires for the missions in Paraguay accompanied by 340 Guaraní. Eight days up the Río de la Plata, smallpox appeared among the latter. All but forty contracted the infection, and for two months the disease raged, at the end of which 121 were convalescing and 179 were dead. The Jesuits, a group more given to numerical precision than most, reckoned that 50,000 had died in the Paraguayan missions in the 1718 smallpox, 30,000 in the Guaraní villages in 1734, and 12,000 in 1765. Out of how many at risk? We shall have to leave that to the demographic historians.[21]

We shall never know how many died among the tribes roaming the pampa. Their ability to flee at short notice must have saved them from some epidemics, but the longer they avoided the infection, the more pulverizing its impact when it did strike. For instance, there is the case of the Chechehets, in 1700 one of the more numerous of the peoples of the grasslands, and therefore probably a tribe that had dodged the worst epidemics. When this tribe acquired smallpox near Buenos Aires early in the eighteenth century, it suffered near obliteration. The Chechehets tried to fly from this danger, which this time only increased their losses: "During the journey they daily left behind them their sick friends and relations, forsaken and alone, with no other assistance than a hide reared up against the wind, and a pitcher of water." They even killed their own shamans "to see if by this means the distemper would cease." The Chechehets never recovered as an autonomous people. By the end of the century, even their language was gone. Today we have fifteen of their words and some place-names, barely as much as we have of the language of the Guanches.*[22]

This disease continued to periodically ravage the pampean tribes, terminating only with the spread of vaccination and the destruction, incarceration, or expulsion of the last peoples of the Argentine steppe. Dr Eliseo Cantón, physician, scientist, and medical historian of Argentina, stated flatly that the extermination of the Amerindians as an effective force on the pampa was due not to the Argentinian army and its Remingtons, but to smallpox.[23]

The impact of smallpox on the indigenes of the Americas was more deadly, more bewildering, more devastating than we, who live in a world from which the smallpox virus has been scientifically exterminated, can ever fully realize. The statistics of demographic decline are cold, the eyewitness accounts at first moving but eventually only macabre. The impact was so awesome that only a writer with the capabilities of a Milton at the height of his powers could have been equal to the subject, and there was no one like him on Española in 1519. We are obliged to turn not to the witnesses but to the sufferers for enlightenment, and they made legends, not epic poems. The Kiowa of the southern Great Plains of North America, who suffered at least three and probably four epidemics of smallpox in the nineteenth century, have a legend about the disease. Saynday, the mythic hero of the tribe, comes upon a stranger dressed in a black suit and a tall hat, like a missionary. The stranger speaks first:

"Who are you?"
"I'm Saynday. I'm the Kiowa's Old Uncle Saynday. I'm the one who's always coming along. Who are you?"
"I'm smallpox."

---

* The Guanches were the indigenous population of the Canary Islands.

"Where do you come from and what do you do and why are you here?"

"I come from far away, across the Eastern Ocean. I am one with the white men – they are my people as the Kiowas are yours. Sometimes I travel ahead of them, and sometimes I lurk behind. But I am always their companion and you will find me in their camps and in their houses."

"What do you do?"

"I bring death. My breath causes children to wither like young plants in the spring snow. I bring destruction. No matter how beautiful a woman is, once she has looked at me she becomes as ugly as death. And to men I bring not death alone but the destruction of their children and the blighting of their wives. The strongest warriors go down before me. No people who have looked at me will ever be the same."[24]

The Whites took a sunnier view of imported diseases. John Winthrop, first governor of Massachusetts Bay Colony and a lawyer by training, noted on 22 May 1634, "For the natives, they are neere all dead of small Poxe, so as the Lord hathe cleared our title to what we possess."[25]

Smallpox was only one of the diseases the *marinheiros* let loose on the native peoples overseas – perhaps the most destructive, certainly the most spectacular – but only one. We have not dealt at all with respiratory infections, the "hectic" fevers so often prevalent among the indigenes after contact with the strangers from over the horizon. We have said nothing of enteric infections, which unquestionably have killed more humans in the last few millennia than any other class of diseases, and still are doing so. Cabeza de Vaca,* staggering lost and desperate across Texas *c*.1530, unintentionally presented his Amerindian masters with some sort of dysenteric disease that killed one-half of them and elevated him and his comrades to the status of priestly physicians, ironically saving their lives.[26] We have said nothing of the insect-borne diseases, though in the nineteenth century malaria was the most impor-

* Alvar Nuñez Cabeza de Vaca (*c*.1490–*c*.1557) was a Spanish explorer. He was captured by Amerindians along the Gulf Coast of North America. After his release, he wandered for several years in Texas and Northern Mexico. He eventually became Governor of Río de la Plata (Paraguay) in 1540.

tant sickness in the entire Mississippi Valley.[27] We have said nothing of the venereal infections, which depressed the indigenes' birth rates as they raised death rates. Old World pathogens in their dismal variety spread widely beyond the seams of Pangaea and weakened, crippled, or killed millions of the geographical vanguard of the human race. The world's greatest demographic disaster was initiated by Columbus and the other *marinheiros*, and Europe's overseas colonies were, in the first stage of their modern development, charnel houses. Afterward, mixed European, African, and indigene societies quite unlike any that had ever existed before grew up in the colonies in the torrid zone, with the single major exception of northern Australia. The temperate-zone colonies developed less distinctively; they became Neo-European, with only minorities of non-Whites.[28]

We accept that Mexico and Peru were full of indigenous peoples prior to European arrival, because their ancient monuments of stone are too huge to ignore and because their descendants still live in these lands in large numbers. But to imagine the Neo-Europes, now chock-full of Neo-Europeans and other Old World peoples, as once having had large native populations that were wiped out by imported diseases calls for a long leap of historical imagination. Let us examine one specific case of depopulation of a Neo-Europe.

Let us select a Neo-European region where indigenous agriculturalists of an advanced culture lived: the portion of the eastern United States between the Atlantic and the Great Plains, the Ohio Valley and the Gulf of Mexico. By the time Europeans had quartered that region, had traversed it up and down, back and forth, often enough in search of new Aztec Empires, routes to Cathay, and gold and furs to have acquainted themselves with its major features – by 1700 or so – the native inhabitants were the familiar Amerindians of the United States history text-books: Cherokee, Creek, Shawnee, Choctaw, and so forth. These and all the others, with only one or two exceptions, were peoples without pronounced social stratification, without the advanced arts and crafts that aristocracies and priesthoods elicit, and without great public works comparable to the temples and pyramids of Meso-America. Their populations were no greater than one would expect of part-time farmers and hunters and gatherers, and in many areas less. Very few tribes numbered in the tens of thousands, and most were much smaller.

The scene in this part of North America had been very different in 1492. The Mound Builders (a general title for a hundred different peoples of a dozen different cultures spread over thousands of square kilometers and most of a millennium) had raised and were raising up multitudes of burial and temple mounds, many no more than knee- or hip-high, but some among the largest earthen structures ever created by humans anywhere. The largest, Monks Mound, one of 120 at Cahokia, Illinois, is 623,000 cubic meters in volume and covers six and a half hectares.[29] Every particle of this enormous mass was carried and put into place by human beings without the help of any domesticated animals. The only pre-Columbian structures in the Americas that are larger are the Pyramid of the Sun at Teotihuacán and the great pyramid at Cholula.* Cahokia, in its heyday, about AD 1200, was one of the great ceremonial centers of the world, served by a village with a population estimated by some archeologists as upward of 40,000. (The largest city in the United States in 1790 was Philadelphia, with a population of 42,000.)[30] Graves at Cahokia and other such sites contain copper from Lake Superior, chert from Arkansas and Oklahoma, sheets of mica probably from North Carolina, and many art objects of superb quality. They also contain, in addition to the skeletons of the honored dead, those of men and women apparently sacrificed at the time of burial. One burial pit at Cahokia contains the remains of four men, all with heads and hands missing, and about fifty women, all between eighteen and twenty-three years of age. Surely this assemblage is evidence for a grim religion and a severely hierarchical class structure – this last a key factor in the origins of civilization everywhere.

When Whites and Blacks settled near the site of Cahokia and similar centers (Moundsville, Alabama; Etowah, Georgia) in the eighteenth and nineteenth centuries, the local Amerindian societies were relatively egalitarian, their population sparse, their arts and crafts admirable but no longer superb, their trade networks regional; these people knew nothing of the mounds and ceremonial centers, abandoned generations before. The

* In Aztec Mexico.

Whites credited them to Vikings, or to the lost tribes of Israel, or to prehistoric races now gone from the earth.[31]

The builders of the mounds had been Amerindians, of course – in some cases, no doubt, the ancestors of the people who were living near the sites when the Old World settlers arrived. These ancestors had been alive in large numbers when the Europeans first approached the coasts of the Americas. They were the people through whose lands and bodies Hernando de Soto* hacked a path from 1539 to 1542 in his search for wealth equal to what he had seen in Peru. His chroniclers give us a clear impression of regions of dense population and many villages in the midst of vast cultivated fields, of stratified societies rules with an iron hand from the top, and of scores of temples resting on truncated pyramids, which though often stubby and made of earth rather than masonry, remind one of similar structures in Teotihuacán and Chichén Itzá.[†]

Where in the images of North American native societies that we share today is there a place for De Soto's wily opponent, the "Señora of Cofachiqui," a province that probably contained the present site of Augusta, Georgia? She traveled by sedan chair borne by noblemen and was accompanied by a retinue of slaves. For a distance of 100 leagues "she was greatly obeyed, whatsoever she ordered being performed with diligence and efficacy."[32] Seeking to deflect the greed of the Spaniards away from her living subjects, she sent the former off to sack a burial house or temple that was 30 meters long and 12 or so wide, with a roof decorated with marine shells and fresh-water pearls, which "made a splendid sight in the brilliance of the sun." Inside were chests containing the dead, and for each chest a statue carved in the likeness of the deceased. The walls and ceiling were hung with artwork, and the rooms filled with finely carved maces, battle-axes, pikes, bows, and arrows inlaid with freshwater pearls. The building and its contents were, in the opinion of one of the grave robbers, Alonso de Carmona, who had lived in both Mexico and Peru, among the finest things he had ever seen in the New World.[33]

The Amerindians of Cofachiqui and of much of what is now the southeastern United States were impressive country

* Spanish conquistador, who lived c.1500–42.
† Chichen Itza is a Mayan site in Yucatan, Mexico.

cousins of the civilized Mexicans, and there were a lot of them. The latest scholarly work estimates that the population of one marginal area, Florida, may have been as high as 900,000 at the beginning of the sixteenth century.[34] Even if we skeptically subtract one-half from that figure, the remainder is impressively large. The southeastern United States, relative to what it had been, was vacant c.1700 when the French came to stay.

Something eliminated or drove off most of the population of Cofachiqui by the eighteenth century, as well as of a number of other areas where heavy populations of people of similar cultural achievements had lived two centuries before: along the Gulf Coast between Mobile Bay and Tampa Bay, along the Georgia coast, and on the banks of the Mississippi above the mouth of the Red River. In eastern and southern Arkansas and northeastern Louisiana, where De Soto had found thirty towns and provinces, the French found only a handful of villages. Where De Soto had been able to stand on one temple mound and see several villages with their mounds and little else but fields of maize between, there was now wilderness. Whatever had afflicted the country through which he had passed may have reached far to the north as well. The region of southern Ohio and northern Kentucky, among the richest in natural food resources on the continent, was nearly deserted when Whites first penetrated from New France and Virginia.[35]

There had even been a major ecological change in the regions adjacent to the Gulf of Mexico and for tens of kilometers back from the coast, a change paralleling and probably associated with the decline in Amerindian numbers. In the sixteenth century, De Soto's chroniclers saw no buffalo along their route from Florida to Tennessee and back to the coast, or if they did see these wonderful beasts, they did not mention them – which seems highly improbable. Archeological evidence and examination of Amerindian placenames also indicate that there were no buffalo along the De Soto route, nor between it and salt water. A century and a half later, when the French and English arrived, they found the shaggy animals present in at least scattered herds from the mountains almost to the Gulf and even to the Atlantic. What had happened in the interim is easy to explain in the abstract: an econiche opened up, and the buffalo moved into it. Something had kept these animals out of the expanses of park-like clearings in the forest that periodic Amerindian use of fire and hoe had created. That something declined or disappeared after 1540. That something was, in all likelihood, the Amerindians themselves, who naturally would have killed the buffalo for food and to protect their crops.[36]

The cause of that decline and disappearance was probably epidemic disease. No other factor seems capable of having exterminated so many people over such a large part of North America. The dismal genocidal process had already begun before De Soto arrived in Cofachiqui. A year or two before, a pestilence had threshed through that province, killing many. Talomeco, where the Spanish raided the burial temple mentioned earlier, was one of several towns without inhabitants because an epidemic had killed and driven off so many. The intruders found four large houses there filled with the bodies of people who had perished of the pestilence. The Spanish judged Cofachiqui heavily populated, but its citizens said their number had been much greater before the epidemic. De Soto entered Cofachiqui on the heels of a medical disaster, just as he had with Pizarro in Peru.[37]

How could this pestilence have reached so far into the interior from European settlements, presuming that it was an Old World importation? Any epidemic in Mexico could have swung around the Gulf through the medium of the coastal tribes and plunged inland along the thickly populated waterways. A number of ships riding the Gulf Stream from Havana were driven by hurricanes on to the shoals along the Florida coast, and their survivors, struggling ashore, could have brought infectious disease with them. And there were Whites, a few of them, living on the mainland already. De Soto obtained one as an interpreter at the beginning of his invasion in Florida, a survivor of the same abortive expedition that had left Cabeza de Vaca to wander off across Texas. De Soto's men found in Cofachiqui a Christian dirk, two Castilian axes, and a rosary, which presumably had found their way there via Amerindian trade routes from the coast or even from Mexico. Infectious disease can tag along with commerce just as effectively as with any other kind of human intercourse. The Old World and many of her creatures had already penetrated the interior of North America by the time De Soto's men sprang into the surf and dragged their boats ashore.[38]

The epidemics continued to arrive and to do their work of extermination, as they did in every part of the Americas we know anything about in the sixteenth and seventeenth centuries. To cite but one, in 1585–6, Sir Francis Drake led a large fleet to the Cape Verde islands, where his men picked up a dangerous communicable disease, and then sailed off to raid the Spanish Main, but so many of the English were sick and dying that the venture failed miserably. Seeking redress, he attacked the Spanish colony at St Augustine, Florida, infecting the local people with the Cape Verde epidemic. The Amerindians, "at first coming of our men died very fast, and said amongst themselves, it was the English god that made them die so fast." Presumably the disease proceeded on into the interior.[39]

When the French penetrated into the hinterlands behind the coast of the Gulf of Mexico, where De Soto had fought so many battles with so many peoples, they found few to oppose their intrusion. And the decline in Amerindian numbers continued; indeed, it probably accelerated. In 6 years, the last of the Mound Builders, the Natchez, with their pyramid-top temples and their supreme leader, the Great Sun, diminished by one-third. One of the Frenchmen wrote, unintentionally echoing the Protestant, John Winthrop: "Touching these savages, there is a thing that I cannot omit to remark to you, it is that it appears visibly that God wishes that they yield their place to new peoples."[40]

The exchange of infectious diseases – that is, of germs, of living things having geographical points of origin just like visible creatures – between the Old World and its American colonies has been wondrously one-sided, as one-sided and one-way as the exchanges of people, weeds, and animals. The Americas do have their own distinctive pathogens, those of at least Carrion's disease and Chagas's disease. Oddly, these very unpleasant and sometimes fatal diseases do not travel well and have never established themselves in the Old World.[41] Venereal syphilis may be the New World's only important disease export, and it has, for all its notoriety, never stopped population growth in the Old World.[42] *Niguas*, as Fernándo de Oviedo called the tropical American chigger causing barefoot Spaniards so much trouble in the sixteenth century, reached Africa in 1872 and spread across the continent as an epidemic of lost toes and fatal secondary infections of tetanus, but it has since retreated to the nuisance category and has never changed the Old World's demographic history.[43] Europe was magnanimous in the quantity and quality of the torments it sent across the seams of Pangaea. By contrast, its colonies, epidemiologically impecunious to begin with, were hesitant to export even the pathogens they did have. The unevenness of the exchange operated to the overwhelming advantage of the European invaders, and to the crushing disadvantage of the peoples whose ancestral homes were on the losing side of the seams of Pangaea.

NOTES

This essay is reprinted from *Ecological Imperialism: The Biological Expansion of Europe, 900–1900* (Cambridge, 1986), by permission of Cambridge University Press.

1 Alfred W. Crosby, "Virgin Soil Epidemics as a Factor in the Aboriginal Depopulation in America," *William and Mary Quarterly*, 3rd ser., 33 (April 1976):293–4.
2 Donald Joralemon, "New World Depopulation and the Case of Disease," *Journal of Anthropological Research* 38 (Spring 1982):118.
3 This is, of course, a matter of ambiguities and controversies. See Calvin Martin, *Keepers of the Game. Indian-Animal Relationships and the Fur Trade* (Berkeley: University of California Press, 1978), 48; William Denevan, "Introduction," *The Native Population of the Americas in 1492*, ed. William Denevan (Madison: University of Wisconsin Press, 1976), 5; Marshall T. Newman, "Aboriginal New World Epidemiology and Medical Care, and the Impact of Old World Disease Imports," *American Journal of Physical Anthropolgy* 45 (November 1976):671; Henry R. Dobyns, *Their Number Become Thinned, Native American Population Dynamics in Eastern North America* (Knoxville: University of Tennessee Press, 1983), 34.
4 Bartolomé de las Casas, *Historia de las Indias*, ed. Agustín Millares Carlo (México: Fondo de Cultura Economica, 1951), 1:332; *Journals and Other Documents of the Life and Voyages of Christopher Columbus*, trans. Samuel Eliot Morison (New York: Heritage Press, 1963), 68, 93; *The Four Voyages of Christopher Columbus*, trans. J. M. Cohen (Baltimore, Md: Penguin Books, 1969), 151. For slightly different numbers, see Peter Martyr D'Anghera, *De orbo novo*, trans. F. A. MacNutt (New York: Putnam, 1912), 1:66; Andrés Bernáldez, *Historia de los reyes católicos don Fernando y doña Isabel*, in *Crónicas de los reyes de Castilla desde don Alfonso el Sabio, hasta los católicos don Fernando y doña Isabel* (Madrid: M. Rivadeneyra, 1878), 3:660.

5 Bernáldez, *Historia de los reyes católicos*, 3:668; *Journals and Other Documents of Columbus*, 226–7.

6 Macfarlane Burnet and David O. White, *Natural History of Infectious Disease* (Cambridge: Cambridge University Press, 1972), 100.

7 There are sequels galore to this story. For instance, Jacques Cartier returned to France from his 1534 voyage to Canada with 10 Amerindians on board. In 7 years all had died of European diseases but one, a young girl. See Bruce G. Trigger, *The Children of Aataentsic, A History of the Huron People to 1660* (Montreal: McGill-Queen's University Press, 1976), 1:200–1.

8 I shall always be referring to the often fatal variola major smallpox. The mild variola minor did not appear until late in the nineteenth century. See Donald R. Hopkins, *Princes and Peasants, Smallpox in History* (Chicago: University of Chicago Press, 1983), 5–6.

9 Michael W. Flinn, *The European Demographic System 1500–1800* (Baltimore, Md: Johns Hopkins Press, 1981), 62–3; Ann G. Carmichael, "Infection, Hidden Hunger, and History," in *Hunger and History, The Impact of Changing Food Production and Consumption Patterns on Society*, ed. Robert I. Rotberg and Theodore K. Rabb (Cambridge: Cambridge University Press, 1985), 57.

10 Alfred W. Crosby, *The Columbian Exchange, Biological and Cultural Consequences of 1492* (Westport, Conn.: Greenwood Press, 1972), 47–58.

11 Harold E. Driver, *Indians of North America* (Chicago: University of Chicago Press, 1969), map 6; Jane Pyle, "A Reexamination of Aboriginal Population Claims for Argentina," in *The Native Population of the Americas in 1492*, ed. William Denevan (Madison: University of Wisconsin Press, 1976), 184–204; Dobyns, *Their Number Become Thinned*, 259.

12 *The Merck Manual*, 12th edn (Rahway, NJ: Merck Sharp & Dohme Research Laboratories, 1972), 37–9; Martin Dobrizhoffer, *An Account of the Abipones, an Equestrial People of Paraguay* (London: John Murray, 1822), 2:338.

13 John Duffy, "Smallpox and the Indians in the American Colonies," *Bulletin of the History of Medicine* 25 (July–August 1951):327.

14 William Bradford, *Of Plymouth Plantation*, ed. Samuel Eliot Morison (New York: Knopf, 1952), 271.

15 Trigger, *Children of Aataenstic*, 2:588–602.

16 Dobyns, *Their Number Become Thinned*, 15.

17 Crosby, "Virgin Soil Epidemics," 290–1.

18 Juan López de Velasco, *Geografía y descripción universal de las Indias desde el año de 1571 al de 1574* (Madrid: Establecimiento Tipográfico de Fortanet, 1894), 552.

19 Pedro Lautaro Ferrer, *Historia general de la medicina en Chile*, vol. 1, *Desde 1535 hasta la inauguración de la Universidad de Chile en 1843* (Santiago de Chile: Talca, de J. Martín Garrido C., 1904), 254–5; José Luis Molinari, *Historia de la medicina Argentina* (Buenos Aires: Imprenta López, 1937), 98; Dauril Alden and Joseph C. Miller,

"Unwanted Cargoes" (unpublished manuscript, University of Washington, Seattle).

20 Roberto H. Marfany, *El Indio en la colonización de Buenos Aires* (Buenos Aires: Talleres Gráficos de la Penitenciaría Nacional de Buenos Aires, 1940), 24; Molinari, *Historia de la medicina Argentina,* 98–9; Pedro Leon Luque, "La medicina en la epoca Hispanica," *Historia general de la medicina Argentina* (Córdoba: Dirección General de Publicaciones, 1976), 50–1; Eliseo Cantón, *Historia de la medicina en el Río de la Plata* (Madrid: Imp. G. Hernández y Galo Saez, 1928), 1:369–74; Alden and Miller, "Unwanted Cargoes."

21 Rafael Schiaffino, *Historia de la medicina en el Uruguay* (Montevideo: Imprenta Nacional, 1927–52), 1:416–17, 419; Dobrizhoffer, *Abipones,* 240.

22 Thomas Falkner, *A Description of Patagonia* (Chicago: Armann & Armann, 1935), 98, 102–3, 117; *Handbook of South American Indians,* ed. Julian H. Steward (Washington DC: United States Government Printing Office, 1946–59), 6:309–10. See also Guillermo Fúrlong, *Entre las pampas de Buenos Aires* (Buenos Aires: Talleres Gráficos "San pablo," 1938), 59.

23 Cantón, *Historia de la medicina,* 1:373–4.

24 Quoted in abbreviated form from Alice Marriott and Carol Rachlin, *American Indian Mythology* (New York: New American Library, 1968), 174–5.

25 *Winthrop Papers,* 1631–1637 (Boston: Massachusetts Historical Society, 1943), 3:167.

26 Alvar Nuñez Cabeza de Vaca, *Relation of Nuñez Cabeza de Vaca* (United States: Readex Microprint Corp., 1966), 74–5, 80.

27 Daniel Drake, *Malaria in the Interior Valley of North America, a Selection,* ed. Norman D. Levine (Urbana: University of Illinois Press, 1964), *passim.*

28 This is as good a place as any to deal with the old legend of intentional European bacteriological warfare. The colonists certainly would have liked to wage such a war and did talk about giving infected blankets and such to the indigenes, and they may even have done so a few times, but by and large the legend is just that, a legend. Before the development of modern bacteriology at the end of the nineteenth century, diseases did not come in ampules, and there were no refrigerators in which to store the ampules. Disease was, in practical terms, people who were sick – an awkward weapon to aim at anyone. As for infected blankets, they might or might not work. Furthermore, and most important, the intentionally transmitted disease might swing back on the white population. As Whites lived longer and longer in the colonies, more and more of them were born there and did *not* go through the full gauntlet of Old World childhood diseases. These people were dedicated to quarantining smallpox, not to spreading it.

29 Jacquetta Hawkes, ed., *Atlas of Ancient Archeology* (New York: McGraw-Hill, 1974), 234.

30 Richard B. Morris, ed., *Encyclopedia of American History* (New York: Harper & Bros. 1953), 442.

31 Jesse D. Jennings, *Prehistory of North America* (New York: McGraw-Hill, 1974), 220–65; Melvin L. Fowler, "A Pre-Columbian Urban Center on the Mississippi," *Scientific American* 223 (August 1975):93–101; Robert Silverberg, *The Mound Builders* (New York: Ballantine Books, 1974), 3, 16–81.

32 *Narratives of the Career of Hernando de Soto*, trans. Buckingham Smith (New York: Allerton Book Co., 1922), 1:65, 70–1.

33 Garcilaso de la Vega, *The Florida of the Inca*, trans. John Varner and Jeannette Varner (Austin: University of Texas Press, 1962), 315–25.

34 Dobyns, *Their Number Become Thinned*, 294.

35 John R. Swanton, *The Indians of the Southeastern United States*, Smithsonian Institution, Bureau of American Ethnology Bulletin no. 137 (Washington DC, 1946), 11–21; Driver, *Indians of North America*, map 6; Alfred Kroeber, *Cultural and Natural Areas of Native North America* (Berkeley: University of California Press, 1963), 88–91; William G. Haag, "A Prehistory of Mississippi," *Journal of Mississippi History* 17 (April 1955):107; Dobyns, *Their Number Become Thinned*, 298.

36 Erhard Rostlund, "The Geographical Range of the Historic Bison in the Southeast," *Annals of the Association of American Geographers* 50 (December 1970):395–407.

37 *Narratives of the Career of De Soto*, 1:66–7; Garcilaso de la Vega, *Florida of the Inca*, 298, 300, 302, 315, 325.

38 *Narratives of the Career of De Soto*, 1:27, 67; 2:14.

39 Charles Creighton, *A History of Epidemics in Britain* (Cambridge: Cambridge University Press, 1891), 1:585–9; Julian S. Corbett, ed., *Papers Relating to the Navy during the Spanish War, 1585–1587*, Navy Records no. 11 (London, 1898) 11:26.

40 John R. Swanton, *Indian Tribes of the Lower Mississippi Valley and Adjacent Coast of the Gulf of Mexico*, Smithsonian Institution, Bureau of American Ethnology Bulletin no. 43 (Washington DC, 1911), 39. See also Dobyns, *Their Number Become Thinned*, 247–90; George R. Milner, "Epidemic Disease in the Postcontact Southeast: A Reappraisal," *Mid-Continent Journal of Archeology* 5, no. 1 (1980):39–56. The archeologists are beginning to produce physical evidence that supports the hypothesis of fierce epidemics, swift population decline, and radical cultural change in the Gulf region in the sixteenth century. See Caleb Curren, *The Protohistoric Period in Central Alabama* (Camden, Ala.: Alabama Tombigbee Regional Commission, 1984), 54, 240, 242.

41 T. D. Stewart, "A Physical Anthropologist's View of the Peopling of the New World," *Southwest Journal of Anthropology* 16 (Autumn 1960):266–7; Philip H. Manson-Bahr, *Manson's Tropical Diseases* (Baltimore, Md: Williams & Wilkins, 1972), 108–9, 143, 579–82, 633–4. See also Newman, "Aboriginal New World Epidemiology," *American Journal of Physical Anthropology* 45 (November 1976):669.

42 Crosby, *Columbian Exchange*, 122–64.
43 Crosby, *Columbian Exchange*, 209; J. R. Audy, "Medical Ecology in Relation to Geography," *British Journal of Clinical Practice* 12 (February 1958):109–10.

3

TRAGEDY AND SACRIFICE IN THE HISTORY OF SLAVERY

Patrick Manning

Slavery in the Americas had its roots both in Africa and in Europe. In his 1990 book Slavery and African Life, *Patrick Manning explores the African origins of American slavery as well as the impact which the transatlantic demand for slaves had upon Africa. Manning, although primarily an economic and demographic historian, wrestles with the philosophical and historical meaning of slavery and the slave trade in the first pages of this selection. His book treats both the Occidental slave trade (meaning chiefly the transatlantic one, but also the smaller current of slave sales from Africa to Europe) and the Oriental slave trade (from sub-Saharan Africa to the Middle East). Here we have excised most of his remarks on the Oriental slave trade, which had little bearing on the Atlantic world.*

In slave-trade and African slavery studies, inevitably, information is far richer for the more recent centuries. In many cases Manning, like other scholars, must rely on eighteenth- and nineteenth-century data – when the slave trade was at its apogee. But, unlike other scholars, he is careful not to project these modern data on to the more distant past.

From the American side of the Atlantic, slavery arose as a result of several factors. Foremost among them was the Europeans' desire not to work (Edmund Morgan will show this in exquisite detail in our next selection.) In trying to implant new societies in the Americas, they searched for alternative sources of labor. The Amerindians could not be counted upon, so attention focused upon Africa, where, by the fifteenth century, Europeans had begun to establish trading outposts. Manning's narrative traces the way in which the Europeans changed the nature and magnitude of the existing African slave trade as well as the way in which slavery contributed the labor essential to implanting European societies in the Americas. Race is not Patrick Manning's

40

central concern, but students would do well to consider it as they read this essay. There is no denying that the Europeans were white and the Africans were not. To what extent did this influence the Europeans' decision to enslave Africans?

* * *

Tragedy is an imitation of an action that is serious, complete, and possessing magnitude . . . and effecting through pity and fear the catharsis of such emotions . . .

There are in tragedy . . . six constituent elements, viz. Plot, Character, Language, Thought, Spectacle and Melody.

Aristotle, *Poetics*[1]

To perform a sacrifice is, primarily, to try to outwit death . . .

When war becomes the servant of sacrifice, when a people decides to appropriate the lives of others in order to incessantly feed its gods, the religious system is lost in madness.

Luc de Heusch, *Sacrifice in Africa*[2]

The spectacle of slavery – with its chains, slave ships, and broken families – touched on every century of the modern era, including our own. This study of African slavery in the modern world focuses primarily on economic history. Yet the influence of slavery has extended beyond the economy to transform human emotions and trouble the human spirit. For this reason I have chosen to integrate spiritual and dramatic terms into this tale of costs and benefits: slavery was a sacrifice of Africans for the transformation of the wider world, and slavery was a tragedy for the people of Africa.

African slavery is of magnitude not only for its moral and philosophical meaning, but for its significance in modern economic history. I shall make no attempt to segregate logic from passion. Instead, I shall seek directly to confront the moral conflicts, the pain and suffering, in order to draw out of the reader pity – or empathy, to use the more modern term – for the victims of slavery on all sides, and fear that we may ourselves fall into a similar dilemma. The experiencing of these emotions, however, will arise from the context of a cold, hard analysis of demographic and economic facts.

The tragic experience of slavery in the modern world left

41

Africans depleted in population, divided irremediably among themselves, retarded economically, and despised as an inferior race in a world which had built a vision of racial hierarchy based on the inspiration of their enslavement.

To portray the history of slavery as a tragedy is to emphasize that it is no morality play, medieval or modern. The cast of characters is not divided into innocent Africans pursued by evil Europeans; nor do I divide Africans themselves into the moral and the immoral. There were many innocents, particularly the children, and there were those who, overcome by consistent temptation, became truly evil exploiters of slaves. The protagonists here, however, are those who lived normal African lives and who, in so doing, involved themselves in slavery and in the slave trade. By removing African individuals and societies from any presumption of innocence, we bring them on to the stage as fully drawn historical actors: protagonists with the full range of emotions, goals, interests, flaws, insights, and blindness expected of tragic heroes.

The mistake of our African protagonists was their willingness to participate in slavery and in the slave trade, even if they did so only to dispose of enemies in revenge, or in hopes of securing a fortune which might enable their family or their kingdom to grow and profit. The tragic results of these attempts to advance themselves at the expense of others emerge out of the logic of the plot itself, though over a period of more than a century rather than in a single episode. Developments in the story included the decline in the African population, the disruption of countless families, and the individual falls of the mighty.

If the enslavement of Africans was a tragedy for Africa, it was also, from the standpoint of the wider world, a sacrifice. Africa's loss was the gain of the Occident – and of the Orient.

Sacrifice takes place in many ways and on many levels. African families performed sacrifices in memory of ancestors, to renew the earth's fertility, and to pay tribute to their rulers. Merchants and planters in Africa and elsewhere sacrificed the enjoyment of their current wealth for investments intended to bring later profit. Christians celebrated the ritual of the Eucharist, to participate in God's sacrifice of his son for the salvation of man. The meanings of these and other sacrifices came to overlap inextricably through the experience of slavery.[3]

42

An act of sacrifice entails distinct roles: the sacrificer who performs the act, the authority to whom the sacrifice is made, and – in the case of human sacrifice – the victim. The sacrificer offers up something of value in order to survive a threat, or to improve the conditions of a community. The victim gives up his or her life, but may leave behind the memory of having made a contribution to the community. The authority in whose honor the sacrifice is made receives it physically or symbolically, and benefits from the prestige of recognition.

If all could agree that slavery involved sacrifice, each tended to see his own sacrifice as central, and each tended to define the sacrificing community rather narrowly. African parents sacrificed their children involuntarily to the attacks of slave raiders, and reluctantly but sometimes voluntarily to the assault of famine and the demands of tax collectors. African monarchs and merchants handed their slaves over to European merchants, and accepted money and gifts in return. But they too could claim to be acting out the will of the gods. They could claim to be using their compensation to provide nourishment and hope for their communities, just as, in time of famine, one might sacrifice an ox in honor of the gods, yet divide the meat among the community.

The slaves themselves – the millions sentenced to death or transportation – were clearly and uniquely the sacrificial victims. Yet in another sense, those slaves who survived were also sacrificers, for they had to contribute their energies to the wealth of a new community. As the same time, plantation owners saw the sacrifice as their own, considering the sums they had to pay and the food they had to advance for slaves before they could achieve any profit. The fact that they defined the slaves as outside their community made it easy to ignore slave contributions either as victims or as sacrificers. Through such reasoning the planters, much like African merchants and monarchs, could see themselves as sacrificers rather than as exploiters.

The authorities on whose altars slaves were sacrificed were both temporal and spiritual. Slaves taken by the Aro, an elite religious clan of eastern Nigeria, were sacrificed to the great oracle of Arochukwu – "eaten" by it – as the first step of their journey to the coast. Secular African authorities – monarchs and warlords – benefited as much as did African gods. In the

New World, slaves were sacrificed to the worldly ambitions of merchants and planters. The victims, once baptized, contributed as well to the glory of the Christian God.

In this complex web of need and greed, the nature, the meaning, and the effectiveness of the sacrifice are seen to shift with the standpoint of the participants. Sacrifice, at its best, strengthens and ultimately rewards a community, brings honor to the victim, ennobles the act of sacrifice, and propitiates the authority for whom it is performed. But sacrifice need not achieve its aims. There is the waste of an investment with no return, and the waste of a human sacrifice which brings neither honor to the victim nor recognition to the sacrificer.

Slavery brought material benefit – growth, if not equitable distribution – to the New World. More than 10 million slave immigrants reached the New World, where they performed much of the earliest, dirtiest, and most exhausting work of constructing an economic system which has since prospered enormously.[4] Slavery brought material benefits to Africa as well: not only in the form of goods purchased in exchange for slaves, but also through centers of manufacture and culture such as the city of Kano in the Nigerian savanna, whose nineteenth-century brilliance was due to the labor of slaves. In each of these cases the sacrifice yielded a tangible gain, but with a disproportionate level of waste: the devastation of the areas raided for slaves, the many lives lost in transit to the New World, and the many more lives brought to an early end in bondage.

The spiritual benefits and costs of slavery are more difficult to trace, but are no less important. They were distributed inequitably and with ironic consequences. For a time, the sacrifice of Africans did contribute to the glory of the Christian God, to worship of the idol of the market-place, and to prostration before the secular icons of Western civilization. Yet as time went on, the continued enslavement of Africans brought each of these into question. Leaders of the Christian faith, prophets of the new industrial order, and philosophers of civilization's development each turned against slavery as the eighteenth century came to an end. Thus the sacrifice of slavery ultimately brought about its own repudiation and a change in the ideals of the Western world. Ironically, however, in the course of their enlightenment Western leaders forgot the contributions of slaves to Christian faith, to economic progress, and to civilization's advance. The very term "Western civilization" serves to arrogate full credit for the present economic supremacy of the Atlantic nations to its European ancestors. Once the African sacrifice was forgotten, the rise of racism followed logically upon the end of slavery. Yet a further irony is that African gods and African ideals, having succumbed to the confusion of slavery, yielded for a time to conquest.

Why were Africans enslaved in such large numbers, and over such a wide area, that there grew up in Western thought an almost automatic connection between black people and slave status? Why did the European conquerors of the New World need to import so much labor? Why did it have to be African labor? And why, finally, did the laborers have to be in slave status?

In fact, the connection that has been made between Africans and slavery is often overdrawn. Slavery has been an institution common to many – perhaps most – societies in recorded history. What distinguishes Africa and Africans with regard to slavery, however, is *modernity*. The enslavement of Africans increased in the modern period, a time when enslavement of most other peoples was dying out. This was true in the Occidental and Oriental areas which imported African slaves; it was also true in Africa, where slavery expanded from a somewhat marginal institution to one of central importance during the modern period.

Orlando Patterson, in his cross-cultural, transhistorical study of slavery, demonstrates the near-universality of the slave condition, touching on ancient Mesopotamia, classical Greece, medieval Korea, the Vikings of Europe, and native North Americans, to name but a few of the societies he discusses.[5] Let us investigate this universality of slavery a bit further, in order to set African slavery in a broader context.*

During the Crusades – the Mediterranean religious wars of the eleventh through fifteenth centuries – Christians enslaved Moslems and Moslems enslaved Christians. These Crusades continued longest in the west, where the long Christian *reconquista* of the Iberian peninsula, along with wars in North Africa and piracy in the Mediterranean, served to keep slavery alive

---

* Manning proceeds to discuss slavery in the ancient Mediterranean, Asia, medieval Europe, and the Islamic world.

and well. Indeed, the Spanish and Portuguese voyages of discovery may be seen, in part, as extensions of the Crusades.

Meanwhile, the association between sugar and slavery took form in the medieval Mediterranean, and spread slowly from east to west. The Belgian historian Charles Verlinden has provided magnificent documentation of the early days of sugar production in Syria and Palestine, of its adoption by European Crusaders, of the use of slaves to perform the heavy labor of planting, cutting, and refining, and of the concentration of sugar prodution on islands, beginning with Cyprus, and then moving to Malta, the Balearic islands and later, with the early Atlantic voyages, the Canaries, the Madeiras, and particularly São Tomé.[6]

With the modern period, after 1500, slavery contracted in some areas of the world, in Europe, in China, and in parts of the Islamic world. One outstanding exception to this regression of slavery was Russia. Russian slavery was unusual in several respects: the slaves were Russian slaves of Russian masters, and they were often self-enslaved. That is, persons without land and unable to gain an existence sold themselves into slavery as a last resort. This system expanded greatly in the sixteenth and seventeenth centuries, and was replaced by the "second serfdom" of Russian peasants.[7] Another case of modern expansion of slavery was in the Dutch East Indies, where Dutch planters enslaved Indonesians for work on sugar and coffee plantations. Slavery, however, was gradually replaced with other forms of servile labor as the Dutch regime proceeded.[8] The demand for slaves in the Islamic heartland of the Middle East and North Africa remained at much the same level as the medieval era shaded into the modern, but the points of origin of the slaves moved southward: Black Sea slaves tended to be replaced by African slaves. In the New World, Spanish and Portuguese conquerors enslaved Indians as well as Africans in Central and South America during the sixteenth century, but by the seventeenth century almost all slaves in the Americas were of African origin.

The net result of all these transformations in the extent of slavery can be summarized by saying that in 1500 Africans and persons of African descent were a clear minority of the world's slave population, but that by 1700 Africans and persons of African descent had become the majority of the world's slave population. African slavery is a phenomenon of the modern world.

To explain why African slavery grew to such an extent in the modern period, and why it lasted so long, we will turn first to a narrative of its expansion, and then draw from the narrative some specific consideration of the demand for and the supply of African slaves.

THE OCCIDENTAL DEMAND FOR AFRICAN SLAVES

As the Portuguese first worked their way along the African coast from around 1440, they captured and purchased slaves which they took to Portugal and to such Atlantic islands as the Azores, the Madeira islands, the Cape Verde islands, the Canaries, and São Tomé. The slaves in Portugal were surprisingly numerous, but they were only part of a larger slave labor force including Arab and Andalusian (or Spanish Moslem) captives. The islands, on the other hand, which had been generally unpopulated, became miniature models of what was to develop in the New World.[9]

It is only with the New World that one can explain the European demand for large numbers of slaves. As the Spanish and Portuguese *conquistadores* strode across the Americas, they expropriated wealth and shipped it home until there was little left to seize. Soon enough, they found that they would have to satisfy their thirst for wealth by going beyond expropriation: they would have to *produce* wealth. But since these *conquistadores* had no intention of performing the work themselves, their desire to produce entailed the creation of a labor force under their control. Such a labor force would have to be both productive and cheap, for otherwise the cost of production and transportation would prevent the resulting goods from being sold on the distant markets of Europe, and no profit would be realized. The first impulse of the Spanish was to enslave the native Americans, but their high mortality and their continuing hope of escape made them unsatisfactory slaves.[10]

Epidemiology is one major factor which pointed toward a demand for African labor. The introduction of Old World diseases to the isolated New World populations decimated them. Smallpox, plague, typhus, yellow fever, and influenza carried away large numbers. While one may doubt the very high estimates of pre-Columbian population proposed by Dobyns and Borah (they estimate as many as 100 million inhabitants of the New World in 1492),* their estimated low point of some 5 million native Americans in the early seventeenth century can be accepted as plausible.[11] With such a rate of extinction, it is remarkable that the cultures and societies of the New World survived.

Of the Old World populations, the Africans had the misfortune and the advantage of living in the most disease-ridden area.[12] Malarial mortality rates for African children took a very heavy toll, but those who survived to maturity had near-immunity from malaria, from other African diseases, and also from many of the diseases known in Europe. For European adults not previously exposed to African malaria, on the other hand, the death rate in the first year of exposure ranged from 30 per cent to 50 per cent; death rates from New World malaria were slightly lower. So it was that Africans, all other things being equal, had the lowest mortality rate of any population in the New World.†

All other things were not equal, of course. The full picture of the Occidental demand for slaves must include not only this epidemiological factor, but other aspects of demography, institutional factors, and such economic factors as labor cost and the demand for slave produce, especially sugar. Since the slaves were given the heaviest work, a minimum of physical care, and poor social conditions, they died in large numbers and failed to bear enough children to reproduce themselves.

This leads us to consider the nature of the work as a cause for the demand for African labor and the demand for slaves in particular. Much of the work done by slaves was on sugar plantations and in mines, though they also provided a great deal of domestic service. We have already seen for the Mediterranean how the particular intensity of labor in sugar production always seemed to point to slavery. For mines as well, a coerced labor force presented great advantages for the

* More recent estimates by Noble David Cook, as yet unpublished, put the hemispheric population of Amerindians at about 35–40 million in 1492.
† Africans had the lowest mortality of any population in the New World wherever malaria (and yellow fever) prevailed; Manning's argument does not apply to the cooler zones, where tropical diseases had no influence.

owners. Africans mined gold in Brazil and various minerals in lowland Spanish territories.[13] (In one important exception, the silver mines of the *altiplano*, the Spanish relied on a workforce drawn from the local population – miners whose descendants are now the tin miners of Bolivia.)

Slaves did more than cut cane and mine gold: there was always a range of agricultural, domestic, and artisanal tasks to be performed. This range of tasks is one of the reasons for the remarkable stability in the age and sex composition of slaves purchased by Europeans from the fifteenth through the nineteenth centuries. For example, sixteenth-century Spanish settlers in the Canaries bought slaves ranging widely in age but averaging just over 20 years of age, of whom just over 60 per cent were male; prices of male slaves averaged 5 per cent higher than those of females.[14] These figures were similar to those for African slave exports over two centuries later. While the range of slave tasks was wide, the slaves were often prevented from becoming skilled artisans. But from manumitted slaves and free mulattos in sixteenth-century Peru and Mexico, for instance, there grew up classes of artisans whose ambitions and competitiveness brought down upon them wrath and restrictions from their Spanish competitors. This ethnic competition among Whites, mulattos, and free Blacks for artisanal work was to show up repeatedly in New World colonies.[15]

African disease resistance, the economic advantages of slavery in sugar and mine work, and the need to replenish lost slaves with new ones set the pattern for the demand for slaves. But new developments were required for the amplitude of this demand to increase. Among these was the entry of the Northern European powers into competition for power on the oceans. Early in the seventeenth century the Dutch, followed by the English and French, as well as the Danes, Swedes, and Brandenburgers,* scoured the oceans for treasure, trade, and colonies.[16] When the Dutch took much of Brazil in 1630, they showed little interest in European settlement and instead got right to work on extending Brazilian sugar plantations, implementing a number of significant and cost-saving technical improvements as they did so. They also began to seek out new sources of African slaves. The Dutch experience in Brazil,

---

* The Brandenburgers were (and are) Prussian Germans.

while it ended with their expulsion at the hands of the Portuguese in 1654, was the harbinger of the new order. British and
French colonies in the West Indian islands began with the
settlement of Europeans but within a generation sugar showed
itself to be the most remunerative crop and a slave population
progressively crowded out the white settlers.[17]

One may ask why the European demand for sugar increased
so rapidly at this time. Part of it was the reduction of the cost
in sugar brought by improved technology and perhaps cheaper
shipping. More importantly, European consumption habits
were changing, with the advance of urbanization. With
changes in the countryside, bee-keeping had been undercut
and production of honey reduced.[18]

With these factors now in place, sugar plantations expanded
steadily, and with them increased their need for slave labor.
The flow of slaves to the New World, which came to exceed
the number going to the Orient in about 1650, continued to
increase for a century at a rate of about 2 per cent per year.

THE SUPPLY OF AFRICAN SLAVES

This continuing upward spiral of slave purchases was possible,
however, only because of the relatively low prices at which
African slaves could be bought. Transportation costs for
moving Africans to the New World were lower than for Europeans, but this was not a major factor. So the explanation for
the concentration of modern slavery on Africans is not complete until it accounts for the supply of slaves from Africa.

Could it be, as some have argued, that Africa was simply
burdened with a surplus population? Was Africa overpopulated in relation to its resources? Were thousands – ultimately
millions – of Africans incapable of making valuable contributions to their societies? Or, to put it more gently, is it possible that the captives were removed from Africa without significantly reducing African levels of production?[19] The error
in such approaches becomes apparent immediately when one
considers Africa's relative abundance of land and labor, the
two great factors of production in agricultural societies. For
most parts of precolonial Africa, land, rather than labor, was
abundant. African patterns of shifting cultivation, preserved
well into the twentieth century, demonstrate the ready avail-

ability of land. Farmers typically opened up new fields every second year, and left their previous fields in fallow for ten years or more. Labor, by comparison to land, was relatively scarce, and its utilization involved difficult choices. The opening of new fields was limited not so much by the shortage of land as by the shortage of labor. And if labor was not initially in short supply, it certainly should have become so in the wake of the disorientation and depopulation that was to come in the eighteenth and nineteenth centuries.[20]

To argue in this way, however, is to propose a paradox: if labor was the limiting resource in Africa, why did Africans agree to sell so many million able-bodied persons to be carried away from their homes? A clue to the solution is suggested in a cynical old saw: "Every man has his price." Or, to update the language a little, European slave buyers were able to make African merchants an offer they could not refuse.

The resolution of this paradox relies on an insight offered by Jack Goody in one of his wide-ranging, cross-cultural studies. Goody divided the peoples of the world according to their technology, into peoples of the plow and peoples of the hoe. Peoples of the plow – in Europe, North Africa, and the Middle East – were able, thanks to an efficient technology, to produce a relatively large amount of agricultural output and to support relatively large urban populations. Peoples of the hoe, regardless of their individual levels of energy and initiative, were doomed by their technology to produce smaller amounts of agricultural output. The reasons for the technical inferiority of African agriculture, in turn, were technical rather than social – the difficulty of using draft animals because of tsetse fly and sleeping sickness; and lateritic tropical soils, easily leached, which generally respond poorly to plowing.[21]

Thus, to the degree that a person is valued in terms of the value of goods he or she can produce, the value of an African in African society – even where labor was the limiting resource – was less than that of a European in European society. Since agricultural labor was the primary producer of value in early modern society (in Africa, Europe, and elsewhere) the value of an agricultural worker's productivity set the value of labor in general in a given society.[22]

The logic of African supply of slaves depends, therefore, on the notion that slaves in the New World were more productive than free producers in Africa, with a margin large enough that New World slave owners could pay for the costs of transportation, mortality, and seasoning of their slaves. As long as African agricultural technology, constricted by the limits of the hoe, was trapped at a level of productivity below that of Europeans, European buyers were able to pay consistently more than the value of an African person's produce at home.[23]

So far I have argued that the value of a person (in this case the price of a slave) is determined most fundamentally by his or her productivity: the additional value that person can produce. But every price is a compromise, accepted provisionally by buyer and seller, and prices of slaves were influenced by many more factors than productivity. These additional factors in price determination can generally be classified either as market factors or as institutional factors.

Normally a key element in the price of a commodity is the cost of its production. The problem here is that slaves were "produced" by their families, but were then carried off without the family ever gaining compensation. That is, the economics of slave capture, as Philip Curtin has noted, are the economics of theft.[24] To the captors, the "cost" of a captive was the cost of turning a free person into a captive (that is the cost of capturing, transporting, and sustaining the captive), rather than the much higher cost of "producing" the captive (that is, the cost of raising and educating a person, borne by his or her family). The initial captors sold their captives at low prices precisely because of their low costs in acquiring slaves. This was a market factor, in the sense that these captives were sold at prices well below the normal value of a laborer because they were stolen. But it was also an institutional factor, in the sense that the institutions of enslavement – the structures permitting the theft of humans from their families – made labor appear cheap.[25]

Prices of slaves in Africa were also held down by the limited demand for slave labor or for slave-produced produce: while monarchs relied on slaves to produce for the palace entourage, few other Africans had the wealth to sustain many slaves, nor could they find purchasers for goods the slaves might produce. Yet another type of market factor was the relative preference of European buyers for male slaves, and the preference of African buyers for female slaves.

One key institutional factor keeping African slave prices low was the political fragmentation of the continent. For, even given the attractive prices slave purchasers might offer African merchants, there can be no doubt that many Africans, arguing on the basis of personal and societal welfare, opposed the enslavement and export of slaves. Such reactions are reflected in the policy statements and the actions of sixteenth-century kings in Jolof, Benin, and Congo.[26] Yet they were insufficient. One way or another, European slave buyers could always find an African who would supply them with slaves. It only required a few greedy or opportunistic persons, who felt they should enrich themselves rather than resist the inexorable pressures of supply and demand, to keep the slave trade alive. Those suppliers, in turn, rapidly became wealthy enough to become a focus of power to whom others had to accommodate.

On the other hand, big men, slave merchants, warlords, all had, through their own greed, inspired feelings of cupidity and revenge in their allies and enemies. So the fortunes built up by slave exporters, while impressive, were often short-lived, as their allies or enemies expropriated them. In yet another reversal, however, the leaders of a successful movement of revenge against African slavers found themselves in control of captives, and then found it to their advantage to sell these captives as slaves for export.[27]

There are, however, records of efforts – some successful – to restrict the scope of enslavement. The rise of the kingdom of Asante in the Gold Coast region, for instance, brought a virtual end to the export of slaves from the area it governed. On the other hand, the state was active in buying and capturing slaves from surrounding areas, with the result that the total volume of Gold Coast slave exports grew in the decades following the rise of Asante. Similarly, the Oyo empire of the Bight of Benin was able to prevent the export of slaves from within its borders as long as it remained strong. However, with the nineteenth-century decline and collapse of Oyo, exports of Yoruba slaves skyrocketed. The nearby but smaller kingdom of Danhomè expanded dramatically at the beginning of the eighteenth century, and at least discussed the policy of attempting to halt slave exports – a policy that was certainly relevant for a region whose population was declining as a result of slave exports. But Danhomè itself was rendered tributary by Oyo and prevented from conquering its whole region, so that the situation was frozen for a century with implacable enemies within easy reach of one another, and the toll in warfare and slave exports continued to be inordinately high.[28]

These examples of the relentless growth of slave exports show that slave exports in many ways fit the model of primary exports from Third World countries in recent years: as prices rose, so did the quantity of slaves supplied. But slaves were unlike exports of rice or palm-oil, in that the "producers" of slaves could not simply plant more of their resource to meet increases in demand. The expansion of the slave trade can more accurately be compared to the case of overfishing, where the resource is ultimately unable to renew itself, especially given the long time required to bring a human to adulthood. Those who harvested the slaves were motivated by the higher prices, but the real producers – the families of those to be enslaved – received nothing in reward.[29]

If African agricultural productivity had been as high as that in the Occident, prices for African labor would have been bid up until only a trickling stream of laborers flowed across the Atlantic, rather than the great rush of laborers who crossed the ocean in the holds of slave ships. But the low level of African productivity did not in itself make the slave trade inevitable. Indeed, it is at least an interesting thought experiment – a counterfactual – to consider what would have happened if Europeans had engaged Africans as wage or contract laborers, i.e. if African political fragmentation had not been a factor. African workers would still have been cheaper than Europeans and might have emigrated if offered a sufficiently high remuneration. The Europeans engaging this labor, in paying a higher remuneration, would have earned lower profit levels, which would have reduced the growth rate and the extent of the New World economic system to that degree. African merchants would not have received the earnings from the sale of slaves. On the other hand, after a time African families would have received remittances from the migrants to the New World (much as European families of the nineteenth and twentieth centuries received remittances from sons and daughters in the Americas). Further, most of the mortality and disorder accompanying enslavement might have been avoided; more generally, Africa would have experienced in much less severe form the contradiction between the grasping for private gain and the achievement of public social welfare. The great private gains to be won through slavery, however, meant that this contract-labor alternative was passed by.

Yet perhaps (the reader may argue) it was not economic logic that brought Africans to sell slaves, but rather social tradition. After all, had not Africans sold slaves across the Sahara for centuries? Was not African participation in the Occidental trade but the continuation of an established pattern? Indeed, Paul Lovejoy has emphasized the Islamic links in the earliest Portuguese slave trade along the west coast of Africa.[30] This set of facts might encourage us to treat the slave trade not as an economically or socially rational (if inhuman) activity, but as an addiction or a contagion, a behavior based on non-rational motivation. In such a view slavery, once begun, continues to replicate itself until it runs out its course, regardless of economic or social consequences. While it does help to explain the propagation of slavery, it cannot explain slavery's origins. The motivation of revenge and the logic of contagion served to catalyze the spread of enslavement, but did not cause it.

We have considered the causes of the slave trade, particularly that linking Africa and the Occident. This combination of forces for the European demand for slave labor and African willingness to supply slaves at a relatively low price set in place, by the end of the seventeenth century, a powerful mechanism for large-scale slave migration.

SOCIAL PRESSURES TO PARTICIPATE IN SLAVERY*

As the continental volume of African slave exports grew toward a peak sometimes exceeding 100,000 slaves per year, more and more social institutions were developed and refined to facilitate the collection and transportation of the slaves. Here we will categorize those as institutions of capture, institutions of enslavement, mercantile institutions of transport and com-

---

* Moving from his discussion of the causes of the slave trade to the social pressures upon Africans to participate in the slave trade, Manning shifts his focus from the seventeenth century to the eighteenth and nineteenth centuries. He does so because of the paucity of historical sources for earlier centuries.

merce, and state institutions of protection, regulation, and taxation. In addition, the African societies incorporating slaves required structures for that incorporation, institutions which paralleled the New World process of "seasoning."[31]

The recruitment of slaves – that is, the enslavement of persons in Africa – took place in many different ways. One important means of recruitment is that many people were born into slavery. Sometimes, but not always, being born into slavery provided the slave with some added rights and protections by comparison to those enslaved after birth, who were usually foreigners. In other cases, non-slave relations of dependency shifted subtly into slavery. Of the many loyal dependants of Angolan rulers, for instance, some suddenly found themselves shackled and exported when their lord's debts were called in by merchants. In most cases, however, the act of enslavement was explicit and forcible. Meanwhile, the slave populations of Africa, the Occident, and the Orient were almost never able to maintain themselves. The result was a continuing demand for new slaves.[32]

The mechanisms of capture were many. They included (in rough order of their significance) warfare, in which the slaves resulted as prisoners of war and booty; *razzia* or raids, aimed particularly at the capture of slaves, but also of other booty; kidnapping on an individual level; court proceedings in which persons were enslaved for violating the rules of society; witchcraft accusations in which persons were enslaved for carrying on illicit supernatural activities; exactions of tribute, in which tributaries were required to render up some of their own to a higher authority; and self-enslavement or sale of one's kin in the wake of famine or epidemic. These mechanisms were of varied importance in different times and climes. Further, the various mechanisms of capture entailed different dynamics of capture, enslaving different types of persons, and imposing different levels of mortality on the captives.

Warfare was the most prominent means for the capture of slaves. For the Bight of Benin, for instance, the seemingly endless wars of the late seventeenth and early eighteenth centuries coincided with the heaviest export of slaves from that region. For seventeenth-century Angola, John Thornton has retrieved descriptions of wars involving armies of several thousand on each side, with a baggage train enclosed within each army consisting mainly of women, so that each side represented, in Thornton's phrase, a "preselected population" ready for export. Slave merchants waited nearby to purchase the vanquished from the victors.[33]

On a different scale from wars were slave raids. Here the balance of forces was less equal, and less effort went into political justification for the raid. The wanderings of the Ngoni in nineteenth-century East Africa may be classified as half conquest, half raid. The annual wars of Danhomè in the nineteenth century were mostly great slave raids. The razzias of Bambara kings and of smaller groups in the western Sudan brought in a large number of slaves. For a detailed description of a slave raid, we may turn to Gustav Nachtigal's 1872 description of a Baghirmi raid on the village of Kôli.[34] There were cases where Europeans led the raids – in Senegambia, Upper Guinea, and Angola – but European-led raids counted for little in the aggregate.[35]

A still smaller scale of slave procurement was kidnapping. Here isolated individuals, usually young and particularly female, were captured and whisked off for sale by small bands. This is the way in which Olaudah Equiano* was enslaved in Igbo country in the eighteenth century, and it was perhaps the main method of slave procurement in the Bight of Biafra. The price of venturing out alone could be high. Kidnapping took place to some degree all over the continent. It would seem that the level of captive mortality in kidnapping was less than in warfare and raiding.[36]

Quite a different mechanism of enslavement was judicial enslavement. The more prominent slavery became, the more common it became for the punishment of enslavement to be meted out to serious offenders, for murder, incest, or threats to authority. The most famous such institution was the Aro oracle of the Bight of Biafra, where the oracle rendered decisions in great disputations brought before it, but consumed the defeated party. That is, those condemned were eaten† by the oracle and were then spewed out as slaves and marched

---

* Olaudah Equiano wrote his memoirs, a valuable document for slavery and slave-trade history: *The Interesting Narrative of the Life of Olaudah Equiano or Gustavus Vassa the African* (London, 1789). A recent abridgment, edited by Paul Edwards, was published by Heinemann International (London, 1989 [1967])

† Symbolically.

to the coast for export. In Portuguese Angola, which Jan Vansina has described as an African state, plaintiffs in any court case who wished to appeal to the next level were called upon to pay a fee in slaves in order to get a hearing.[37]

Tribute and taxation represented another method of slave recruitment. The famous *baqt* paid by Dongola to the rulers of Egypt for several centuries included some 400 slaves per year. The tribute paid by Danhomè to Oyo from the 1730s to 1818 included eighty-two slaves per year. Tribute-payers sometimes enslaved strangers to pay as tribute, but at other times they were forced to choose among their own. Those condemned to judicial enslavement when they were influential, sometimes arranged to send substitutes.[38]

Accusations of witchcraft could also end in the enslavement of the accused, and this mechanism of enslavement was relatively common in the areas of Loango and Angola. Indeed, once slave exports from the area ended, the general level of anxiety about witches seems to have risen, since they could not be disposed of so easily, and the tendency was to execute them instead. Condemnations for witchcraft were thus, in effect, decisions made by popular courts.[39]

Famines and epidemics led families to such desperation that they offered children, adults, or whole families into slavery as a last hope for survival. This self-sacrificing method of enslavement, normally kept to a minimum, rose to importance when hunger became severe. In Angola, repeated famine and associated epidemics drove down the prices of slaves and increased their flow to the coast. The same is true for eighteenth-century Senegambia and for the central Sudan. These famines, of course, were more than simple natural disasters: the previous conditions of the slave trade caused enough dislocation of agriculture to make famines more common.[40]

Warfare and *razzia* tended to capture a cross-section of the source population, though the death rate of young male captives was relatively high because they were most heavily involved in fighting. Kidnapping tended to result in the capture of young and economically active (because mobile) persons, captured while away from centers of population. Court proceedings and witchcraft accusations were more likely to yield mature adults. Tribute exaction probably resulted in the enslavement of persons who were physically or socially marginal, except to the degree that the overlords were able to insist on the supply of slaves meeting specific criteria. Famine and epidemic resulted in the enslavement of a high proportion of children.

Finally, there are cases where enslavement can be seen as a form of voluntary emigration. European observers on the Horn in the nineteenth century found large groups of young Oromo women walking to the coast, guarded only by a few men. They announced themselves to be looking for husbands, and most would go to Arabia. Behind them they left some villages with overwhelmingly male populations. A somewhat similar case is to be found in the Ivory Coast and Burkina Faso, where the nineteenth-century pattern of Voltaic women going south as slaves to marry men of the lagoon region has been succeeded by a twentieth-century movement which, except for the abolition of slavery, is the same.[41]

The act of capture put the captive into the hands of a captor. The process of rendering a captive into a slave involved the imposition of both distance and socialization. Only rarely did the captor become the owner of the captive. A captive of war, *razzia*, or even kidnapping might still be ransomed, and captives of high social standing were often ransomed. More commonly, the captor sold the captive to a merchant, or rendered the captive over to a higher authority, as when soldiers passed their captives over to the agents of their king. The need to feed captives, in particular, was a factor encouraging captors to pass their captives on rapidly and for modest compensation. Assuming, however, that the captors sought to profit from their booty, their gain from the sale of captives should not have been less than the physical and monetary cost of their making the capture.

This cheap captive became a more expensive slave after several conditions were satisfied. As Claude Meillassoux has written for the case of the western Sudan, the captive was desocialized, depersonalized, degendered, and decivilized upon capture. Once the captive was too distant from home to hope for escape, cut off from family, and dependent on the whim of the owner, he or she was forced to accept a subordinate role in the adoptive society. The captive, now reborn as a slave, took up a new trade: as laborer, concubine, or domestic. He or she was held within a family group, but had no rights: slaves became and remained the *other*.[42] These new slaves now acquired a higher value, based on the level of their productivity.

The function of merchants involved transporting captives from the areas of supply to areas of demand, and passing them off as slaves at their next point of sale. This merchant function was performed most obviously by large-scale merchants, such as the Ovimbundu merchants of Angola and the Maraka merchants of the middle Niger valley. But the function was also performed by small operators, who passed individual slaves from hand to hand in numerous transactions; and it was performed by state trading agencies and by states acting on their own account. The sale price at the completion of the merchant's function reflected the value of the slave to the purchaser, and this depended most fundamentally on the social and economic productivity of the slave. At the same time, this slave selling-price had to cover the merchants' cost of transporting, feeding, and perhaps even clothing the slaves. Very likely, however, for the eighteenth century and some of the nineteenth century, the selling-price of the slave exceeded the purchase-price of the captive by a substantial amount, thus allowing for a margin of mercantile profit.[43]

The most striking evidence for this thesis of African commercial profit on slave exports lies in the increase of slave prices on the Atlantic coast. Prices in the late eighteenth century were five or six times higher than in the mid-seventeenth century. The cost of capture may have risen, but not at this rate. That is, slaves were marched a longer average distance to the coast in the eighteenth century than in the seventeenth, but not five or six times longer. One is left to conclude that African profits rose. I do not wish to argue, however, that merchants collected all of this windfall profit: state authorities, for instance, were able to intervene with tolls and taxes, in exchange for protection of the trade, which diverted a significant portion of the profits from merchants to monarchs. For the moment, it is difficult to assess the share of this profit which went to each, or the mechanisms and institutions through which this division was achieved.

Trade in slaves, more than that in non-human commodities, required the support and protection of political authorities. Where states defended the property rights of slave merchants and defended their caravans, it was difficult for slaves to escape or for their families to rescue them. Similarly, to hold a servile population within an African society required political authority to maintain order and subjugation. But state regulation of slavery, that is, state protection of private slave traders' and masters' rights over their slaves, is not the same as state monopoly of the slave trade or state ownership of all slaves. Thus in Asante and Danhomè, the kings exercised rights and responsibilities over all slaves, but they did not own all the slaves within their realms.[44]

These structures of capture and distribution provided the social pressures encouraging new generations of Africans to participate in enslavement. Alongside the institutions of enslavement developed the institutions of slavery itself. African institutions for the social and economic exploitation of slavery also began as innovations, but were passed on to later generations as rules of society: slavery and the slave trade became "traditional."

YIELDING TO TEMPTATION: SLAVERY AND MONEY

According to a story which is still told today along the lagoons of the republic of Bénin, cowries were obtained by the use of slaves. A slave was thrown into the sea and allowed to drown. Then cowries would grow on the body of the slave, and after a time the body would be dredged up and the cowries collected from it.[45]

The story is both true and untrue. Cowrie shells, of course, were money here and in a wide area of West Africa. The story is untrue in that cowries grow in the Indian Ocean, not in the Atlantic or the lagoons edging it, and untrue also in that slaves were not drowned in order to get them. But the story is true as well as picturesque in its presentation of the sacrifice made in order to gain money in exchange. It is a stark example of the ideology justifying slavery in Africa. Africans seemed to throw away a precious resource, young men and women, in exchange for money – for cash. Further, the slaves who remained in Africa did the work of carrying sacks of cowries inland to the sellers.

I will give particular scrutiny to imported cowries and other monies in this section, though they were only a portion of

African imports in the slave-trade era. Chief among imported goods were textiles: cottons, woolens, velvets, silks, and linens of all descriptions, bleached, dyed, and embroidered. The textiles were mostly of Indian origin until the end of the eighteenth century, and mostly manufactured in Europe thereafter. Next in importance were alcoholic beverages (especially rum, but including a wide variety) and tobacco, mostly grown in Brazil and prepared in rolls. Of lesser but still strategic importance were guns and gunpowder, salt, and iron and copper bars used by smiths. The wide array of remaining goods – shoes, umbrellas, kitchenware, beads, jewelry, sedan chairs and so on – was important to the continuation of the trade, but comprised only a small part of its total value.[46]

The pattern of African imports reveals two contradictory dimensions of the export slave trade: its elite and mass characteristics. On the one hand, the slave trade served the interests of an elite. The slave-trading elite grasped the best cloths and liquor, the most prestigious luxury goods, and most of the firearms. These imported goods served to reflect and to reinforce the dominant positions of monarchs, big men, and great merchants. On the other hand, the slave trade involved all levels of society. The plainer textiles and much of the tobacco and alcoholic beverages passed into the hands of the common people. Some of these commoners had sold one or two slaves themselves; some purchased imports with income they gained otherwise.

The import of money in Africa is of particular interest because it reveals the contrast between the elite and mass dimensions of the slave trade, and because it illustrates the tightness of economic ties among Africa, the Occident, and the Orient. The imported money took the varying forms of Africa's commodity monies – cowrie shells, brass manillas in horseshoe shape, squares of cloth, iron bars, copper wire, brass pans, but also gold dust and silver dollars (Maria Theresa thalers,* and Spanish, American, and Latin American dollars of roughly equal value) – but it was money nonetheless. Large and small squares of imported cloth corresponded to different denominations of currency in Angola, and served as working capital for inland slave merchants. In total, these currency

---

* From Austria.

imports ranked relatively high on the list of African imports. In the eighteenth-century Bight of Benin, cowries sometimes amounted to one-third of the value of imports. More generally, money imports may be estimated at from 10 to 15 per cent of the value of African imports.[47]

The money supplies of Africa were thus constituted through foreign trade. Africans exported slaves and other goods whose value exceeded that of the goods they imported. They imported money to pay for this export surplus, and added this money to the currency already circulating in their domestic economies. The work of Jan Hogendorn and Marion Johnson has quantified the immense imports of cowries in the Bight of Benin and neighboring regions. These imports led by the end of the eighteenth century to a money supply whose value may have reached £2 million shared among perhaps 8 million people.[48] By the same mechanism, Maria Theresa thalers became widely used as currency across much of Africa during the nineteenth century. Indeed, precisely the same system for constituting the money supply remained in force in twentieth-century Africa. The currencies were now British, French, and Portuguese, but the only means of obtaining them was through export surpluses. Only after World War II did modern central banks gain control of the money supply.

According to certain sorts of monetary reasoning, it may be possible that the addition to the African money supply resulting from the slave trade brought forth a more efficient commercial system and even some new sources of supply of goods and services. As the money supply increased, cash transactions became easier, a larger proportion of output was oriented toward the market, and goods and services flowed more smoothly and over a wider area than before. The sixteenth through the eighteenth centuries along the western coast, and the nineteenth century along the eastern coast, were times of considerable expansion of money supply and trading activities generally, as a direct result of the slave trade.[49]

On the other hand, and in a remarkable parallel to the European experience of importing large quantities of gold and silver from the Americas (plus African gold), the result of importing so much money into Africa was simply to redistribute the ownership of existing goods and services. In the African case, further, this exchange resulted in the emigration of millions of prime workers, and left behind a declining population and a disordered society. Overall, the imports into Africa allowed first of all for the redistribution of existing wealth, then for the satisfaction of short-term consumer desires, and only lastly for production and creation of new wealth. Some of this was inevitable and natural in the conditions of world trade from the seventeenth through the nineteenth centuries. But much of it was a more specific result of the fact that the African slave trade was based on theft and piracy, that is, on the redistribution of wealth already created rather than on the creation of new wealth. So while it seems certain that the slave trade brought an expansion in the African money supply and a displacement of self-sufficient production by production for the market, it is by no means certain that this type of market expansion brought an improvement in African economic welfare.[50]

The desire for money posed the temptation that drew many Africans into the slave trade. There were other things to be gained from selling and holding slaves – imported goods, social prestige, family and political power, a life of ease – but money was an important part of the total, and it crystallizes the crassness of the trade in slaves. Any person could be reduced to a monetary value. African complicity in the slave trade systematically reinforced the primacy of narrow self-interest and of short-term economic calculations. The future in a world with so many reversals could never be certain, so that long-term investment seemed like a poor bet as compared to the possibility of immediate profit and immediate consumption of those profits. The myth of collecting cowries from the cadavers of slaves evokes the crass and cruel mentality of the era. Yet the participants in the slave trade could never escape the humanity of their captives.

Instead, slave raiders, slave merchants, and slave owners devised ways to distance themselves from the fact that they were dealing in bodies for cash. They needed to clothe their greedy motivations and justify the suffering they propagated; they needed to protect themselves against the retribution of men in this world and gods in the next. They lubricated and disguised the flow of slaves with a hundred euphemisms, proverbs, equivocations, and outright lies. European merchants at the coast were told that the slaves had been brought from the far interior, and that each kingdom or ethnic group had a prohibition on enslaving people of their own group: these were half-truths, often stretched very far to preserve the integrity of the sellers of slaves. Slaves brought down the Zaire river by Bobangi merchants were told not that they would be sold, but rather that they were being left for a few days in one village while their owners did business in another. Or, as European and African merchants said to each other about the slaves they shipped off, they would have died otherwise in warfare or sacrifice.[51] Thus did the slave trade influence the ideas and the discourse of African peoples.

The steady growth in the Occidental slave trade from its fifteenth-century beginnings brought it, in about 1650, to the same annual volume as the Oriental trade. For the next two centuries, the Occidental trade dominated the commerce in African slaves. From the moment of its emergence to its dominance, the Occidental slave trade began to affect social conditions in Western Africa generally, no longer just in isolated areas of the coast.

Although the growth in the Occidental slave trade was steady and gradual, averaging a 2 per cent increase per year, its seventeenth-century eclipse of the Oriental trade was accompanied by some dramatic new developments. The Northern European powers had joined the struggle for maritime power, and now the Dutch, English, and French, not to mention the Danes, Swedes, and Brandenburgers, plied the seas in search of colonies, booty, commerce, and slaves. New maritime power relationships and technology combined with improved efficiency in plantation operation and with changes in European demand. The result was a rapid expansion in the New World sugar plantations and an equivalent increase in demand for African labor.[52]

Gradually and systematically, if not consciously, Africans made institutional changes which led to a more regular stream of slave deliveries. Overall, that is, Africans decided to supply slaves to meet the new European demand: this conclusion is supported by the fact that the number of slaves exported in 1690 was nearly double that of 1640, but the price of slaves had not increased. In the previous forty years, the volume of slave exports had grown while prices fell.

It would be naive, however, to assume that slave exports expanded as a result of an easily formed African consensus. This decision to participate in the slave trade was contested. The documents do tell us most clearly of the monarchs who opposed the slave trade, as in Jolof, and of the slaves who rebelled against their condition, but one must presume that there was a broader discussion of the opportunities and dangers inherent in expanding the slave trade. Overall the opportunists – those determined to profit in the short run from slavery – won out, but it is surely the case that the dimensions and conditions of the slave trade were affected by those critical of it.

Warfare became more frequent and more deadly in the areas contributing the largest number of slaves: the growth in warring activity can be traced clearly for the Bight of Benin and the Gold Coast; Angola's earlier domination of slave exports is reflected in mid-century warfare there.[53]

With this steady expansion of the slave trade, the African market for female slaves came into existence. As the sale of slaves to Europeans caused many young women to pass through the hands of slave traders, these merchants gradually developed a desire to hold on to some of them. For those men who avoided slavery and remained in Africa, the potential reward of this new demographic imbalance was multiple wives, female servants, and a position as beneficiary of the developing system of "family slavery." So the bifurcated price system in the Atlantic slave trade expanded in the seventeenth century: European prices for men became slightly higher than for women (reflecting higher male productivity in a situation where men could be controlled), and African prices for women became higher than for men (reflecting their sexuality, their slightly greater productivity in domestic labor under conditions of a restricted market for slave produce, and the difficulty of controlling men under African conditions). As a result, most male captives went to the Europeans, and over one-half of the women went to the Africans, with the difference that the male fraction of slave exports grew as slaves were drawn from further inland.[54]

All of these seventeenth-century changes are best described by the "societal" image: the development of New World plantations, the expansion of African slave supply, the development of African demand for female slaves, all were cases of the development of a new logic and new social institutions. This new logic, once set in place, dominated the western coast for nearly two centuries.

NOTES

This chapter is reprinted from *Slavery and African Life* (Cambridge, 1990), by permission of Cambridge University Press.

1 James Hutton, ed. and trans., *Aristotle's Poetics* (New York, 1982), 50–1.

2 Luc de Heusch, *Sacrifice in Africa: A Structuralist Approach*, trans. Lindo O'Brien and Alice Morton (Bloomington, Ind., 1985).

3 De Heusch, *Sacrifice in Africa*; M. F. C. Bourdillon and Meyer Fortes, eds, *Sacrifice* (London, 1980). Academic economists speak not of *sacrifice* but of the *cost* of investment and production. In contrast, practicing members of business communities – personally and emotionally involved in their enterprises – have often portrayed their ventures as sacrifices.

4 David Eltis's magisterial study of the nineteenth-century Atlantic slave trade has demonstrated in exceptional detail and clarity the contribution of slavery to New World economic growth, and it has the additional merit of addressing African aspects of slavery in detail. Nevertheless, since his approach centers on the calculations of slave owners, he under-estimates the cost and the waste involved in the slave system: Eltis, *Economic Growth and the Ending of the Transatlantic Slave Trade* (New York, 1987).

5 Orlando Patterson, *Slavery and Social Death: A Comparative Study* (Cambridge, Mass., 1982).

6 Charles Verlinden, *L'Esclavage dans l'Europe médiévale*, vol. 1 (Bruges, 1955), vol. 2 (Ghent, 1977). By contrast, Phillips has more recently emphasized the Mediterranean tradition of small-scale slavery (in contrast to the large-scale or gang slavery of New World plantations), and has expressed skepticism about the importance of slave labor in the sugar plantations of the medieval Mediterranean: William D. Phillips, *Slavery from Roman Times to the Early Transatlantic Trade* (Minneapolis, Minn., 1985).

7 Richard Hellie, *Slavery in Russia, 1450–1725* (Chicago, 1982).

8 H. J. Nieboer, *Slavery as an Industrial System* (The Hague, 1910).

9 Charles Verlinden, *Les Origines de la civilisation atlantique. De la Renaissance à l'âge des lumières* (Neuchâtel, 1966); Manuel Lobo Cabrera, *La esclavitud en las Canarias orientales en el siglo XVI* (Gran Canaria, 1982); A. C. de M. Saunders, *A Social History of Black Slaves and Freedmen in Portugal, 1441–1555* (Cambridge, 1982).

10 Frederick Bowser, *The African Slave in Colonial Peru, 1524–1650* (Stanford, Calif., 1973); Colin Palmer, *Slaves of the White God: Blacks*

in Mexico, 1570–1650 (Cambridge, Mass., 1976); Herbert Klein, *African Slavery in Latin America* (Oxford, 1986).

An influential economic model of the demand for slaves is that of Domar, who focuses on the relative shortage of labor (in comparison to land) as the principal cause of demand for slaves; Domar acknowledged his debt to Nieboer's earlier statement of this view: Evsey Domar, "The Causes of Slavery or Serfdom: A Hypothesis," *Journal of Economic History* 30, no. 1 (1970):18–32; H. J. Nieboer, *Slavery as an Industrial System* (The Hague, 1910). See also Frederic L. Pryor, "A Comparative Study of Slave Societies," *Journal of Comparative Economics* 1 (1977):25–49.

11 Sherburne F. Cook and Woodrow Wilson Borah, *Essays in Population History: Mexico and the Caribbean*, 3 vols (Berkeley, Calif., 1971–9); Henry F. Dobyns, "Estimating Aboriginal American Population: An Appraisal of Techniques with a New Hemispheric Estimate," *Current Anthropology* 7 (1966): 395–416; William N. Deneven, ed., *The Native Population of the Americas in 1492* (Madison, Wis., 1976); Noble David Cook, *Demographic Collapse: Indian Peru, 1520–1620* (Cambridge, 1981); Alfred W. Crosby, *The Columbian Exchange: Biological and Cultural Consequences of 1492* (Westport, Conn., 1972).

12 Philip D. Curtin, "Epidemiology and the Slave Trade," *Political Science Quarterly* 83 (1968): 190–216; Kenneth F. Kiple and Virginia Himmelsteib King, *Another Dimension to the Black Diaspora: Diet, Disease, and Racism* (Cambridge, 1981).

13 A. J. R. Russell-Wood, "Technology and Society: The Impact of Gold Mining on the Institution of Slavery in Portuguese America," *Journal of Economic History* 37, no. 1 (1977):59–86.

14 Lobo Cabrera, *La esclavitud en las Canarias orientales*, 141–78.

15 Bowser, *The African Slave in Colonial Peru*; Palmer, *Slaves of the White God*; Edmund Morgan, *American Slavery, American Freedom: The Ordeal of Colonial Virginia* (New York, 1975).

16 J. H. Parry, *The Age of Reconnaissance* (London, 1963); C. R. Boxer, *The Dutch in Brazil, 1624–1654* (Oxford, 1957); *The Portuguese Seaborne Empire 1415–1825* (New York, 1969).

17 Richard N. Bean and Robert P. Thomas, "The adoption of slave labor in British America" in Henry A. Gemery and Jan S. Hogendorn (eds), *The Uncommon Market: Essays in the Economic History of the Atlantic Slave Trade* (New York, 1979) 377–98; Richard S. Dunn, *Sugar and Slaves: The Rise of the Planter Class in the English West Indies, 1624–1713* (Chapel Hill, 1972); David Galenson, *White Servitude in Colonial America, An Economic Analysis* (Cambridge, 1981); Richard B. Sheridan, *Sugar and Slavery: An Economic History of the British West Indies* (Bridgetown, Barbados, 1974).

For a detailed description of Portuguese trading practices of the seventeenth century in Africa, see Joseph C. Miller, "Capitalism and slaving: the financial and commercial organization of the Angolan slave trade, according to the accounts of Antonio Coelho

Guerreiro (1684–1692)," *International Journal of African Historical Studies* 17, no. 1 (1984):1–56.

18 Sidney Mintz, *Sweetness and Power: The Place of Sugar in Modern History* (Harmondsworth, 1985); J.-L. Vellut, "Diversification de l'économie de cueillette: miel et cire dans les sociétés de la forêt claire d'Afrique centrale (*c.*1750–1950)," *African Economic History* 7 (1979):93–112.

19 Some defenders of the slave trade argued that Africa had a population surplus. John D. Fage comes close to the same conclusion in his argument that, for West Africa, "the effect may have been no more than to cream-off surplus population" (John D. Fage, "The effect of the Export Slave trade on African populations" in R. P. Ross and R. J. A. Rathbone (eds), *The Population Factor in African Studies* (London, 1975) 15–23. Henry Gemery and Jan Hogendorn developed a well-known model of slave supply based on the vent-for-surplus model popularized by the development economist Hla Myint. See H. A. Gemery and J. S. Hogendorn, "The Atlantic Slave Trade: A Tentative Economic Model," *Journal of African History* 15, no. 2 (1974): 233–46; and Hla Myint, *The Economics of the Developing Countries* (New York, 1964). The model does not actually require a labor surplus, but only requires that labor be underutilized. Gemery and Hogendorn do, however, use the term "surplus capacity available for export" (for instance on pp. 237–9, 246). LeVeen labeled his analogus model an "excess supply" model: E. Phillip LeVeen, *British Slave Trade Suppression Policies, 1821–1865* (New York, 1977), 128.

20 For a classic study of shifting cultivation, see Pierre de Schlippe, *Shifting Cultivation in Africa: The Zande System of Agriculture* (London, 1956).

21 Jack Goody, *Technology, Tradition and the State in Africa* (Cambridge, 1971), 25.

22 De Vries has demonstrated this principle nicely for Holland in the early modern period, where the high productivity of agricultural labor (which resulted from capital improvements in the land) raised the general level of wages so high that industrial firms chose to locate in other areas, with the result that Dutch industry never became as brilliant as Dutch commerce: Jan de Vries, *The Dutch Rural Economy in the Golden Age, 1500–1700* (New Haven, Conn., 1974), 182–6, 238–40; "Labor in the Dutch golden age" (unpublished paper, Berkeley, 1980), 14–15.

Asian producers of rice, it may be noted, occupied a level of technical efficiency intermediate between those of Europe and Africa. This factor, in addition to the extra distance from Asia to the New World colonies, tended to isolate Asians from being drawn into European-dominated plantation work. There were, nevertheless, important cases of enslavement and plantation work in Asia, notably Dutch slave plantations in Indonesia and Dutch importation of Malaysian slaves into South Africa. Further, as African slave exports came to an end in the nineteenth century, millions of Indian and Chinese workers were recruited as cheap contract laborers for plantations and mines in the Caribbean, the Indian Ocean, Pacific islands, and elsewhere: A. J. H. Latham, *The International Economy and the Undeveloped World 1865–1914* (London, 1978), 105–16.

23 Fenoaltea has constructed an alternative explanation for slave exports on the assumption that African productivity equaled that in Europe. His model is driven by price differences resulting from African demand for imports. While his assumption on productivity is probably ill-founded, his observations on the relative costs of transporting gold, slaves, and agricultural goods are of importance in explaining the changing nature of African exports in the seventeenth, eighteenth, and nineteenth centuries: Stefano Fenoaltea, "Europe in the African Mirror: The Slave Trade and the Rise of Feudalism" (unpublished paper, Princeton University, 1988).

24 Philip D. Curtin, "The African Diaspora," in *Roots and Branches: Current Directions in Slave Studies*, ed. Michael Craton (Toronto, 1979), 15–16.

25 This reasoning has some analogies to Marx's discussion of cost and productivity in wage labor, in which he argued that employers pay workers the cost of their reproduction but keep the difference between that and the value of their output. For the American south, there are numerous studies of the value of slaves: these are based both on the value of goods produced by slaves, and on the cost of raising a slave (in a situation where, by contrast to the case of African captives, slaves were born into the master's household): Robert William Fogel and Stanley L. Engerman, *Time on the Cross*, 2 vols (Boston, Mass., 1974).

26 Philip D. Curtin, Stephen Feierman, Leonard M. Thompson, and Jan Vansina, *African History* (Boston, Mass., 1978), 188–9; Basil Davidson, *Black Mother: The Years of the African Slave Trade* (Boston, Mass., 1961).

27 Fenoaltea has implicitly demonstrated the importance of African political and social fragmentation in sustaining slave exports by asking why more slaves were not ransomed by their families or by their own efforts: Fenoaltea, "Europe in the African mirror."

28 Christopher Udry, "The Akan transitional zone" (unpublished paper, Yale University, 1985); Robin Law, *The Oyo Empire, c.1600–c.1836* (Oxford, 1977), 158–61; Patrick Manning, *Slavery, Colonialism and Economic Growth in Dahomey, 1640–1960* (Cambridge, 1982), 27–46.

29 Thomas and Bean have used the image of fishing on the high seas to emphasize the competitiveness of the African slave trade; here I offer instead the image of fishing in a river or lake to emphasize the limits on renewing resources. Robert Paul Thomas and Richard Bean, "The fishers of men – the profits of the slave trade," *Journal of Economic History* 34, no. 4 (1974), 885–914.

30 Paul E. Lovejoy, *Transformations in Slavery: A History of Slavery in Africa* (Cambridge, 1983), 35–40.

31 Cooper, *Plantation Slavery*, 215–28; K. Nwachukwu-Ogedengbe, "Slavery in Nineteenth-Century Aboh (Nigeria)," in Miers and Kopytoff, *Slavery in Africa*, 143–7.

32 Miller, *Way of Death*, 106; Curtin, *Atlantic Slave Trade*, 28–30; Meillassoux, *Anthropologie de l'esclavage*, 79–85; Austen, "Trans-Saharan slave trade." The outstanding exception to naturally declining slave populations was that of the south of the United States, where slave populations became self-sustaining from the early eighteenth century.

33 John Thornton, "The Military Operations of the Slave Trade in Angola, 1600–1670: the social, economic and demographic impact" (unpublished paper, Montreal, 1985). Of 142 slaves drawn from all over Western Africa and interviewed in Sierra Leone by S. W. Koelle in 1850, 34 per cent said they had been enslaved in war, 30 per cent said they had been kidnapped, 7 per cent said they were sold by relatives or superiors, 7 per cent were sold to pay debts, and 11 per cent admitted to having been condemned by judicial process. Hair, in summarizing Koelle's data, did not report the cause of enslavement for the remaining 11 per cent: P. E. H. Hair, "The Enslavement of Koelle's Informants," *Journal of African History* 6, no. 2 (1965):193–203.

34 Gustav Nachtigal, *Sahara and Sudan*, ed. and trans. Allan G. B. Fisher and Humphrey J. Fisher, 4 vols (London, 1971–). This section is from vol. 3, which still awaits publication. See also Jan S. Hogendorn, "Slave Acquisition and Delivery in Precolonial Hausaland," in *West African Culture Dynamics*, ed. B. K. Swartz, Jr, and Raymond E. Dumett (The Hague, 1980), 477–93.

35 Davidson, *Black Mother*.

36 G. I. Jones, "Olaudah Equiano of the Niger Ibo," in *Africa Remembered*, ed. Philip D. Curtin (Madison, Wis., 1962), 85–7; Northrup, *Trade Without Rulers*, 69–73, 75–6.

37 Vansina, *Kingdoms of the Savanna*.

38 Austen, "Trans-Saharan Slave Trade," 31; Law, *The Oyo Empire*, 226.

39 Wyatt MacGaffey, "Economic and Social Dimensions of Kongo Slavery," in *Slavery in Africa*, ed. Miers and Kopytoff, 247; Joseph C. Miller (personal communication).

40 Cooper, *Plantation Slavery*, 126–7; Miller, "Significance of drought"; Becker, "Conditions écologiques"; Lovejoy and Baier, "Desert-side economy."

41 G. Prunier (personal communication).

42 Meillassoux, *Anthropologie de l'esclavage*, 100. Miller notes that the sheer incapacitation of the captives in transit was one of the means of their subordination to masters: Miller, *Way of Death*, 380–1.

43 The Congo merchants operating from Cabinda were seen as suffering from affliction because of the anomaly of the commitment to material wealth in slaves and imported goods, in contrast to their agricultural kin. They joined in the *lemba* cult to provide therapy

for their affliction: Miller, *Way of Death*, 202. See also Curtin, "The African diaspora," 15–16.

44 Robin Law, "Royal Monopoly and Private Enterprise in the Atlantic Trade: The Case of Dahomey," *Journal of African History* 18, no. 4 (1977):555–77.

45 Felix Iroko, "Cauris et esclaves en Afrique occidentale entre les XVIe et XIXe siècles," in Daget, *De la traite à l'esclavage* 1:193–204.

46 David Eltis and Lawrence C. Jennings, "Trade between Western Africa and the Atlantic World in the Pre-Colonial Era," *American Historical Review* 93, no. 4 (1988):936–59.

47 Paul E. Lovejoy, "Interregional Monetary Flows in the Precolonial Trade of Nigeria," *Journal of African History* 15, no. 4 (1974):563–85; Miller, *Way of Death*, 80–1, 180–3; Harms, *River of Wealth*, 85–92; Jan S. Hogendorn and Henry A. Gemery, "Abolition and its impact on monies imported to West Africa," in *Abolition*, ed. Eltis and Walvin, 99–115; Manning, *Slavery, Colonialism and Economic Growth*, 44; Eltis, *Transatlantic Slave Trade*.

48 Jan Hogendorn and Marion Johnson, *The Shell Money of the Slave Trade* (Cambridge, 1986). The estimate of an aggregate £2 million in cowries by 1800 is my own, based on assumed rates of replacement of lost and broken cowries.

49 It should be emphasized that African moneys – whether gold, cowries, or cloth – were general-purpose moneys usable in a wide range of transactions. For a contrary view, once influential, see Paul Bohannan, "Some Principles of Exchange and Investment among the Tiv," *American Anthropologist* 57 (1955):60–70. For an analysis spanning both mercantile generality and institutional specificity, see Miller, *Way of Death*, 173–88.

50 Hogendorn and Gemery, "Abolition and its impact on monies," 101–3.

51 Harms, *River of Wealth*, 37–9; Dalzel, *History of Dahomy*.

52 Parry, *The Age of Reconnaissance*.

53 Kea, *Settlements, Trade and Politics*, 164–6, 286; Akinjogbin, *Dahomey and its Neighbours*, 39.

54 See Patrick Manning, *Slavery and African Life* (Cambridge, 1990), ch. 5.

4

THE LABOR PROBLEM AT JAMESTOWN

Edmund Morgan

*Edmund Morgan's classic article, "The Labor Problem at Jamestown"
(1971) addresses how European colonists – in this case, the English
– intended to survive in their new circumstances. Morgan transports
us to early modern England and Virginia, in order to demonstrate
that English settlers behaved very much as they would have at home.
The example of the earlier Spanish conquest of the Americas led the
English to expect the Indians to labor for them. When that proved
hard to arrange, the English colonists nearly starved. It was only
after tobacco took off in 1618 that the colonists had sufficient incentive
– the promise of profit – to work. Even then, they constantly sought
others to perform their labor for them.*

*Morgan's argument is important for several reasons. In the first
place, he is particularly adept at teasing out the connections between
the New and the Old Worlds by examining Englishmen at home and
abroad. In the second place, he shows us that these Englishmen had
no clearly defined idea about what to do after they had conquered
their particular territories. Their view of the world was naive, and
they did not have a firm grasp of just what was going on around
them. His subjects are demonstrably human; they are full of foibles
and failings. We feel as if we know them. His article shows just how
haphazard was the process of implantation and how ill-prepared the
English colonists were. Finally, Morgan suggests that a combination
of a cash crop and a cheap labor force, in the form of slavery, combined
to save the Englishmen from destroying themselves.*

*This formula for economic mobility shaped much of Atlantic
America during the implantation phase. Each colonist encountered a
new environment which he or she needed to manipulate in order to
earn a sufficient living. In the process of doing so, most Europeans
were unwilling to change their own behavior in order to accommodate*

a set of physical conditions which fundamentally differed from those which they had known at home. Rather, they sought to implant their way of doing things throughout the hemisphere. In this sense, implantation meant the attempted Europeanization of the Americas.

* * *

The story of Jamestown, the first permanent English settlement in America, has a familiar place in the history of the United States. We all know of the tribulations that kept the colony on the point of expiring: the shortage of supplies, the hostility of the Indians, the quarrels among the leaders, the reckless search for gold, the pathetic search for a passage to the Pacific, and the neglect of the crucial business of growing food to stay alive. Through the scene moves the figure of Captain John Smith, a little larger than life, trading for corn among the Indians and driving the feckless crew to work. His departure in October 1609 results in near disaster. The settlers fritter away their time and energy, squander their provisions, and starve. Sir Thomas Gates, arriving after the settlement's third winter, finds only sixty men out of six hundred still alive, and those sixty scarcely able to walk.

In the summer of 1610 Gates and Lord La Warr get things moving again with a new supply of men and provisions, a new absolute form of government, and a new set of laws designed to keep everybody at work. But when Gates and La Warr leave for a time, the settlers fall to their old ways. Sir Thomas Dale, upon his arrival in May 1611, finds them at "their daily and usuall workes, bowling in the streetes."[1] But Dale brings order out of chaos. By enlarging and enforcing the colony's new law code (the famous *Lawes Divine, Morall and Martiall*) he starts the settlers working again and rescues them from starvation by making them plant corn. By 1618 the colony is getting on its feet and ready to carry on without the stern regimen of a Smith or a Dale. There are still evil days ahead, as the Virginia Company sends over men more rapidly than the infant colony can absorb them. But the settlers, having found in tobacco a valuable crop for export, have at last gone to work with a will, and Virginia's future is assured.

The story probably fits the facts insofar as they can be known. But it does not quite explain them. The colony's long period of starvation and failure may well be attributed to the idleness of the first settlers, but idleness is more an accusation than an explanation. Why did men spend their time bowling in the streets when their lives depended on work? Were they lunatics, preferring to play games rather than clear and plow and plant the crops that could have kept them alive?

The mystery only deepens if we look more closely at the efforts of Smith, Gates, La Warr, and Dale to set things right. In 1612 John Smith described his work program of 1608: "the company [being] divided into tennes, fifteenes, or as the businesse required, 4 hours each day was spent in worke, the rest in pastimes and merry exercise." Twelve years later Smith rewrote this passage and changed the figure of four hours to six hours.[2] But even so, what are we to make of a six-hour day in a colony teetering on the verge of extinction?

The program of Gates and La Warr in the summer of 1610 was no more strenuous. William Strachey described it:

> it is to be understood that such as labor are not yet so taxed but that easily they perform the same and ever by ten of the clock have done their morning's work: at what time they have their allowances [of food] set out ready for them, and until it be three of the clock again they take their own pleasure, and afterward, with the sunset, their day's labor is finished.[3]

The Virginia Company offered much the same account of this period. According to a tract issued late in 1610, "the setled times of working (to effect all themselves, or the Adventurers neede desire) [requires] no more pains than from sixe of clocke in the morning untill ten, and from two of the clocke in the afternoone till foure."[4] The long lunch period described for 1610 was also a feature of the *Lawes Divine, Morall and Martiall* as enforced by Dale. The total working hours prescribed in the *Lawes* amounted to roughly five to eight hours a day in summer and three to six hours in winter.[5]

It is difficult, then, to escape the conclusion that there was a great deal of unemployment or underemployment at Jamestown, whether it was the idleness of the undisciplined in the absence of strong government or the idleness of the disciplined in the presence of strong government. How are we to account for this fact? By our standards the situation at Jamestown demanded hard and continuous work. Why was the response so feeble?

One answer, given by the leaders of the colony, is that the settlers included too many ne'er-do-wells and too many gentlemen who "never did know what a dayes work was."[6] Hard work had to wait until harder men were sent. Another answer may be that the Jamestown settlers were debilitated by hunger and disease. The victims of scurvy, malaria, typhoid, and diphtheria may have been left without the will or the energy to work. Still another answer, which has echoed through the pages of our history books, attributed the difficulty to the fact that the settlement was conducted on a communal basis: everybody worked for the Virginia Company and everybody was fed (while supplies lasted) by the company, regardless of how much he worked or failed to work. Once land was distributed to individuals and men were allowed to work for themselves, they gained the familiar incentives of private enterprise and bent their shoulders to the wheel.[7] These explanations are surely all valid – they are all supported by the testimony of contemporaries – and they go far toward explaining the lazy pioneers of Jamestown. But they do not reach to a dimension of the problem that contemporaries would have overlooked because they would have taken it for granted. They do not tell us what ideas and attitudes about work, carried from England, would have led the first English settlers to expect so little of themselves in a situation that demanded so much. The Jamestown settlers did not leave us the kind of private papers that would enable us to examine directly their ideas and attitudes, as we can those of the Puritans who settled New England a few years later. But in the absence of direct evidence we may discover among the ideas current in late sixteenth- and early seventeenth-century England some clues to the probable state of mind of the first Virginians, clues to the way they felt about work, whether in the Old World or the New, clues to habits of thinking that may have conditioned their perceptions of what confronted them at Jamestown, clues even to the tangled web of motives that made later Virginians masters of slaves.

Englishmen's ideas about the New World at the opening of the seventeenth century were based on a century of European exploration and settlement. The Spanish, whose exploits surpassed all others, had not attempted to keep their success a secret, and by the middle of the sixteenth century Englishmen interested in America had begun translating Spanish histories and memoirs in an effort to rouse their countrymen to emulation.[8] The land that emerged from these writings was, except in the Arctic regions, an Eden, teeming with gentle and generous people who, before the Spanish conquest, had lived without labor, or with very little, from the fruits of a bountiful nature.[9] There were admittedly some unfriendly exceptions who made a habit of eating their more attractive neighbors; but they were a minority, confined to a few localities, and in spite of their ferocity were scarcely a match for Europeans armed with guns.[10] Englishmen who visited the New World confirmed the reports of natural abundance. Arthur Barlowe, for example, reconnoitering the North Carolina coast for Walter Raleigh, observed that "the earth bringeth foorth all things in aboundance, as in the first creation, without toile or labour," while the people were "most gentle, loving, and faithfull, void of all guile, and treason, and such as lived after the manner of the golden age. . . . "[11]

English and European readers may have discounted the more extravagant reports of American abundance, for the same authors who praised the land often gave contradictory accounts of the hardships they had suffered in it. But anyone who doubted that riches were waiting to be plucked from Virginia's trees had reason to expect that a good deal might be plucked from the people of the land. Spanish experience had shown that Europeans could thrive in the New World without undue effort by exploiting the natives. With a mere handful of men the Spanish had conquered an enormous population of Indians in the Caribbean, Mexico, and Peru and had put them to work. In the chronicles of Peter Martyr, Englishmen learned how it was done. Apart from the fact that the Indians were naturally gentle, their division into a multitude of kingdoms, frequently at odds with one another, made it easy to play off one against another. By aiding one group against its enemies, the Spaniards had made themselves masters of both.[12]

The story of English plans to imitate and improve on the Spanish strategy is a long one. It begins at least as early as Francis Drake's foray in Panama in 1572–3, when he allied with a band of runaway slaves to rob a Spanish mule train carrying treasure from Peru across the isthmus to Nombre de

Dios on the Caribbean.[13] The idea of joining with dissident natives or slaves either against their Spanish masters or against their wicked cannibalistic neighbors became an important ingredient in English plans for colonizing the New World. Martin Frobisher's experiences with the Eskimos in Baffin Land and Ralph Lane's with the Indians at Roanoke[14] should perhaps have disabused the English of their expectations; but they found it difficult to believe that any group of natives, and especially the noble savages of North America, would fail to welcome what they called with honest pride (and some myopia) the "gentle government" of the English.[15] If the savages first encountered by a colonizing expedition proved unfriendly, the thing to do was to make contact with their milder neighbors and rescue them from the tyranny of the unfriendly tribe, who must be their enemies and were probably cannibals to boot.[16]

The settlers at Jamestown tried to follow the strategy, locating their settlement as the plan called for, near the mouth of a navigable river, so that they would have access to the interior tribes if the coastal ones were hostile. But as luck would have it, they picked an area with a more powerful, more extensive, and more effective Indian government than existed anywhere else on the Atlantic Coast. King Powhatan had his enemies, the Monacans of the interior, but he felt no great need of English assistance against them, and he rightly suspected that the English constituted a larger threat to his hegemony than the Monacans did. He submitted with ill grace and no evident comprehension to the coronation ceremony that the Virginia Company arranged for him, and he kept his distance from Jamestown. Those of his warriors who visited the settlement showed no disposition to work for the English. The Monacans, on the other hand, lived too far inland (beyond the falls) to serve as substitute allies, and the English were thus deprived of their anticipated native labor.[17]

They did not, however, give up their expectations of getting it eventually. In 1615 Ralph Hamor still thought the Indians would come around "as they are easily taught and may be lenitie and faire usage . . . be brought, being naturally though ingenious, yet idlely given, to be no lesse industrious, nay to exceede our English."[18] Even after the massacre of 1622 Virginians continued to dream of an Indian labor supply, though there was no longer to be any gentleness in obtaining it. Captain John Martin thought it better to exploit than to exterminate the Indians, if only because they could be made to work in the heat of the day, when Englishmen would not. And William Claiborne in 1626 invented a device (whether mechanical or political is not clear) that he claimed would make it possible to keep Indians safely in the settlements and put them to work. The governor and council gave him what looks like the first American patent or copyright, namely a three-year monopoly, to "have holde and enjoy all the benefitt use and profitt of this his project or inventione," and they also assigned him a recently captured Indian, "for his better experience and tryall of his inventione."[19]

English expectations of the New World and its inhabitants died hard. America was supposed to be a land of abundance, peopled by natives who would not only share that abundance with the English but increase it under English direction. Englishmen simply did not envisage a need to work for the mere purpose of staying alive. The problem of survival as they saw it was at best political and at worst military.

Although Englishmen long remained under the illusion that the Indians would eventually become useful English subjects, it became apparent fairly early that Indian labor was not going to sustain the founders of Jamestown. The company in England was convinced by 1609 that the settlers would have to grow at least part of their own food.[20] Yet the settlers themselves had to be driven to that life-saving task. To understand their ineffectiveness in coping with a situation that their pioneering descendants would take in stride, it may be helpful next to inquire into some of the attitudes toward work that these first English pioneers took for granted. How much work and what kind of work did Englishmen at the opening of the seventeenth century consider normal?

The laboring population of England, by law at least, was required to work much harder than the regimen at Jamestown might lead us to expect. The famous Statute of Artificers of 1563 (re-enacting similar provisions from the Statute of Laborers of 1495) required all laborers to work from 5:00 in the morning to 7:00 or 8:00 at night from mid-March to mid-September, and during the remaining months of the year from daybreak to night. Time out for eating, drinking, and rest was not to exceed two and a half hours a day.[21] But these were injunctions, not descriptions. The Statute of Laborers of 1495 is preceded by the complaint that laborers "waste much part of the day . . . in late coming unto their work, early departing therefrom, long sitting at their breakfast, at their dinner and noon-meat, and long time of sleeping after noon."[22] Whether this statute or that of 1563 (still in effect when Jamestown was founded) corrected the situation is doubtful.[23] The records of local courts show varying efforts to enforce other provisions of the statute of 1563, but they are almost wholly silent about this provision,[24] in spite of the often-expressed despair of masters over their lazy and negligent laborers.[25]

It may be said that complaints of the laziness and irresponsibility of workmen can be met with in any century. Were such complaints in fact justified in sixteenth- and early seventeenth-century England? There is some reason to believe that they were, that life during those years was characterized by a large amount of idleness or underemployment.[26] The outstanding economic fact of the sixteenth and early seventeenth centuries in England was a rapid and more or less steady rise in prices, followed at some distance by a much smaller rise in wages, both in industry and in agriculture. The price of provisions used by a laborer's family rose faster than wages during the whole period from 1500 to 1640.[27] The government made an effort to narrow the gap by requiring the justices in each county to readjust maximum wages at regular intervals. But the wages established by the justices reflected their own nostalgic notions of what a day's work ought to be worth in money, rather than a realistic estimate of what a man could buy with his wages. In those counties, at least, where records survive, the level of wages set by the justices crept upward very slowly before 1630.[28]

Wages were so inadequate that productivity was probably impaired by malnutrition. From one-quarter to one-half of the population lived below the level recognized at the time to constitute poverty. Few of the poor could count on regular meals at home, and in years when the wheat crop failed, they were close to starvation.[29] It is not surprising that men living under these conditions showed no great energy for work and that much of the population was, by modern standards, idle much of the time. The health manuals of the day recognized that people normally slept after eating, and the laws even prescribed a siesta for laborers in the summer time.[30] If they slept longer and more often than the laws allowed or the physicians recommended, if they loafed on the job and took unauthorized holidays, if they worked slowly and ineffectively when they did work, it may have been due at least in part to undernourishment and to the variety of chronic diseases that undernourishment brings in its train.[31]

Thus low wages may have begot low productivity that in turn justified low wages.[32] The reaction of employers was to blame the trouble on deficiencies, not of diet or wages, but of character. A prosperous yeoman like Robert Loder, who kept close track of his expenses and profits, was always bemoaning the indolence of his servants. Men who had large amounts of land that they could either rent out or work with hired labor generally preferred to rent because labor was so inefficient and irresponsible.[33]

Even the division of labor, which economists have customarily regarded as a means of increased productivity, could be a source of idleness. Plowing, for example, seems to have been a special skill – a plowman was paid at a higher rate than ordinary farm workers. But the ordinary laborer's work might have to be synchronized with the plowman's, and a whole crew of men might be kept idle by a plowman's failure to get his job done at the appropriate time. It is difficult to say whether this type of idleness, resulting from failure to synchronize the performance of related tasks, was rising or declining; but cheap, inefficient, irresponsible labor would be unlikely to generate pressures for the careful planning of time.

The government, while seeking to discourage idleness through laws requiring long hours of work, also passed laws that inadvertently discouraged industry. A policy that might be characterized as the conservation of employment frustrated those who wanted to do more work than others. English economic policy seems to have rested on the assumption that the total amount of work for which society could pay was strictly limited and must be rationed so that everyone could have a little,[34] and those with family responsibilities could have a little more. It was against the law for a man to practice more than one trade or one craft.[35] And although large numbers of farmers took up some handicraft on the side, this was to be discouraged, because "for one man to be both an husbandman and an Artificer is a gatheringe of divers mens livinges into one mans hand."[36] So as not to take work away from his elders, a man could not independently practice most trades until he had become a master through seven years of apprenticeship. Even then, until he was thirty years old or married, he was supposed to serve some other master of the trade. A typical example is the case of John Pikeman of Barking, Essex, a tailor who was presented by the grand jury because he "being a singleman and not above 25 years of age, does take in work of tailoring and works by himself to the hindrance of other poor occupiers, contrary to the law."[37]

These measures doubtless helped to maintain social stability in the face of a rapid population increase, from under three million in 1500 to a probable 4½ million in 1640 (an increase reflected in the gap between wages and prices).[38] But in its efforts to spread employment so that every able-bodied person would have a means of support, the government in effect discouraged energetic labor and nurtured the workingman's low expectations of himself. By requiring masters to engage apprentices for seven-year terms and servants (in agriculture and in most trades) for the whole year rather than the day, it prevented employers from hiring labor only when there was work to be done and prevented the diligent and effective worker from replacing the ineffective. The intention to spread work is apparent in the observation of the Essex justices that labor by the day caused "the great depauperization of other labourers."[39] But labor by the year meant that work could be strung out to occupy an unnecessary amount of time, because whether or not a master had enough work to occupy his servants they had to stay and he had to keep them. The records show many instances of masters attempting to turn away a servant or apprentice before the stipulated term was up, only to have him sent back by the courts with orders that the master "entertain" him for the full period.[40] We even have the extraordinary spectacle of the runaway master, the man who illegally fled from his servants and thus evaded his responsibility to employ and support them.[41]

In pursuit of its policy of full employment in the face of an expanding population, the government often had to create jobs in cases where society offered none. Sometimes men were obliged to take on a poor boy as a servant whether they needed him or not. The parish might lighten the burden by paying a fee, but it might also fine a man who refused to take a boy assigned to him.[42] To provide for men and women who could not be foisted off on unwilling employers, the government established houses of correction in every county, where the inmates toiled at turning wool, flax, and hemp into thread or yarn, receiving nothing but their food and lodging for their efforts. By all these means the government probably did succeed in spreading employment. But in the long run its policy, insofar as it was effective, tended to depress wages and to diminish the amount of work expected from any one man.

Above and beyond the idleness and underemployment that we may blame on the lethargy and irresponsibility of underpaid labor, on the failure to synchronize the performance of related tasks, and on the policy of spreading work as thinly as possible, the very nature of the jobs to be done prevented the systematic use of time that characterizes modern industrialized economies. Men could seldom work steadily, because they could work only at the tasks that could be done at the moment; and in sixteenth- and seventeenth-century England the tasks to be done often depended on forces beyond human control: on the weather and the seasons, on the winds, on the tides, on the maturing of crops. In the countryside work from dawn to dusk with scarcely an intermission might be normal at harvest time, but there were bound to be times when there was very little to do. When it rained or snowed, most farming operations had to be stopped altogether (and so did some of the stages of cloth manufacture). As late as 1705 John Law, imagining a typical economy established on a newly discovered island, assumed that the persons engaged in agriculture would necessarily be idle, for one reason or another, half the time.[43]

To be sure, side by side with idleness and inefficiency, England exhibited the first signs of a rationalized economy. Professor J. U. Nef has described the many large-scale industrial enterprises that were inaugurated in England in the late sixteenth and early seventeenth centuries.[44] And if the development of systematic agricultural production was advancing less rapidly than historians once supposed, the very existence of men like Robert Loder, the very complaints of the idleness and irresponsibility of laborers, the very laws prescribing hours of work all testify to the beginnings of a rationalized economy. But these were beginnings only, and not widely felt. The laborer who seemed idle or irresponsible to a Robert Loder probably did not seem so to himself or to his peers. His England was not a machine for producing wool or corn. His England included activities and pleasures and relationships that systematic-minded employers would resent and that modern economists would classify as uneconomic. At the opening of the seventeenth century, England was giving him fewer economic benefits than she had given his grandfathers, so that he was often ready to pull up stakes and look for a better life in another county or another country.[45] But a life devoted to more and harder work than he had known at home might not have been his idea of a better life.

Perhaps we may now view Jamestown with somewhat less surprise at the idle and hungry people occupying the place: idleness and hunger were the rule in much of England much of the time; they were facts of life to be taken for granted. And if we next ask what the settlers thought they had come to America to do, what they thought they were up to in Virginia, we can find several English enterprises comparable to their own that may have served as models and that would not have led them to think of hard, continuous, disciplined work as a necessary ingredient in their undertaking.

If they thought of themselves as settling a wilderness, they could look for guidance to what was going on in the northern and western parts of England and in the high parts of the south and east.[46] Here were the regions, mostly wooded, where wastelands still abounded, the goal of many in the large migrant population of England. Those who had settled down were scattered widely over the countryside in isolated hovels and hamlets and lived by pasture farming, that is, they cultivated only small plots of ground and ran a few sheep or cattle on the common land. Since the gardens required little attention and the cattle hardly any, they had most of their time to themselves. Some spent their spare hours on handicrafts. In fact, they supplied the labor for most of England's minor industries, which tended to locate in pasture-farming regions, where agriculture made fewer demands on the inhabitants than in regions devoted to market crops. But the pasture farmers seem to have offered their labor sporadically and reluctantly.[47] They had the reputation of being both idle and independent. They might travel to the richer arable farming regions to pick up a few shillings in field work at harvest time, but their own harvests were small. They did not even grow the wheat or rye for their own bread, and made shift to live in hard times from the nuts and berries and herbs that they gathered in the woods.

Jamestown was mostly wooded, like the pasture-farming areas of England and Wales; and since Englishmen used the greater part of their own country for pasture farming, that was the obvious way to use the wasteland of the New World. If this was the Virginians' idea of what they were about, we should expect them to be idle much of the time and to get grain for bread by trading rather than planting (in this case not wheat or rye but maize from the Indians); we should even expect them to get a good deal of their food, as they did, by scouring the woods for nuts and berries.

As the colony developed, a pasture-farming population would have been quite in keeping with the company's expectation of profit from a variety of products. The Spaniards' phenomenal success with raising cattle in the West Indies was well known. And the proposed employment of the settlers of Virginia in a variety of industrial pursuits (iron works, silk works, glass works, shipbuilding) was entirely fitting for a pasture-farming community. The small gardens assigned for cultivation by Governor Dale in 1614 will also make sense: three acres would have been far too small a plot of land to occupy a farmer in the arable regions of England, where a single man could handle thirty acres without assistance.[48] But it would be not at all inappropriate as the garden of a pasture farmer. In Virginia three acres would produce more than enough corn to sustain a man for a year and still leave him with time to make a profit for the company or himself at some other job – if he could be persuaded to work.

Apart from the movement of migrant workers into wastelands, the most obvious English analogy to the Jamestown settlement was that of a military expedition. The settlers may have had in mind not only the expeditions that subdued the Irish[49] but also those dispatched to the European continent in

England's wars. The Virginia Company itself seems at first to have envisaged the enterprise as partly military, and the *Lawes Divine, Morall and Martiall* were mostly martial. But the conception carried unfortunate implications for the company's expectations of profit. Military expeditions were staffed from top to bottom with men unlikely to work. The nucleus of sixteenth-century English armies was the nobility and the gangs of genteel ruffians they kept in their service, in wartime to accompany them into the field (or to go in their stead), in peacetime to follow them about as living insignia of their rank.[50] Work was not for the nobility or for those who wore their livery. According to the keenest student of the aristocracy in this period, "the rich and well-born were idle almost by definition." Moreover they kept "a huge labor force . . . absorbed in slothful and parasitic personal service." Aside from the gentlemen retainers of the nobility and their slothful servants, the military expeditions that England sent abroad were filled out by misfits and thieves whom the local constables wished to be rid of. It was, in fact, government policy to keep the able-bodied and upright at home and to send the lame, the halt, the blind, and the criminal abroad.[51]

The combination of gentlemen and ne'er-do-wells of which the leaders at Jamestown complained may well have been the result of the company's using a military model for guidance. The Virginia Company was loaded with noblemen (thirty-two present or future earls, four countesses, three viscounts, and nineteen barons).[52] Is it possible that the large number of Jamestown settlers listed as gentlemen and captains came from among the retainers of these lordly stockholders and that the rest of the settlers included some of the gentlemen's personal servants as well as a group of hapless vagabonds or migratory farm laborers who had been either impressed or lured into the enterprise by tales of the New World's abundance? We are told, at least, that persons designated in the colony's roster as "laborers" were "for most part footmen, and such as they that were Adventurers brought to attend them, or such as they could perswade to goe with them, that never did know what a dayes work was."[53]

If these men thought they were engaged in a military expedition, military precedent pointed to idleness, hunger, and death, not to the effective organization of labor. Soldiers on campaign were not expected to grow their own food. On the other hand they *were* expected to go hungry often and to die like flies even if they never saw an enemy. The casualty rates on European expeditions resembled those at Jamestown and probably from the same causes: disease and undernourishment.[54]

But the highest conception of the enterprise, often expressed by the leaders, was that of a new commonwealth on the model of England itself. Yet this, too, while it touched the heart, was not likely to turn men toward hard, effective, and continuous work.[55] The England that Englishmen were saddled with as a model for new commonwealths abroad was a highly complex society in which the governing consideration in accomplishing a particular piece of work was not how to do it efficiently but who had the right or the duty to do it, by custom, law, or privilege. We know that the labor shortage in the New World quickly diminished considerations of custom, privilege, and specialization in the organization of labor. But the English model the settlers carried with them made them think initially of a society like the one at home, in which each of them would perform his own special task and not encroach on the rights of other men to do other tasks. We may grasp some of the assumptions about labor that went into the most intelligent planning of a new commonwealth by considering Richard Hakluyt's recommendation that settlers include both carpenters and joiners, tallow chandlers and wax chandlers, bowyers and fletchers, men to rough-hew pikestaffs and other men to finish them.[56]

If Jamestown was not actually troubled by this great an excess of specialization, it was not the Virginia Company's fault. The company wanted to establish at once an economy more complex than England's, an economy that would include not only all the trades that catered to ordinary domestic needs of Englishmen but also industries that were unknown or uncommon in England: a list of artisans the company wanted for the colony in 1611 included such specialists as hemp planters and hemp dressers, gun makers and gunstock makers, spinners of pack thread and upholsterers of feathers.[57] Whatever idleness arose from the specialization of labor in English society was multiplied in the New World by the presence of unneeded skills and the absence or shortage of essential skills.

Jamestown had an oversupply of glassmakers and not enough carpenters or blacksmiths, an oversupply of gentlemen and not enough plowmen. These were Englishmen temporarily baffled by missing links in the economic structure of their primitive community. The later jack-of-all-trades American frontiersman was as yet unthought of. As late as 1618 Governor Argall complained that they lacked the men "to set their Ploughs on worke." Although they had the oxen to pull them, "they wanted men to bring them to labour, and Irons for the Ploughs, and harnesse for the Cattell." And the next year John Rolfe noted that they still needed "Carpenters to build and make Carts and Ploughs, and skilfull men that know how to use them, and traine up our cattell to draw them; which though we indeavour to effect, yet our want of experience brings but little to perfection but planting Tobacco."[58]

Tobacco, as we know, was what they kept on planting. The first shipload of it, sent to England in 1617, brought such high prices that the Virginians stopped bowling in the streets and planted tobacco in them. They did it without benefit of plows, and somehow at the same time they managed to grow corn, probably also without plows. Seventeenth-century Englishmen, it turned out, could adapt themselves to hard and varied work if there was sufficient incentive.

But we may well ask whether the habits and attitudes we have been examining had suddenly expired altogether. Did tobacco really solve the labor problem in Virginia? Did the economy that developed after 1618 represent a totally new set of social and economic attitudes? Did greater opportunities for profit completely erase the old attitudes and furnish the incentives to labor that were needed to make Virginia a success? The study of labor in modern underdeveloped countries should make us pause before we say yes. The mere opportunity to earn high wages has not always proved adequate to recruit labour in underdeveloped countries. Something more in the way of expanded needs or political authority or national consciousness or ethical imperatives has been required.[59] Surely Virginia, in some sense, became a success. But how did it succeed? What kind of success did it have? Without attempting to answer, I should like very diffidently to offer a suggestion, a way of looking ahead at what happened in the years after the settlement of Jamestown.

The founders of Virginia, having discovered in tobacco a substitute for the sugar of the West Indies and the silver of Peru, still felt the lack of a native labor force with which to exploit the new crop. At first they turned to their own overpopulated country for labor, but English indentured servants brought with them the same haphazard habits of work as their masters. Also like their masters, they were apt to be unruly if pressed. And when their terms of servitude expired – if they themselves had not expired in the "seasoning" that carried away most immigrants to Virginia – they could be persuaded to continue working for their betters only at exorbitant rates. Instead they struck out for themselves and joined the ranks of those demanding rather than supplying labor. But there was a way out. The Spanish and Portuguese had already demonstrated what could be done in the New World when a local labor force became inadequate: they brought in the natives of Africa.

For most of the seventeenth century Virginians were unable to compete for the limited supply of slaves hauled across the ocean to man the sugar plantations of the Americas. Sugar was a more profitable way to use slaves than tobacco. Moreover, the heavy mortality of newcomers to Virginia made an investment in Africans bound for a lifetime more risky than the same amount invested in a larger number of Englishmen bound for a term that was likely to prove longer than a Virginia lifetime.

But Virginians continued to be Englishmen: the more enterprising continued to yearn for a cheaper, more docile, more stable supply of labor, while their servants loafed on the job, ran away, and claimed the traditional long lunch hour. As the century wore on, punctuated in Virginia by depression, discontent, and rebellion, Virginia's position in the market for men gradually improved: the price of sugar fell, making it less competitive with tobacco; the heavy mortality in the colony declined, making the initial outlay of capital on slaves less risky; and American and European traders expanded their infamous activities in Africa. The world supply of slaves, which had fallen off in the second quarter of the seventeenth century, rose sharply in the third quarter and continued to rise.[60]

With these developments the Virginians at last were able to acquire substitute natives for their colony and begin, in their own English way, to Hispanize Virginia. By the middle of the eighteenth century Africans constituted the great majority of the colony's entire labor force.[61] This is not to say that plantation slavery in Virginia or elsewhere can be understood simply as a result of inherited attitudes toward work confronting the economic opportunities of the New World. The forces that determined the character of plantation slavery were complex. But perhaps an institution so archaic and at the same time so modern as the plantation cannot be fully understood without taking into consideration the attitudes that helped to starve the first settlers of the colony where the southern plantation began.*

* Morgan's book, *American Slavery, American Freedom* (New York, 1975) has dealt with this important theme in rich detail.

NOTES

This was originally published as an article in the *American Historical Review* (1971), and is reprinted by permission of the author.

1 Ralph Hamor, *A True Discourse of the Present State of Virginia* (London, 1615; Richmond, 1957), 26.
2 John Smith, *Travels and Works*, ed. Edward Arber and A. G. Bradley (Edinburgh, 1910) 1:149; 2:466.
3 L. B. Wright, ed., *A Voyage to Virginia in 1609* (Charlottesville, Va, 1964), 69–70.
4 *A True Declaration of the Estate of the Colonie in Virginia* (London, 1610), reprinted in Peter Force, ed., *Tracts and Other Papers* (Washington DC, 1844), 3, no. 1, 20; Smith, *Travels and Works* 2:502. Captain Daniel Tucker maintained a similar program in Bermuda in 1616: "according to the Virginia order, hee set every one [that] was with him at Saint Georges, to his taske, to cleere grounds, fell trees, set corne, square timber, plant vines and other fruits brought out of England. These by their taske-Masters by breake a day repaired to the wharfe, from thence to be imployed to the place of their imployment, till nine of the clocke, and then in the after-noone from three till Sunneset." ibid., 653.
5 *For the Colony in Virginia Brittania: Lawes Divine, Morall and Martiall* (London, 1612), 61–2.
6 Smith, *Travels and Works* 2:487.

7 A much more sophisticated version of this explanation is suggested by Professor Sigmund Diamond in his discussion of the development of social relationships in Virginia, "From Organization to Society: Virginia in the Seventeenth Century," *American Journal of Sociology* 63 (1958): 457–75; see also his "Values as an Obstacle to Economic Growth: The American Colonies," *Journal of Economic History* 27 (1967): 561–75.

8 See especially the translation of Peter Martyr, in Richard Eden, *The Decades of the new worlde or west India* (London, 1555); a useful bibliographical history is John Parker, *Books to Build an Empire* (Amsterdam, 1966).

9 Gustav H. Blanke, *Amerika im Englishen Schrifttum des 16. und 17. Jahrhunderts*, Beiträge Zur Englischen Philologie, no. 46 (Bochum-Langendreer, 1962), 98–104.

10 Since Peter Martyr, the principal Spanish chronicler, identified most Indians who resisted the Spaniards as cannibals, this became the familiar sixteenth-century epithet for unfriendly Indians. It is doubtful that many tribes actually practiced cannibalism, though some certainly did.

11 D. B. Quinn, ed., *The Roanoke Voyages 1584–1590*, Works issued by the Hakluyt Society, 2d ser., 104, 105 (London, 1955) 1:108.

12 Eden, *Decades, passim*. For English awareness of the Spanish example, see Smith, *Travels and Works* 2:578–81, 600–3, 955–6; and Susan M. Kingsbury, ed., *The Records of the Virginia Company of London* (Washington DC, 1906–35), 3:558, 560–2.

13 Irene A. Wright, ed., *Documents concerning English Voyages to the Spanish Main 1569–1580*, Works issued by the Hakluyt Society, 2d ser., 71 (London, 1932), gives the original sources, both English and Spanish.

14 Richard Collinson, ed., *The Three Voyages of Martin Frobisher*, Works issued by the Hakluyt Society, 1st ser., 38 (London, 1867), 131, 141–2, 145–50, 269, 271, 280–9; Quinn, *Roanoke Voyages* 1:275–88.

15 The phrase "gentle government" is the younger Hakluyt's, in a proposal to make use of Drake's Negro allies from Panama for a colony at the Straits of Magellan: E. G. R. Taylor, ed., *The Original Writings and Correspondence of the two Richard Hakluyts*, Works issued by the Hakluyt Society, 2d ser., 76, 77 (London, 1935), 1:142.

16 *Writings of the Hakluyts*, 121, 2:241–2, 246–9, 257–65, 275, 318, 342.

17 The secondary literature on the Indians of Virginia is voluminous, but see especially Nancy O. Lurie, "Indian Cultural Adjustment to European Civilization," in *Seventeenth-Century America*, ed. J. M. Smith (Chapel Hill, NC, 1959), 33–60. The most helpful original sources, on which most of our information is necessarily based, are Smith, *Travels and Works*, and William Strachey, *The Historie of Travell into Virginia Britania* (composed 1612), ed. L. B. Wright and V. Freund, Works issued by the Hakluyt Society, 2d ser., 103 (London, 1953), 53–116.

18 *True Discourse*, 2. See also Strachey, *Historie of Travell*, 91–4; Alexander Whitaker, *Good Newes from Virginia* (London, 1613), 40.
19 Susan M. Kingsbury, ed., *The Records of the Virginia Company of London* (Washington DC, 1906–35) 3:705–6; H. R. McIlwaine, ed., *Minutes of the Council and General Court of Colonial Virginia* (Richmond, Va, 1924), 111.
20 *Records of the Virginia Company*, 3:17, 27.
21 R. H. Tawney and Eileen Power, eds, *Tudor Economic Documents* (London, 3 vols, 1924), 1:342. For some seventeenth-century prescriptions of long working hours, see Gervase Markham, *A Way to get Wealth*, 13th edn (London, 1676), 115–17; Henry Best, *Rural Economy in Yorkshire in 1641*, Surtees Society, Publications, no. 33 (Durham, 1857), 44. See also L. F. Salzman, *Building in England down to 1540* (Oxford, 1952), 61–5.
22 11 Henry 7, cap. 22, sec. 4; Douglas Knoop and G. P. Jones, *The Medieval Mason* (Manchester, 1933), 117.
23 Tawney and Power, *Tudor Economic Documents* 1:352–63.
24 A minor exception is in J. H. E. Bennett and J. C. Dewhurst, eds, *Quarter Sessions Records . . . for the County Palatine of Chester, 1559–1760*, Publications of the Record Society for the Publication of Original Documents relating to Lancashire and Cheshire, no. 94 (Chester, 1940), 95–6, where a master alleged that his apprentice, John Dodd, "hath negligently behaved him selfe in his service in idleinge and sleepinge in severalle places where he hath been comanded to work." But sleeping (from 8:00 in the morning till 2:00 in the afternoon and beyond) was only one of Dodd's offenses. On the enforcement of other provisions in the statute, see Margaret G. Davies, *The Enforcement of English Apprenticeship . . . 1563–1642* (Cambridge, Mass., 1956); R. K. Kelsall, *Wage Regulation under the Statute of Artificers* (London, 1938); and R. H. Tawney, "The Assessment of Wages in England by Justices of the Peace," *Vierteljahrshrift für Sozial- und Wirtschaftsgeschichte* 11 (1913):307–37, 533–64.
25 E. S. Furniss, *The Position of the Laborer in a System of Nationalism* (Boston, Mass., 1920), 117–34; E. P. Thompson, "Time, Work-Discipline, and Industrial Capitalism," *Past and Present* 38 (1967):56–97.
26 D. C. Coleman, "Labour in the English Economy of the Sixteenth Century," *Economic History Review*, 2d ser., 8 (1956); repr. in E. M. Carus Wilson, ed., *Essays in Economic History* (London, 3 vols, 1954–62) 2:291–308.
27 E. H. Phelps Brown and Sheila V. Hopkins, "Seven Centuries of Building Wages," *Economica*, 2d ser., 22 (1955):95–206, "Seven Centuries of the Prices of Consumables, compared with Builders' Wage-Rates," ibid., 2d ser., 23 (1956):296–314, "Wage Rates and Prices: Evidence for Population Pressure in the Sixteenth Century," ibid., 2nd ser., 24 (1957):289–306; H. P. R. Finberg, ed., *The Agrarian History of England and Wales*, 4, *1500–1640*, ed. Joan Thirsk (Cambridge, 1967), 435–57, 531, 583–695.

28 Tawney, "Assessment of Wages," 555–64; Kelsall, *Wage Regulation*, 67–86. Tawney and Kelsall both argue that the enforcement of maximum wages according to the statute of 1563 demonstrates a shortage of labor; but except in a few isolated instances (there may well have been local temporary shortages), the evidence comes from the period after the middle of the seventeenth century.

29 Coleman, "Labour in the English Economy," 295; Laslett adduces figures to show that actual starvation was probably rare among English peasants: Peter Laslett, *The World We Have Lost* (London, 1965), 107–27; but there can be little doubt that they were frequently close to it and chronically undernourished. See Carl Bridenbaugh, *Vexed and Troubled Englishmen* (New York, 1968), 91–8.

30 Thomas Elyot, *The Castel of Helthe* (London, 1541), fols. 45–6; Thomas Cogan, *The Haven of Health* (London, 1589), 231–9; *The Englishmans Doctor, or The School of Salerne* (London, 1608) (New York, 1920), 77.

31 E. P. Thompson, "Time, Work-Discipline, and Industrial Capitalism."

32 On the prevalence of such a vicious circle in pre-industrial countries, see W. F. Moore, *Industrialization and Labor* (Ithaca, NY, 1951), 106–13, 308. But see also E. J. Berg, "Backward-Sloping Labor Supply Functions in Dual Economies – The Africa Case," *Quarterly Journal of Economics* 75 (1961):468–92. For a comparison of Tudor and Stuart England with modern underdeveloped countries, see F. J. Fisher, "The Sixteenth and Seventeenth Centuries: The Dark Ages in English Economic History," *Economica*, 2d ser., 24 (1957):2–18.

33 G. E. Fussell, ed., *Robert Loder's Farm Accounts 1610–1620*, Camden Society, 3d ser., no. 53 (London, 1936); Lawrence Stone, *The Crisis of the Aristocracy, 1558–1641* (New York, 1965), 295–7; Thirsk, *Agrarian History*, 198.

34 Compare Bert F. Hoselitz, *Sociological Aspects of Economic Growth* (Glencoe, Illinois, 1960), 33–4.

35 37 Edward 3, c.6. *A Collection in English of the Statutes now in Force* (London, 1594), fols. 22–3; Calendar of Essex Quarter Session Rolls (microfilm in the University of Wisconsin Library) 4:228; 17:124.

36 Tawney and Power, *Tudor Economic Documents* 1:353.

37 April 1594. Calendar of Essex Quarter Sessions Rolls 16:165. See also the indictment (1589) of four bachelors for taking up the trade of poulterer, which "hindreth other powre men:" ibid. 15:54. While the statute seems to allow single men and women under thirty to set up in trade unless their services are demanded by a master, the courts, in Essex County at least (where the earliest and most extensive records are preserved), required such persons to find themselves a master. Moreover, the court was already issuing such orders before the statute of 1563: ibid. 1:85, 116.

38 See note 27 above.

39 Calendar of Essex Quarter Sessions Rolls 4:128.

40 For examples: William LeHardy, ed., *Hertfordshire County Records*,

vol. 5 (Hertford, 1928): 191–2, 451; E. H. Bates, ed., *Quarter Sessions Records for the County of Somerset*, vol. 1, Somerset Record Society, no. 23 (London, 1907), 11–12, 21; B. C. Redwood, ed., *Quarter Sessions Order Book 1642–1649*, Sussex Record Society, no. 54 (1954), 34, 44, 46, 128, 145–6, 188, 190.

41 For examples: LeHardy, *Hertfordshire County Records* 5:376; Bates, *Quarter Sessions Records for Somerset*, 1:97, 193, 258, 325.

42 Bates, *Quarter Sessions Records for Somerset*, 114, 300; Redwood, *Order Book*, 96, 146, 194; W. L. Sachse, ed., *Minutes of the Norwich Court of Mayoralty*, Norfolk Record Society, no. 15 (Norwich, 1942), 78, 216.

43 Coleman, "Labour in the English Economy"; E. P. Thompson, "Time, Work-Discipline, and Industrial Capitalism"; Keith Thomas, "Work and Leisure in Pre-Industrial Society," *Past and Present* 29 (1964):50–66.

44 J. U. Nef, *The Conquest of the Material World* (Chicago, 1964), 121–328.

45 On the geographical mobility of the English population, see E. E. Rich, "The Population of Elizabethan England," *Economic History Review*, 2d ser., 2 (1949–56):249–65; and Peter Laslett and John Harrison, "Clayworth and Cogenhoe," in *Historical Essays 1600–1750 presented to David Ogg*, ed. H. E. Bell and R. L. Ollard (New York, 1963), 157–84.

46 This paragraph and the one that follows are based on the excellent chapters by Joan Thirsk and by Alan Everitt in Thirsk, *Agrarian History*.

47 Thirsk, *Agrarian History*, 417–29; Joan Thirsk, "Industries in the Countryside," in *Essays in the Economic and Social History of Tudor and Stuart England*, ed. F. J. Fisher (London, 1961), 70–88. See also E. L. Jones, "Agricultural Origins of Industry," *Past and Present* 40 (1968):58–71; Lawrence Stone, "An Elizabethan Coalmine," *Economic History Review*, 2d ser., 3 (1950):97–106, especially 101–2; Thirsk, *Agrarian History*, 35, 111.

48 Hamor, *True Discourse*, 16–17; Peter Bowden, in Thirsk, *Agrarian History*, 652. It is impossible to determine whether the settlers had had direct experience in pasture farming, but the likelihood that they were following familiar pasture-farming procedures and may have been expected to do so by the company is indicated by the kind of cattle they brought with them: swine, goats, neat cattle, and relatively few horses. When they proposed to set plows going, they were to be drawn by oxen as was the custom in pasture-farming areas. In arable farming areas it was more common to use horses. The company's concern to establish substantial herds is evident in the *Lawes Divine, Morall and Martiall* in the provisions forbidding slaughter without government permission.

49 See Howard M. Jones, *O Strange New World* (New York, 1964), 167–79; David B. Quinn, "Ireland and Sixteenth Century European Expansion," in *Historical Studies*, ed. T. D. Williams, Papers Read at the Second Conference of Irish Historians (London, 1958); *The*

Elizabethans and the Irish (Ithaca, NY, 1966), 106–22. Professors Quinn and Jones have both demonstrated how the subjugation of Ireland served as a model for the colonization of America. Ireland must have been in the minds of many of the settlers at Jamestown.

50 W. H. Dunham, *Lord Hastings' Indentured Retainers 1461–1483*, Connecticut Academy of Arts and Sciences, Transactions, no. 39 (New Haven, Conn., 1955); Gladys S. Thompson, *Lords Lieutenants in the Sixteenth Century* (London, 1923); Stone, *Crisis of the Aristocracy*, 199–270.

51 Stone, *Crisis of the Aristocracy*, 331; Lindsay Boynton, *The Elizabethan Militia 1558–1638* (Toronto, 1967); Thompson, *Lords Lieutenants*, 115.

52 Stone, *Crisis of the Aristocracy*, 372. About 50 per cent of the other members were gentry: Theodore K. Rabb, *Enterprise and Empire: Merchant and Gentry Investment in the Expansion of England 1575–1630* (Cambridge, Mass., 1967).

53 Smith, *Travels and Works* 2:486–7.

54 The expedition of the Earl of Essex in 1591 to assist Henry IV of France met with only a few skirmishes, but only 800 men out of 3,400 returned: Thompson, *Lords Lieutenants*, 111. Even the naval forces mustered to meet the Armada in 1588 suffered appalling losses from disease. In 10 of the largest ships, in spite of heavy replacements, only 2,195 out of the original complement of 3,325 men were on the payroll by September. The total loss was probably equal to the entire original number: Lawrence Stone, "The Armada Campaign of 1588," *History* 29 (1944):120–43, especially 37–41.

55 For typical statements implying that Virginia is a new commonwealth on the English model, see *Lawes Divine, Morall and Martiall*, 47–8; Robert Johnson, *The New Life of Virginia*, in Force, *Tracts*, 1, no. 7: 17–18.

56 Taylor, *Writings of the two Richard Hakluyts* 2:323, 327–38.

57 Alexander Brown, *The Genesis of the United States* (Boston, Mass., 1890), 1:469–70.

58 Smith, *Travels and Works* 2:538, 541.

59 Moore, *Industrialization and Labor*, 14–47; Melville J. Herskovits, "The Problem of Adapting Societies to New Tasks," in *The Progress of Underdeveloped Areas*, ed. Bert F. Hoselitz (Chicago, 1952), especially 91–2. See also William O. Jones, "Labor and Leisure in Traditional African Societies," Social Science Research Council, *Items*, no. 23 (1968), 1–6.

60 On the last point, see Philip D. Curtin, *The Atlantic Slave Trade: A Census* (Madison, Wisc., 1969), 119.

61 In 1755 the total number of white tithables in the colony was 43,329, of black tithables 59,999: Evarts B. Greene and Virginia D. Harrington, *American Population before the Federal Census of 1790* (New York, 1932), 150–1. Tithables were white men and black men and women over 16. Black women were tithable because they were made to work like men.

Part II

MATURITY
c.1650–*c*.1770

5

THE COSMIC ORDER IN CRISIS

Nancy M. Farriss

Nancy M. Farriss, in her prize-winning book Maya Society Under
Colonial Rule *(1984), describes the ways in which the Yucatec Maya
and Spanish learned to interact with and accommodate each other.
In this selection, Farriss describes both the ways in which Catholic
missionaries attempted to bring Christianity to the local population
and the ways in which this population received the Europeans'
religion. She argues that the Maya did not accept Christian doctrine
as a representation of a single truth; nor did they completely reject it
as implausible. Rather, the Maya incorporated many of Christianity's
ideas into their own cosmological order.*

*If the Maya believed that their own religion with its full pantheon
and the Catholic Trinity imported by Spanish friars were not mutually
exclusive, the Spanish did not understand this. Many believed that
the Maya completely accepted the Spanish brand of Catholicism. They
were invariably puzzled when "pagan idols" turned up in a local
church. They could not understand a religion which had more than
one divinity; yet they did not see that the Trinity (Father, Son, Holy
Ghost) could be perceived by many non-Christians as just such a
religion.*

*Though Farriss is only concerned here with the Maya (and the
Spanish), we believe that her approach can be applied to other societies
in the Atlantic world. The mature colonial societies which emerged
from the implantation phase had come to terms with their Amerindian
populations – where they still existed. In some places, like the Caribbean
islands, the natives had perished through disease and warfare. The
mature colony had no indigenous peoples. In places like British North
America, the Amerindians lived apart from the Europeans, perched
upon a precipice of disaster. Farriss's subjects interacted when necessary. In general, intrusions were kept to a minimum. By studying*

the process of accommodation, it is possible for us to reconstruct one of the most important facets of life in a mature colony.

* * *

In the Maya scheme of things, man's existence depended on a host of sacred beings who controlled the universe and everything in it. The Maya cosmos was neutral. Its sacred forces – let us call them gods – were neither good nor evil, merely capricious; and their whims could be manipulated because they in turn were dependent on human attention for their welfare, if not their very existence. Mesoamerican gods were like extremely powerful infants (indeed the Olmec "Were-Jaguar" god is often portrayed as an infant, though a rather disconcerting one with large fangs)[1] likely to go into terrible tantrums and eventually expire if neglected. They had to be housed and cared for, diverted with music, dance, and colorful paintings and – most especially – fed.[2]

Religion is a highly complex expression of human fears, needs, and desires; and Maya religion no doubt operated at many levels – personal and public, intellectual and emotional, as well as spiritual. I assume that it satisfied the need for meaning, helping to explain why things are the way they are, and provided some comfort for the fact that they are no better. I am concerned here with Maya religion mainly as a social activity designed to keep the cosmos in operation and thereby ensure the continued survival of its human component.

The introduction of Christianity into Yucatan produced a far more serious crisis in the Maya world than the devastation of military warfare and political domination. We have no way of comparing the magnitude of material losses with anything the Maya had suffered in the past. Nothing in the Mesoamerican history of conquests could have prepared them for the Spaniards' determination to obliterate their entire religious system. Acknowledging the political sovereignty of the Spanish king and acknowledging the spiritual sovereignty of the Christian God must have appeared at first as familiar and related acts of vassalage from a defeated people; the symbol of conquest in the Mesoamerican tradition, after all, was a burning temple. The very different meaning that the new conquerors attached to "spiritual" submission would not have been at all clear during the military campaigns. The Montejos (father, son and nephew), who directed the conquest of Yucatan, proceeded with either more prudence or less zeal than Hernán Cortés in his sweep through Mesoamerica to the Aztec capital, which he punctuated with dramatic scenes of idol-smashing. Neither they nor the few clergymen who accompanied them gave much attention, if any, to evangelization. Some of the allied Maya leaders were baptized – at their own request, we are told. What the ceremony signified to them is impossible to say. Only with the arrival of the first group of Franciscan friars in 1545 (or possibly early 1546) to launch the missionary effort in earnest did the intentions of the conquerors become apparent.[3]

It must have been a profound shock to the Maya when they realized that the Christian God was not merely to take precedence over their own gods but to replace them altogether. There is no evidence that the Maya totally rejected this new deity in the sense of refusing to acknowledge his divinity. Their initial acceptance of Christianity; the very early amalgamations of pagan and Christian rituals (including all-too-realistic reenactments of the Crucifixion); the docility with which they received missionaries and later the parish priests, who traveled and lived alone, unarmed and unprotected among them, making a thorough nuisance of themselves (yet producing only one martyr in Yucatan during the entire colonial period, and only a rumored one at that):[4] all these responses could well have derived from a prudent recognition of the Spaniards' superior military power. They could also derive from Maya recognition of the sacred power that the Catholic priests represented. And the two explanations are wholly compatible. The Spaniards' military success could be seen as a sign of divine favor, and it would have been rash, perhaps impossible for the pantheistic Maya, to deny the possibility that the Spanish god was a force to be reckoned with.

To accept this new personage as a sacred being, even as an especially powerful one, was not the same as accepting him as the *only* sacred being in the cosmos. And it was the Judaeo-Christian God's intolerance of rivals that created the crisis in the Maya's corporate relationship with the supernatural. The friars could forbid the new catechumens to worship their deities, but convincing them that such worship was unnecessary or futile was another matter. The Maya believed that a sacred umbilical cord, through which nourishment flowed in both directions, linked heaven and earth.[5] It is not clear whether gods or men would perish first if the life-sustaining cord were cut, as the ban on pagan rituals threatened to do. Regardless of the exact sequence, the existence of the world and everything in it was placed in peril.

IDOLATRY VERSUS SUPERSTITION

The Maya, in common with most people, divided their dealings with the supernatural into public and private spheres. Within the private domestic sphere, involving the everyday concerns of the Maya farmer and his family, Christianity seems to have produced little conflict between behavior and belief, and only minor changes in either. The modern ethnographic literature contains descriptions of many domestic rituals, especially those surrounding childbirth, illness, and death, which could have been copied almost verbatim from colonial documents.[6] The search for animal tracks around a house at the time of a child's birth to determine the identity of his particular guardian spirit; the use of grains of maize for divination and curing, and the characteristically Yucatecan *zaztun*, or crystal, through which the shaman sees hidden causes and events; the ceremony of *kex*, or "exchange," by which food is offered to the spirits of death as ransom for the recovery of a sick person; the placing of work tools appropriate to the sex of the individual (spinning and weaving tools for women, machete and digging-stick for men) on the mat of a deceased family member: these are among a variety of rites that, along with their underlying concepts, have been reported in similar form through the past several centuries.

Some of the elements in this private sphere can be traced back to the pre-Columbian period, and fuller documentation would doubtless reveal many others. It is in fact highly likely that this decidedly folk level of religion has functioned with scant modification from very early times, long before the arrival of the Spanish and probably long before the arrival of earlier invaders who came from central Mexico with their religious cults. It would seem that this humble domain of belief was no more affected by foreign conquest or changing elite fashions than the way of life with which it enmeshed.

This continuity in lifeways and beliefs can be seen most

strongly in the all-important task of food production, with its locus in the *milpa*. A few Christian elements have crept into the complex of ceremonies linked to clearing, planting, and harvesting. The Holy Trinity *(Dios Yumbil, Dios Mehenbil, Dios Espiritu Santo)* is often invoked in the prayers, along with indigenous sacred beings. Among these are the four *pauahtuns* (possibly manifestations of the *chaacs*, or rain spirits), which, although they bear ancient Maya associations with the four cardinal directions and their identifying colors and are embedded in an equally (if not more) ancient complex of symbols centered on rain, have also acquired the names of Christian saints.[7] These elements do not seem to be more than minor accretions. The traditional methods of subsistence, and the beliefs and rituals associated with them, have remained virtually unchallenged. I once asked a Maya farmer why, if he was a Christian, he made offerings to the *chaacs*. He answered, with the air of one stating the obvious, "Because I make *milpa*."

Apart from its close ties to the Maya's immediate physical environment, and to an unchanging agricultural system and associated way of life, the stability of this substratum of traditional Maya religion is mainly due to its lowly and private nature. The Catholic priests in Yucatan, as in other parts of Spanish America, made a convenient distinction between this level – which they labeled superstition – and idolatry.

Superstitious beliefs and practices, confined to the individual and his kinfolk and to the forest, *milpa*, and household, were particularly difficult to detect. Some scholars have seen in the Catholic clergy's greater tolerance for these practices an ill-disguised confession of failure to eradicate pagan ways. But because the rites were domestic and addressed themselves to the humbler spirits in the indigenous cosmology, the clergy also came to regard them as less dangerous. They were only venial sins, arising from ignorance rather than perversity, and they usually elicited no more than an admonition or mild penance when detected. The rites were performed by minor religious practitioners, the village shamans, whom the clergy sometimes called witches *(brujos)* or sorcerers *(hechiceros)* but whom they nevertheless tolerated as long as they did not seem to be creating any mischief.[8]

Superstition might be foolish and futile and even wicked at times. It did not pose the same threat to Christianity as idolatry, nor the same threat to the social and political order on which Christianity rested. The shaman's power, though far from negligible, operated within a very circumscribed sphere. It was the upper level of the Maya priesthood, the deities they served, and the public rituals they and the civil-religious leaders performed – that is, the state religion – with which the friars were in competition and which they sought to replace.

This state religion, which might more aptly be seen as a Weberian "community cult," was linked to the private sphere through the family-owned idols that the Spaniards found in such bewildering and frustrating profusion. References to these idols and to household shrines, and the proliferation of these shrines in the late Postclassic site of Mayapan, have led some scholars to see a fragmentation of Maya religion in this period into almost purely family devotions.[9] But the existence of household icons and shrines does not signify a breakdown of public worship among the Maya any more than it does among Roman Catholic and Orthodox Christians. Spanish accounts and court records make clear that Maya obsequies to their family idols, whether these represented lineage gods or community gods – or both – did not replace but were performed in parallel with the public cults; sometimes the family idols were trotted out to be included in the public ceremonies.[10] Although the Spanish were not always precise in their own verbal distinctions, referring at times to "idolatries" as any kind of ritual involving idols, in practice they focused their evangelical fervor on the public rites that by tradition were performed in temples and plazas and which represented the Maya's collective bond with the supernatural.

We need not question the evangelical sincerity of the missionaries in order to recognize the social and political, and even the military, needs that were served by forced conversion. If the religious underpinnings of the old system had to be destroyed in order to consolidate and preserve the new, that did not negate the moral imperative of preaching the gospel. Nor need we attribute purely political motives to the Maya elite who resisted the change, simply because their own power and prestige were so firmly linked to the idolatry the conquerors wished to eradicate.

Unless we assume that the Maya leaders had been engaged in an elaborate and conscious fraud, they believed that the sacrifices and rogations they made were necessary to ensure the common good as well as to support their own authority.[11] I assume that their subjects shared this belief with more or less conviction, even if they were not initiated into the complex calendrical and astronomical computations and the other esoteric lore with which the specialists sought to understand and control the supernatural forces and, above all, keep the cosmic order from coming apart. Hence the dilemma of external conversion: to worship their deities provoked punishment from the Spaniards; not to worship them courted perhaps less immediate but more terrifying consequences.

This dilemma produced a split within the public or corporate sphere of religion between open observance of Christian ritual and clandestine adherence to the old religion. The Christian ritual took over the towns, just as the churches took over the temple sites, and the friars replaced the *ahkins*, the Maya high priests. The Maya ritual remained as a parallel system driven underground – often literally, into sacred caves. There, in the bush, or in the houses of the *principales*, the idols were hidden and when possible worshiped and fed with copal incense, maize gruel, and the blood of sacrificial victims, including humans.[12]

These furtive rites were not a satisfactory substitute for the old religion. By their nature they could not be public in the same way. In the more remote towns, all or a large part of the community could still participate. Wherever a friar was in residence the rites had to be highly secret, sometimes attended by only the *batab*, the *ahkin* and a few close kinsmen. Even then word sometimes leaked out (thereby entering the historical record) and the cost was high. Investigations were made, the idols smashed, and the idolators severely punished. The lightest sentence was a hundred lashes, and the interrogation techniques the friars had brought with them from Spain were none too gentle. The Church's laws forbade any procedure that involved "effusion of blood" or "loss of life or limb." The water torture and stretching inflicted on the Indians were designed to stay within those limits, but the friars were heavy-handed, perhaps accustomed to the larger, more robust physical specimens the Holy Office dealt with in Spain. Witnesses sometimes died or were crippled or "displayed their cowardice" by committing suicide before the questioning could be completed.[13]

The famous (or infamous) and well-documented idolatry trials conducted under the supervision of Fray Diego de Landa while he was Franciscan Provincial in 1562 revealed a disheartening gap between the Maya's public acceptance of Christianity and their private activities. A substantial portion of the Maya elite of Mani, Sotuta, Hocaba, and the other districts investigated – almost the entire core area of the colony except the territory between Campeche and Merida – were found to have been engaging in sacrificial rituals devoted to their pagan gods. The less densely populated and more supervised areas to the east and south were reported somewhat later to be even more flagrant in their idolatries. They still openly worshiped their gods with the whole community in attendance, and they threatened to provide the Church with a new set of martyrs when the clergy attempted to interfere.[14] But these territories were not yet considered very secure in the faith. What especially dismayed the friars in the 1562 investigations was the evidence of widespread apostasy within the regions where Christianity had seemed to take root so well. They were also deeply horrified. Some of the more gruesome (to Western eyes) rites had been practiced inside the churches and had incorporated Christian elements in what seemed a demonic parody, notably the crucifixion of children. All had gone on right under their noses and not by ignorant commoners either, but by *maestros cantores* and other church assistants, by the native rulers, and by other members of the most illustrious lineages, all of them educated by the friars.[15]

The trials created a double furor in the colony: first over the shocking finds, and next over the harsh methods the inquisitors had used to elicit confessions. Many of them were later retracted under the milder rule of the first resident bishop, Fray Francisco de Toral. The original confessions are, however, too circumstantial, too detailed, and too much in agreement with other evidence to be dismissed as fabrications simply because they were obtained under torture.

Rigged trials are not unknown in the colonial records, but they are easy to spot. The testimonies are monotonously repetitious, all in the same stilted language; and there are no messy details, even confirming ones, to interfere with the neatly concocted and smoothly flowing narrative. The testimony in unrehearsed trials is colloquial, almost conversational in style, as spotty and confused as human memory usually is, with conflicting details and loose ends. If the original testimonies in these idolatry trials were invented, the friars went to unequaled lengths to create an air of verisimilitude, even to coordinating evidence from different trials by different judges in neighboring districts to dovetail into a plausible, if disjointed, picture. Independent documentation, including somewhat later reports in a less hysterical atmosphere by a variety of officials less single-minded in their pursuit of idolatry, lends further credence to the trial. Altogether the evidence leads to the conclusion that for at least the first decades after conquest, the old gods were alive and well behind the public façade of Christianity.

The Christian forms of public worship eventually won out over the rival pagan tradition. One could argue that the steady decline in the number of cases of idolatry reported after the purge of the 1560s meant only that the Maya had become more circumspect or the clergy more relaxed in their vigilance. The clergy did become increasingly tolerant, but they could afford to be. If idolatry had not been entirely extirpated, it had ceased to pose a serious threat to the new state religion. Christianity had taken over the towns, and the Maya, who formerly had infused their whole environment with their own symbols and rituals, were left with the ones associated with the forest: the *milpa* ceremonies for rain and good harvests, hunting rituals, and the rituals related to caves, *cenotes*, wild beehives, and ceiba trees; or at best some furtive offerings in long-abandoned temples.[16]

The boundary between idolatry and superstition became largely obscured. Banished entirely to the *milpas* and forest, the clandestine rites ceased to be a regular community activity and became instead a more or less secret offering made by individuals or families in some out-of-the-way sacred spot. The one quasi-communal rite of which we have any record was the Cha-Chaac ceremony to avert drought. A few images preserved as family heirlooms might be taken from their hiding places and brought to a *milpa*, where a small group of men – certainly no substantial portion of the community – would gather to make their offerings.[17] One gets the impression that in the intervals between these emergencies, so long as the rains came more or less on schedule, the *milpa* gods or spirits received only the private ministrations of each farmer. This does not mean that the Maya abandoned their corporate efforts to maintain the cosmic order, only that the community as a whole, and particularly the civil-religious elite, were channeling their efforts through a new set of sacred beings and sacred rituals. These were the Christian saints and the Christian liturgy. And if they were not an entirely new set, they at least had new names and new houses.

SPANISH AND MAYA MICROCOSMS

The colonial clergy had a conveniently simple explanation for the apparent oscillations in Maya behavior. According to them, the Maya had freely accepted the Christian gospel of salvation, presenting themselves for baptism as they became persuaded of its redemptive power. No one had threatened them with any but otherworldly sanctions if they chose not to undergo this rite of initiation into the Body of Christ (technically this official version is on the whole true).[18] Many of them had then succumbed to Satan's temptations and committed apostasy – that is, defected from their voluntarily professed beliefs. But they recanted when their idolatry was discovered and they returned chastened to the fold, convinced of the essential truth of Christian doctrine. For the more pessimistic among the clergy, the Maya's lack of spiritual fortitude left them perpetually exposed to the danger of apostasy. The zones of refuge served as a constant lure and source of "infection," and the residents in the more isolated hamlets also tended to slide back into old ways. Not all the clergy shared so bleak a view. There were some who thought that in general, and especially in the towns, the Maya had managed to become as good Christians as any ignorant and brutish group of peasants could be.[19]

The main trouble with this explanation is that Christianity and paganism are offered as mutually exclusive alternatives from which the Maya had to choose and between which they might switch back and forth as the forces of light and darkness struggled for their souls. Certainly the friars saw and presented the two systems in that light, but it is far from certain that the Maya perceived them in the same way.

Much of the comparative study of religion is based on the same either/or dichotomy, although the theological categories and value judgments have been replaced by intellectual ones. According to the standard typology derived from Max Weber, traditional (or "primitive" or "magical") religions are contrasted with universal (or "rational") ones such as Islam, Christianity, and Buddhism. When dealing with religious change, this typology easily feeds into an evolutionary model (or perhaps the model itself is the implicit source of the typology) in which rationalized religions arise in a few favored spots and spread at the expense of less enlightened, more primitive ones. The model is not very different from the one presented by the missionaries. One has only to substitute the terms "weak," "incoherent," and "primitive" for "false" and "evil," and "rational" and "sophisticated" for "true" and "good." Neither model is particularly helpful in explaining how or why universal religions replace primitive ones except when implanted by superior physical force, and that sidesteps the issue of whether forced conversion brings about any actual changes in belief.

Robin Horton, in a series of articles based on evidence from sub-Saharan Africa, has developed a model of voluntary conversion from traditional (read primitive) belief systems to a universal religion that, while stimulated by outside contacts, does not depend on the introduction, peaceful or forced, of an alien religious system. The central hypothesis is that all traditional religions contain some latent notion of a universal supreme being. Horton argues that traditional religions (particularistic, segmental, local) are satisfactory explanations of, and modes of dealing with, the microcosmic world of geographically and culturally isolated groups. When the boundaries of that microcosm dissolve or significantly weaken through trade, conquest, or other sustained contact with the outside, the need to deal with this wider reality will stimulate the emergence of a latent concept of a universal supreme being whose power encompasses the world as a whole – that is, the macrocosm. Thus the monotheistic message of Islam and Christianity has been less important in stimulating both conversion and the rise of universalistic sects than the gradual incorporation of the sub-Saharan peoples into a wider political and economic sphere.[20]

For colonial Mesoamerica it would be more useful to abandon altogether the Weberian typology and the evolutionary schema it feeds into. Neither Spanish Catholicism nor Mesoamerican paganism fits neatly into either the universal or the traditional category (nor, I would suggest, do Islam and the French and Portuguese brands of Christianity that were introduced into Africa; only the "disenchanted" Protestantism that served as Weber's touchstone seems to correspond to the pure "universal" type). Both conceived of the divinity as at the same time unified and multiple, a conception that may be more common to religious thought than is generally acknowledged. The complex Mesoamerican iconography and the multiplicity of gods have tended to obscure the fact that these were refractions or manifestations of sacred power emanating from a single source, whether called Hunabku, Itzamna, Ometeotl, or Tezcatlipoca.[21] Faced with this apparent contradiction, Spanish friars postulated a possible descent from some past monotheism;[22] modern scholars have suggested an ascent *toward* monotheism. Both have failed to see that the one could encompass the many and that the imported and indigenous religions possessed certain structural similarities based on this same concept.

Some of the early Spanish missionaries, influenced by the reformist Erasmian humanism of the early sixteenth century, attempted to purge their religion of medieval accretions, which might more properly be called incorporations, and to present to the Amerindian neophytes a pristine form of Christianity (whatever that may be). The version that was transplanted to America fell far short of this ideal. For the mass of the Spanish laity, and the majority of the clergy as well, the uncompromising monotheism of the Old and New Testaments had become tempered in their Mediterranean version of popular Catholicism by the incorporation of a rich variety of sacred beings. Angels, saints, the Prince of Darkness and his minions, and a host of lesser spirits accompanied and aided or sometimes sought to foil the will of the supreme godhead. For most of the Spanish culture-bearers, the Christian cosmos was as densely populated as that of the Maya.[23]

Both Spanish Christianity and Mesoamerican paganism, then, represented richly complex, multilayered systems instead of any one pure type. Only if we recognize that they confronted each other as total systems and interacted at a variety of levels can we begin to make some sense of postconquest religious change, not as a shift from one type to another (the standard model of conversion), nor even necessarily from one level to another (the modified "emergence" model) nor as the superimposition of Christianity on a pagan base (a common syncretistic model applied to Latin America), but as a set of horizontal, mutual exchanges across comparable levels.

In distinguishing among these levels, Horton's microcosm–macrocosm concept serves as a useful ordering principle. To be sure, microcosm and macrocosm are but opposite ends of a continuum. We could find almost an infinity of gradations corresponding to levels of contact with the world "out there": gradations among people, among spheres of activity, among sacred beings, and among religious modes related to them. The more isolated the group and the more private the activity, the more particularistic the religious expression is likely to be. But for the present analysis the gradations can be divided into three broad categories.

Starting with the universal level, I find that Horton defines his upper tier rather narrowly as monotheism or monolatry (the worship of one god while acknowledging the existence of others). A more general, and therefore for our purposes more useful, distinction would be between lesser, localized members of the cosmos and an all-encompassing concept of the divinity, whether seen as single or multiple, or both. Accompanying this concept would be a greater elaboration of a transcendental theology addressing itself to the larger question of where we come from, why we are here, and where we are going when we leave: in other words, questions transcending the immediate concerns of human existence emphasized in the more pragmatic goals of geographically bounded spheres.

Horton's lower, microcosmic tier needs to be divided in two. At the bottom we find what I have identified as the private sphere in Maya religion. Defined by the Spanish clergy as superstition and corresponding to what later taxonomies have come to call magic, this level involves the manipulation of highly discrete and localized supernatural forces for the benefit of the individual and his family. I have created a new middle-level niche for corporate or parochial cults with their patron deities or saints; they are still microcosmic because they are tied to a particular group but are less particularistic than the magical. Although these corporate cults might shade into semiprivate devotions to family patrons, I place them in the public, collective sphere of religious activity referred to earlier in the chapter.

Like many other sixteenth-century Christians, a substantial portion of Spaniards shared with the Maya a belief in magic as a means of controlling one's immediate environment and personal welfare. Considering the private, everyday concerns of this belief, it is not surprising that it has been the least affected by political change or the erosion of cultural boundaries, whether in Spain or in Yucatan. I have suggested that the magical sphere of Maya religion survived Spanish conquest and colonization largely intact. As long as we look only for cultural loss or attrition or the assimilation of Christian elements – that is, vertical influences from orthodox, universalistic Christianity – this appears to be the case. However, we should not ignore the possibility of horizontal enrichment from the Spaniards' own magical world, or even a reciprocal movement. Maya magic and orthodox Christianity did not on the whole impinge on each other, but that does not preclude the possibility of mutual influence at more compatible levels.

From the perspective of a twentieth-century urban dweller, the magical beliefs held by the Maya and the Spanish in Yucatan seem like minor variations on the same theme. It would require a far more detailed comparison than is warranted here, and perhaps much more information than is now available on the preconquest versions of both traditions, to be able to judge how much the similarities are structural and coincidental and how much they derive from mutual influence. The main point is that Spanish religion did not all float like a layer of oil on the surface of Maya magic but had its own magical layer that could blend with the Maya's.

The Spaniards' own magical beliefs help to account for the ambivalence behind the Church's stance on Maya "superstitions." These were not condemned as doctrinal errors, nor even, despite the official label of superstition, always dismissed as fabrications or delusions. How could they be, when so many of the clergy themselves saw the world teeming with demons, imps, and other disembodied spirits and had the same belief in the power of spells and incantations?[24] No distinction seems to have been made in practice between the indigenous and the imported versions of magic. The Church in Yucatan as elsewhere was far more concerned with heterodoxy, whether idolatry or Lutheranism, that challenged its ideological and ritual supremacy. When it did bother with magic, the issue in question was whether a particular person had sought to call upon supernatural forces and to what end. The ethnic identity of the practitioner and his or her familiar spirits were largely irrelevant except in a jurisdictional sense, since Spaniards and *castas* were subject to the Inquisition, while the episcopal courts handled Indian cases.

These cases reveal that Maya and Spanish magic did not operate as separate and equal systems but commingled in a two-way exchange in which the Maya system seems to have been dominant. It was almost as if the political and economic prostration of the Indians was partially compensated for by their superior supernatural powers. Spaniards (including some of the wealthiest and most influential colonists) as well as *castas* acknowledged these powers, feared them, and sought their help in need: to exorcise a bewitched cow, remove the curse from a field, relieve an ailment, or cure infertility.[25] The Indian shamans were the experts from whom an enterprising *mestizo* or mulatto might learn some very useful and marketable skills, though it seems that the magical powers were not always transferable. One unfortunate mulatto ran afoul of the Inquisition because he had bragged to his fellow inmates in the Merida prison that an Indian sorcerer had taught him how to turn himself into a bird and fly.[26] The judges did not take the boast seriously – after all, the man had not managed to fly out of the prison yard, but neither did they find it totally absurd. By the late colonial period the Inquisition had become defunct in all but name. Yet parish clergy still expressed only hesitant doubts about witchcraft accusations on the grounds of insufficient proof. And as late as 1813 one curate reported with half-hearted skepticism a girl's claim that in the guise of a bird she accompanied sorcerers on their nocturnal flights through the countryside, commenting that she had "probably dreamed" these occurrences.[27]

Spaniards and Africans brought their magical beliefs with them to America, but in leaving behind their own microcosms, they had to leave behind the supernatural beings and forces associated with them. The broadening of their geographical and cultural horizons did not preclude their having to deal with their immediate surroundings when they found themselves in the alien microcosms belonging to the Maya and other Indians. This was a different spirit world inhabited by another set of beings and forces, tied to the particular place, with which anyone living in that place would have to reckon. And just as they had to rely on the Indians' knowledge of the physical environment – which plants were edible, which snakes venomous, and what signs presaged the coming of the rains – they must have felt that the Indians understood and could control the local spirits better than outsiders.

Wherever a large African population has replaced the Amerindian, as in parts of Brazil and the Caribbean, it has been able to transplant or reconstruct its own spirit world in the new setting with its own shamanistic specialists. There the same ambivalent attitude that Spaniards displayed toward Indian magic was transferred to Africans.[28] In Yucatan both the Europeans and the Africans deferred to the Maya's superior knowledge of that particular microcosm and its spirits. Even those who chose to ignore these spirits in practice and rely exclusively on the Christian God or the saints to intervene in their daily lives did not therefore deny their reality. And some who had doubts still turned to Maya magic in a kind of hedging of bets, just in case there might be something to it.

Beyond the level of magical beliefs and practices, Maya and Spanish religions appear to diverge sharply. According to the standard models of conversion, the choice between traditional polytheism and universal monotheism is clear, even if not always conscious. The two are antithetical. Thus the choice faced by the Maya would be modified by the superior military power of the Spanish, but it would still be well defined: either accept the new religion as a replacement for their traditional beliefs, or retain these beliefs intact, plus whatever rituals could be carried on *sub rosa*, while submitting only nominally to Christianity's external forms.

A long-standing axiom in Mesoamerican studies is that this choice is precisely what the Indians could not or would not make. Scores of accounts with hundreds of photographs of village fiestas have been published to illustrate the colorful ways in which the Indians have blended the two traditions;[29] all the more quaint because they are almost, but not quite, familiar to the Western eye. It is possible to see this blend as a confused jumble created by accident and ignorance – as the incorporation of whatever ill-understood Christian elements happened to strike the Indians' fancy. Since Christianity and pre-Columbian paganism are incompatible, so the argument goes, confusion must lie at the heart of any amalgamation between the two. Some confusion no doubt did exist, but much of it may disappear if we cease to see polytheism and monotheism as mutually exclusive alternatives. They can represent, as I have suggested earlier, simply two different levels – the parochial and the universal – within the public sphere of religion, which can coexist with each other as well as with the magical level.

The parochial tier, though still microcosmic and particularistic, has wider horizons than the individual or family and the immediate surroundings. It concerns the welfare and identity of the community, be that hamlet, village, province, or city-state, and the community's corporate relationship with the supernatural. And that welfare and identity are the responsibility of one or more particular sacred beings. The Mesoamerican pantheon was inhabited by a host of deities, with multiple attributes, human and anthropomorphic, and shifting identities, represented in rich, many-layered clusters of visual and verbal imagery. The symbolic system, still only partially decoded, that linked this kaleidoscopic profusion of sacred beings into an all-encompassing conception of the divinity need not concern us here, only their role as tutelary gods on which group loyalties were focused.

Each collection of deities was discrete, corresponding to particular geopolitical units and ruling lineages, in addition to the special patrons of occupational groups such as merchants. The nature and astral deities, like the gods of maize, of rain, of the sun and the moon, that regulated and sustained the farmer's central concern – his maize crop – were pan-Mesoamerican. Indeed, their equivalents can be found in any peasant society. But the peasant does not conceive of them as any more universal than the particular ancestral and territorial gods that watch over his own community and with whom some of them may in fact have been associated in the Mesoamerican system as variants or local manifestations.

It was at this parochial or corporate level of religion that the

Maya and Spanish systems competed most directly. This middle tier of the Spanish cosmos was no more a void than the humbler domain of "ghosties, ghoulies, and things that go bump in the night," from which, in the old Scottish Book of Common Prayer, the Good Lord is asked to deliver us. The Christian God reigned supreme but he had not absorbed all lesser beings. And the Christian saints transported across the Atlantic were in their own way as much tutelary deities as the collections of gods that watched over the Maya communities. Each neighborhood, town, and region in Spain had its own patron saint or saints; and the territorial hierarchy culminates in the guardian spirit for the entire Christian nation, Santiago Matamoros (St James the Moor-Killer).

Some of the patrons are historically associated with the locale, like St Isidore, the seventh-century bishop of Seville. The universality of other saints was subordinated to their roles as local manifestations of the sacred and as repositories of local welfare and local pride.[30] Although in theory Mary is the same Mother of God regardless of what physical image represents her, in the popular mind the Virgin of Macarena, say, is the rival of the Virgin of Triana, who resides across the river in Seville. Each set of devotees take corporate pride in extolling the superior beauty, greater pathos of expression, and richer adornments of their own Queen of Heaven, and the rivalry has been known to erupt into physical violence during Holy Week, when the jewel-bedecked images are taken out in candlelit processions through the city streets and partisan fervor reaches its height.

The social as well as the geopolitical map of sixteenth-century Spain could be drawn by plotting out the spaces allocated to their sacred sponsors. Each craft speciality or other occupational group also had its own patron saint – for example, St Joseph for carpenters and Our Lady of Carmen for fishermen. These had no place in the largely undifferentiated peasant society of the postconquest Maya. But the saints rapidly became the focus of corporate identity for the territorial groups – the *parcialidades*, the *pueblos*, and the quasi-*pueblos* or large *haciendas*.

CHRIST, KUKULCAN, AND THE MACROCOSM

In this scheme of consonances at the magical and parochial levels, the third or universal level of religious expression appears to be left dangling. Without any equivalent of the Christian Almighty in the indigenous system, there is no possibility of amalgamation. The Maya would have to make a leap of faith in accepting this alien concept, or fail to make it. Or at best, the arrival of the Spanish and the incorporation of the Maya into a wider universe would stimulate the emergence of such a concept already there in latent form.

Whether the Indians "really" became Christians is one of the more intriguing questions in Latin American history, or so I must assume since I am so frequently asked; and it is a perplexing one, starting with the distinct lack of agreement among Christian theologians over the exact definition of "Christian." I take it to mean whether the Indians genuinely came to believe in "One God, Father Almighty, Maker of Heaven and earth . . ." and so on down the articles of faith in the Nicene Creed. Judging from the words and actions of the colonial Maya, reaching us mainly through the alien perspective of their conquerors and thus subject to double distortion (first the Spaniards' and then our own), the missionaries do not seem to have succeeded in converting more than a handful of their catechumens. The same evidence also points to a more novel proposition: that Maya cosmology became less, not more, universalistic after the conquest.

I have earlier suggested that the pre-Hispanic Maya, in common with the rest of Mesoamerica, already possessed a concept of the all-encompassing divinity of whom the lesser deities were refractions or manifestations. This does not mean that either Hunabku or Itzamna was the exact equivalent of Jehovah. Whether conceived of as an extremely remote being who directed the cosmos only through his multiple manifestations or more in the way of an abstract principle, a creative force, or prime mover,[31] the Maya supreme godhead does not seem to have intervened directly in human affairs. Nor did he figure prominently, in his unitary aspect, in Maya ritual. More to the point is that the Maya, or rather the educated elite, were far from living totally enclosed in a microcosmic world, either mentally or physically. They possessed the leisure and inclination for metaphysical speculation and a consciousness of wider horizons beyond their own locale through their activities in warfare, long-distance trade and diplomacy.[32]

In assessing the impact of Christianity, we have to distinguish between the ordinary Maya villager and the cosmopolitan elite, who were already conscious of and involved in events beyond the boundaries of their own group, who held a more abstract and formalized idea of the divine, and for whom Christianity therefore presented a different challenge. This is not to say that the elite's response would be uniform either. Some of them led resistance movements during and directly following the military conquest that were aimed explicitly against Christianity; others seem to have "converted" with a certain alacrity and even proselytized actively among their followers.[33] Though contrasting, these responses may have been equivalent, the reverse sides of the same intellectual coin. The Maya elites, as distinct from the peasantry, may have found enough theological congruence between Christianity and their own religion to facilitate either an informed acceptance or an equally informed rejection of what they perceived as analogous but rival doctrines. The Christian idea of the Trinity, of a god who is One God but at the same time Three Persons, would be no more incomprehensible to the sophisticated ruling groups among the Maya, whose gods had multiple (although usually 4) identities, than it is to the Christians who routinely repeat their belief in this divine mystery when they recite the Creed.

Whatever other affinities may have existed between the formal theologies elaborated by the two cults, the Christian doctrine of exclusivity gained few if any adherents among Maya priests and rulers. Their inclination to incorporate new elements rather than substitute new for old can be seen clearly on the east coast of Yucatan, an area where Christianity was adopted – or rather adapted – with little coercion, or even supervision, from the Spanish.

The east-coast Maya were brought under Spanish rule with scarcely a battle and then quickly left to their own devices. Their spiritual conquest was, if anything, more relaxed and perfunctory than their military conquest. Cortés was the first to preach the gospel, during his brief stopover on the island of Cozumel in 1519, and perhaps the only ardent proselytizer the area was ever to see. Certainly neither Montejo nor his chaplain showed much interest in converting the inhabitants when the 1527 expedition passed through, and the Franciscans who arrived in the colony in the 1540s could spare no friars for what was by then a thinly populated region isolated from the main colonial centers to the west. It received little attention from either Church or state, and only occasional visitors. Even when a resident curate was appointed in 1582, he could not, from his offshore base on Cozumel, have kept very close watch over a parish scattered along more than 100 kilometers of coast.[34]

Not surprisingly, pagan practices continued barely checked. The *encomendero* was absent and in any case inimical to ecclesiastical incursions, and the few clergymen who did visit the area were totally dependent on the goodwill of the native rulers. What is surprising is that these same Maya who withdrew food supplies and threatened worse to any priest attempting to interfere with their idolatries were at the same time cordially welcoming other clergymen who stuck to purely Christian business; so generous was their support that an enterprising Portuguese sailor thought it worth his while to sojourn there, posing as a priest. They docilely lined up for masses, baptisms, and weddings in fairly substantial Christian churches that must have been built with very little clerical supervision.

Recent excavations in one of these churches, at the coastal site of Tzama (present-day Tancah), unearthed a pagan cache offering under the base of the altar and two pre-Columbian-style burials (flexed position, one with a jade bead in the mouth) under the floor of the nave.[35] Equally significant are the seventeen other burials in the sample, all in standard Christian fashion and all or most presumably interred when no Spaniard was around – unless everyone happened to die during the rare priestly visits. Perhaps they did, but then we have the cross that Cortés erected in one of the main temples of Cozumel, which later visitors found in place alongside the restored traditional deities. Did the Maya hastily reerect the cross every time they spotted a Spanish sail on the horizon? A somewhat less strained explanation for all the assembled evidence is that the Maya were receptive to the new cult, but on their own terms, which meant incorporating it into the existing system.

Neither the written reports nor the archaeological evidence make clear exactly what frame of reference the new symbols and rituals were incorporated into. The cross among the Maya seems to have signified the sacred "first tree of the world" which linked heaven and earth.[36] We also know that the east coast was a center for the cult of Kukulcan, himself an alien deity (Quetzalcoatl) imported from the highlands and blended into the local tradition. The particular focus of the local cult was Quetzalcoatl in the form of Venus as morning star, representing the risen god. Having their own god who died, descended into the underworld, and rose again (as in the cycle of Venus) and who was expected to come again to reclaim his earthly kingdom, the Maya could well have found the teachings on Christ a variation on a familiar theme.[37]

The east coast was part of Yucatan's "Putun" periphery, which on the whole displayed a much more open and flexible attitude toward the Spanish and their new cult than the more geographically and culturally isolated provinces in the interior. As principal links in a pan-Mesoamerican system of commercial exchange, the "Putun" rulers were particularly involved with the wider world beyond their immediate territory. We have no idea how prominent the idea of a supreme being or beings was in "Putun" cosmology. But their cosmopolitan perspective, reflected in their devotion to the "international" cult of Quetzalcoatl, suggests that the receptive responses to Christianity of the east-coast Maya were based on some concept more overarching in scope than the rulers' own ancestral and territorial deities.

One might expect the Spanish conquest to stimulate further elaboration of a universal concept of the divine and to help spread the concept to more isolated regions and to the lower levels of Maya society, even without missionary efforts on behalf of Christianity. The Spanish, after all, were much more foreign to the Maya than their former trading partners and the earlier invaders from the highlands. The Spaniards' arrival thus represented a more drastic erosion of cultural boundaries, a forced awareness of a world far wider than Mesoamerica. This does not seem to have happened. The cause lies partly with the quality of religious instruction. The early missionaries, handicapped by lack of personnel and by ignorance of the language, had to rely on native interpreters and catechists. Even when a Catholic priest was in residence, he would have found it difficult to monitor either covert resistance to the gospel message or unwitting distortions in its transmission. And only a small proportion of congregated towns had resident priests.[38]

If evangelization is measured in terms of architecture, liturgy, and administrative organization, the friars' achievement is most impressive. Within a few decades of their arrival, the entire population under Spanish military control had been congregated into towns and the towns organized into parishes. Grandiose stone churches and friaries had been constructed in the major centers, and even the most remote villages had their stone chapels with pole-and-thatch naves to house the congregations. The vast majority of adults had been baptized; catechism classes were held regularly; and the ordinary parish routine of infant baptism, Christian marriage and burial, and yearly confession and communion was well underway through the tireless activity of the circuit-riding friars. There are signs, however, that the less tangible goal of implanting orthodox Christian doctrine had eluded them.

As the numbers of clergy in the colony increased, the level of enthusiasm declined. Most of them were Creoles and therefore bilingual from infancy, yet by their own admission the vast majority of curates continued to leave the catechism completely to the Maya *maestros cantores* and counted these successful if the catechumens learned to repeat from memory the "Four Prayers" (the Creed, Hail Mary, Our Father, and *Salve regina*) by the time they were ready for first communion.[39] The more conscientious priests reexamined the adult parishioners before admitting them to the sacraments for their annual Easter Duty and sent those with faulty memory back to remedial catechism class on Sunday afternoons. Even so, the bishops who bothered to examine candidates for confirmation during their diocesan tours found the majority grossly ignorant of even these rudiments. And the few clergymen who ventured to inquire whether the rote learning had inculcated any understanding of Christian precepts came to the painful conclusion that the gospel seed had borne little fruit among the Maya.

It must be admitted that the ground was not fertile. It is doubtful that the ordinary Maya peasant had ever possessed more than a hazy notion of Itzamna or Kukulcan or the complex cosmologies in which they were embedded. If the vast majority of colonial Maya found the concept of a distant, all-encompassing god who meted out rewards and punishments in the hereafter meaningless or irrelevant, it was surely the fault as much of the content of the message as of the manner of instruction. The concerns of the Maya peasant, Spanish conquest notwithstanding, were still confined to the welfare of his family and his village, his hunting-grounds and beehives, and above all his *milpa*; and his negotiations were directed to the less awesome beings who were in charge of them. If anything, religious universalism suffered a decline after the conquest.

If rationalization of the sacred is tied to the breakdown of cultural and geographical isolation, then the process must be reversible, ebbing and flowing according to circumstances. By thinking of the magical, the parochial, and the universal as levels or spheres rather than as stages of development, we can consider the possibility of shifts in emphasis in both directions. The Spanish conquest may have provided an initial stimulus toward increased universality, but before long Maya society became more self-contained, more microcosmic in outlook than before.

The colonial Maya texts called the books of Chilam Balam, which blended Christian concepts and biblical lore into the esoteric learning of traditional Maya cosmology, demonstrate that at least for some period after conquest a corps of priestly intellectuals survived for whom Christianity was not an entirely mystifying ragbag of curious notions. Though the meaning of the books is often obscure because of our ignorance of much of the complex Maya symbolic system, enough can be puzzled out to suggest a response to Christian dogma at a highly sophisticated level of interpretation. As I have already suggested, an association of Christ with Kukulcan is not necessarily whimsical. The Church's teachings on Christ's death, rebirth, and prophesied second coming, as mentioned earlier, had more than faint echoes in the pre-Columbian beliefs about Kukulcan. It has been argued that the Maya associated the Virgin with the moon goddess Ixchel because of the Virgin's common depiction on a crescent moon. That may be so. But the moon goddess was also the consort of the creating sun god. And there is no Christian imagery, only meaning, to associate Mary, as she is associated in the Chilam Balam of Chumayel, with the Maya "Cord from Heaven" – the divine umbilical cord that signifies the link between the natural and sacred worlds, between man and God (or the gods).[40]

The priestly corps eventually died out, and along with it the theological sophistication that informed the Chilam Balam texts. It is unlikely that the later colonial scribes added anything of substance to the early postconquest versions of the cosmological sections or even understood much of what they copied.

Christianity did not replace Maya paganism at the upper levels of theology, nor did it even blend with it; they both lost out to the syncretic parochialism of the cult of the tutelary deity-saints, as the Maya elites became reduced to purely local and subordinate status and their horizons shrank to the size of their *macehual* subjects. The functions that had previously taken them beyond their cultural boundaries – warfare, diplomacy, and long-distance trade – were taken over by the conquerors. After the region was pacified, the Spanish for the most part withdrew to the cities, and the Maya, from top to bottom of the sociopolitical hierarchy, turned inward, encapsulated in their microcosmic boundaries, whch they were able to rebuild and even to strengthen after the first shock of conquest.

The increased parochialism of the colonial Maya outlook did not depend on a hermetic seal around each township or parish. Changes of residence from one community to another, temporary migrations to the coastal salt flats, even movement across the colonial frontier either by flight into the unpacified zones or forced repatriation from them, were all within the same self-contained universe of the lowland Maya. Except for references to a few men recruited as seamen in the early postconquest period, no Maya seem to have traveled outside that universe. The Spanish not only took over the long-distance trade but also employed only *castas* to man the *bongos* (large canoes) and other craft that plied the coast and gulf.

The old pilgrimage centers of the east coast of Yucatan died out along with the trade routes to which they had been linked. During the late Postclassic period these shrines, especially the ones on Cozumel, had brought devotees from Campeche, Xicalango, Tabasco, and perhaps more distant parts of Mesoamerica, as well as people from the interior of the peninsula. It would be futile to try to decide whether they came primarily to exchange goods or to make offerings and consult the island's sacred oracles. The two activities mingled, as did the diverse populations of visitors to this cosmopolitan spot. The Spanish asserted that Cozumel retained its importance for decades after the conquest, as the Maya equivalent of Jerusalem or Rome.[41] But its decline to a sparsely populated, rarely visited backwater had already started before the final military campaigns were over. The area was eventually abandoned to the pirates and smugglers who carried on the "Putun" tradition in their own way. It had long been a victim and a symptom of the lowland Maya's isolation within their own cultural and geographical boundaries.

Presumably the perceptual boundaries of the *macehuales* had always been so circumscribed, and the elite's horizons contracted to the same dimensions after conquest. For them as well as the *macehuales* there was little to heighten awareness of the world outside. Even the intermittent presence of the Spaniards, once the Maya had incorporated their demands into their scheme of reality, came to lose its strangeness and be counted among the other common and explicable woes to which human existence was subject. For most Maya the postconquest disintegration of interprovincial and intercommunity ties within Yucatan meant that the social world was confined even more closely to the community in which they had been born or to another barely distinguishable one to which they might migrate.

Colonial Maya religion reflects this increased isolation. The idea of an all-encompassing godhead was not necessarily totally lost. It could have survived and become merged into the remote figure of the Christian *Dios*. But even if deferred to in theory, this vaguely defined and omnipotent being held no prominent place in either the ritual or what we can recover of the cosmology of the colonial Maya.

The implantation of a universalistic religion among any peasant population would seem to be a futile exercise. They may be willing to pay more or less formal homage to the abstract entity of whose divinity the saints or lesser gods are supposed to be mere reflections. But it would be difficult to find a peasant group, whether nominally followers of the Buddha, Shiva, Christ, or Mohammed, who have totally and permanently forsaken the more accessible sacred beings of the locale or group, so long at least as they remain peasants – that is, bound by their microcosmic worlds.

OLD GODS IN NEW GUISES

The colonial Maya continued to concentrate their collective attention on the middle range of the cosmos, on the tutelary beings identified with their own communities. Within this public sphere no shift in emphasis toward universality can be discerned. On the contrary, universality withdrew further into the background once it lost its only class of adherents within Maya society.

The evangelistic zeal of the friars, backed by the military power of the conquerors, ensured that the parochial level of religion would eventually be expressed exclusively within the framework of Christianity. The outward transformation was accomplished rapidly. Within a decade or so after the friars' arrival the pagan temples, except the ones already long abandoned to the bush, had been destroyed and their stones incorporated into the fabric of the Christian churches erected on their platforms. The old idols had also been destroyed or hidden away. Their place had been taken by effigies of Christian saints adorned with European finery and served by foreign priests with a whole new array of vestments, ritual objects, and sacred symbols. Even if the indigenous long-distance trade had not been destroyed, the new temples had no place for the jade masks, the jaguar-pelt draperies, or the iridescent plumage of the quetzal bird. Moreover, the ceremonial round that focused on the new temples, the various feasts and rites that marked the passage of time, were not only new; they also moved to the different rhythm of the Christian calendar.

The pagan cults that had persisted as a clandestine rival were no match for the officially sanctioned cult, for the more stealthy and exclusive the ritual, the less it fulfilled its purpose. Hidden worship can sustain a personal relationship with a supreme deity; secret gifts to the corporate gods that no one else knows about or shares in, although possibly satisfying to the individual, cannot express and sustain an entire community's links with the sacred. The Maya's corporate relationship with the supernatural was triadic, consisting of deities, elite mediators, and the rest of the community. With the third element removed by the vigilance of the friars, the mediators would become superfluous. They might as well cease their intercessions – and, incidentally, renounce their claim to legitimacy – unless they could transfer them elsewhere.

The ancient calendar-round that the gods sustained may have been forgotten; the gods themselves were not. They were transformed into the particular collections of Catholic saints assigned to each town or village according to the whim or special devotion of the friars who established its church. It is unlikely that the neophytes had any say over whether they would be placed under the special protection of SS Cosme and Damian or Santo Bernardino de Sena; or whether the Virgin Mary in their community should have the title of the Immaculate Conception (a special favorite of the Franciscans, which accounts for nearly one-half of the Our Lady cults in the original foundations) rather than the Assumption (the next in popularity), the Rosary, the Visitation, or some other Marian advocation.[42] It did not really matter, except in establishing which annual feast-days the community would henceforth celebrate in honor of its protectors.

Much of the rich lore of Christian hagiography was lost in the transfer to Yucatan. Whatever information may have been transmitted to the Maya about the life-histories, the personalities, the special powers, and other idiosyncrasies of their designated patrons, it seems to have had little impact. There is no evidence that St Antony's power to trace lost objects or cure sore throats was ever appealed to, or that SS Michael, Peter, and Gregory were distinguished in any way other than as patrons of different Maya communities. And their importance, like that of the various local images of the Virgin, was measured purely in terms of the intervillage hierarchy.

The physical images of these saints were as foreign to the Maya as the names and particular miraculous traditions they bore. Few if any were produced in the peninsula, even after Spanish craftsmen had begun to settle there and teach their skills to the Maya. Carved and painted in pure European style, the images were imported from Guatemala and Mexico, to be deposited in the village churches ready-made for local veneration. Although through the centuries silver halos, silk robes and canopies, and other locally made adornments were added, and arms were replaced and faces retouched, none of the later embellishments reveals any influence of local styles or visual symbolism.[43]

Some formal deference was paid to a god who had no Maya name (only the Spanish term *Dios*) and who was invoked either alone or as the Trinity at the beginning of prayers and the most solemn documents, but was otherwise ignored. We can only guess what this god meant to them. The ultimate source from which the other sacred beings derived their powers? The Creator who had withdrawn after setting things in motion? The Maya equivalent of the Athenians' "Unknown God," included as an insurance policy? Some mysterious Spanish divinity who had to be taken into account, just as the people who represented him could not be ignored? Whatever his nature, he did not intervene directly in their lives, and their attention was focused on those who did – the local Virgin and the patron saints, who were with few exceptions male. The Virgin was called *colebil* in Maya, meaning "lady or mistress of servants [or serfs] or slaves."[44] The other saints were referred to as *bolonpixan*, which the Spanish translators rendered as blessed (*bienaventurado*), but which literally means "nine-souled." Nine was a sacred Maya number, and this designation may refer to the nine states of transformation through which the souls passed to achieve their immortality.[45]

Nuances aside, the Virgin and the patron saint were viewed as the proprietors as well as the protectors of the community, rather like lord and lady of the manor, whose manor house was the church. The other holy images that resided there, though also venerated, were accorded a slightly lower rank.

Included in these collections of community guardians was any special image of Christ that the local church might have acquired. Each one was regarded as a separate entity, whether as Christ the King, Jesus the Nazarene, Christ of the Trans-figuration, or the Infant Jesus (*Niño Dios*); and none of them was equated with the second person of the Trinity (called *Dios Mehenbil*), or for that matter with the figure on the crucifix placed above the main altar in every church. None of these separate Christ entities seems to have held any special status above the "other" saints. Each was allotted his particular feast-day in the Christian calendar, in addition to the separate ritual observed everywhere for the "Dead God" on Good Friday, when the descent from the cross was reenacted in each church and a life-sized Christ figure placed on a catafalque before the main altar. The clergy believed the Maya entered into this sacred drama with great devotion, and no doubt they did. However, there is no indication that they regarded the death and resurrection of this particular sacred being in accordance with Christian doctrine as *the* central events that had perma-nently transformed the cosmic order.[46]

Good Friday and Holy Week in general were secondary festi-vals in the yearly calendar of the Yucatec Maya, in sharp con-trast with Hispanic custom and even the postconquest traditions that have developed in highland regions of Mesoamerica. Holy Week fell somewhere on the scale between Christmas, a decidedly minor feast, and All Souls' Day, the Day of the Dead on which the ancestors were especially honored, and well below the feasts of the patron and the Virgin.

As alien as the Iberian saints were originally – in name, in physical appearance, and in the whole devotional apparatus surrounding them – the Maya were able to merge them with their traditional gods. We have no reliable guide to which particular gods might have merged with which saints, or even whether there was a one-to-one correlation. Whatever ordered complexity the popular cosmology of the colonial Maya may have had, we must be content with lumping the saints together into more or less undifferentiated assemblages and concentrate on their collective role as community guardians, rather than on any specialized attributes and powers that might have been assigned to them within that category.

Some have seen in the Christianized religion of postconquest Mesoamerica simply a cover for the old gods, who as "idols behind altars" have remained hidden in the saints' shrines or at least in the minds of the Indians.[47] The evidence suggests a more subtle and complex process of gradual fusion, at least among the Yucatec Maya.

Few areas under Spanish rule had the freedom enjoyed by the east-coast Maya to work out on their own terms a satisfactory combination of the new cult with their pagan practices. In more closely supervised areas those who were prepared to accept the Christian God, even as supreme being, had no easier a time than those who rejected him. The sticking-point was his jealous nature, the idea that all divinity was concentrated in this one remote figure to the exclusion of all the more familiar and more intimate deities that permeated the Maya's world. We can only guess at the disorientation and anxiety the Maya must have suffered as the first shock of conquest became deepened by the friars' assault on their deities, indeed on their whole world-order. One assumes that their earliest reactions were what has been termed "culture shock," or loss of "plausibility structure," or what Anthony Wallace has described in the psychological terms of personal loss as "Disaster Syndrome": the destruction of one's familiar world first brings about disorientation and numbness, followed by a denial of the loss, then severe anxiety, and finally anomie or despair, unless the world can be pieced together again, albeit with an altered configuration.[48]

The creative process of reconstruction, adaptation, and fusion that the Maya pursued in order to adjust their "reality" to the new circumstances created by evangelization is almost as obscure as the earliest responses, since only a few clues surface now and then from the records. The early adaptation of certain ritual elements from Christianity is well documented, such as the famous cases of human sacrifice in the Sotuta region in which the Maya priests added crucifixion to their standard repertoire and performed these and other sacrifices inside the Christian churches.[49] Idols were still being discovered through the first half of the seventeenth century, and, according to the Spanish, as soon as they were smashed the Maya would fashion new ones of clay or wood "over-night" and simply place them in a different cave. There they would continue to nourish them with copal incense, the ritual drink *balche*, maize, and offerings of turkey and deer (apparently the menu had ceased to include human hearts).[50] These might seem to indicate that Christianity and paganism were still perceived and practiced as two entirely separate, parallel cults. In fact, the fusion was already well under way, in the caves as well as in the churches.

Rather than simply addressing their community gods through Christian stand-ins, the Maya had given them a dual identity, smuggling idols into churches and also giving saints' names to the idols that they were at the same time worshiping in the caves, where they had no need for pretense.[51] Indeed, the Catholic clergy found these syncretic mutations, whenever they learned of them, even more offensive than unadulterated paganism. The "chameleon" nature of Maya gods has made the task of sorting out the pre-Columbian pantheon a frustrating puzzle. It may also have facilitated the process of fusion in this early stage of dual identity. The addition of one more guise to the multiple permutations each deity already possessed would hardly have fazed the Maya theologians.[52]

What I suggest is a gradual shift in emphasis from the old, risky, and increasingly dysfunctional (because necessarily secret) idolatry, which itself was becoming infused with Christian elements, to the less obviously syncretic worship of saint-deities in the churches. The shift would have received a major push from Fray Diego de Landa's vigorous campaign against paganism in the 1560s, which included the wholesale destruction of Maya codices as well as the more easily reproduced idols. The loss of the major part of these "books of the devil," the gradual extinction of a priestly class who could interpret them, and the general decline in literacy after the conquest (including a total loss of the ability to decipher the pre-Columbian glyphs) all facilitated innovation and adaptation, as oral tradition began to replace written texts in the transmission of sacred lore. The Chilam Balam books, and perhaps other colonial texts, preserved in Latin script some of the ancient cosmology, and the colonial *maestros cantores*, the *escribanos*, and some other members of the elite were able to read the words. But the ability to understand their full meaning got lost somewhere along the way.

The gradual extension of the colonial frontier also helped to isolate more and more of the pacified Maya from the "contaminating" contacts they maintained with their unconquered brethren even before the last pagan stronghold at Lake Peten Itza was taken in 1697. The clergy believed that this isolation was a major cause of the decline in idolatry in the older territories. I am inclined to think that the main cause was the high psychic as well as social costs of the conscious subterfuges. In any case, by the middle of the seventeenth century the traditional idolatries had been firmly relegated to secondary status, although not totally eclipsed.

By the end of the colonial period the saints had lost whatever surrogate status they may have had. Even when free to reinstate the old gods and rituals, as during the rebellion led by Jacinto Canek in 1761, the Maya did not do so, presumably because the old gods no longer had a separate identity. Indeed, the only insignia left for the supernatural and supreme political authority that Canek claimed for himself were the crown and blue mantle of the local Virgin in the church of Cisteil, both of which he donned for his royal investiture.[53]

Jacinto Canek, the anonymous "authors" of the books of Chilam Balam, and the Caste War Maya of the nineteenth century all expressed strong nativistic sentiments. All wished to restore the remembered cultural and political autonomy of preconquest times by expelling or annihilating the foreign rulers. But as creatures themselves of a centuries-long interchange with the Spanish, and as so often occurs in such nationalistic movements, the Maya were necessarily selective in their repudiation of the alien cultural tradition. They drew ideological support and symbolic elements from Christianity for their opposition to Spanish rule (a rule that did not end for the Maya with formal separation from Spain). Canek sought to reestablish links with the native past by taking the Peten Itza ruler's name of Can Ek, to which he added the name of Chichan (little) Montezuma (it is more likely that Canek learned the name of the last Aztec ruler from his reading in the Franciscan convent library where he was educated than that it was known in local Maya tradition). But in assuming the regalia of the Cisteil Virgin Mary, he acknowledged the special status and power of the Christian saint (regardless of gender). And prominent among the grievances he listed in a speech made to rally supporters was the neglect that *visita* towns like Cisteil suffered from the clergy, who left them for weeks without hearing mass.[54]

However nativistic in purpose, none of the manifestations of anti-Spanish sentiment have been anti-Christian. Nor could they be, since within less than a century after conquest, the Maya had fully incorporated Christian saints, perhaps some vaguely articulated notion of the Christian God, and many Christian symbols and rituals into their own system.

No sharp division need exist between the magical level and the Christianized corporate level. It is only from an external perspective that the Maya appear to shift between paganism and Christianity, as they move back and forth between house and church, village and *milpa*. After the initial conflicts and confusion produced by evangelization, the Maya were able to reintegrate both levels into a single system with no more internal contradictions than most systems of meaning and probably no more many-layered and fragmented than the earlier adaptations to foreign cults. The new system was a creative synthesis that drew mainly on the indigenous tradition for its ideational structure and combined Christianity with paganism in varying strengths to devise new forms.[55]

Conceptual coherence at the corporate, parochial level was achieved by merging the tutelary deities with the saints. The restoration of ritual unity was, however, a more difficult undertaking. As explained earlier, in the Maya scheme of things the maintenance of man's bond with the sacred at the corporate level was a public, collective enterprise. This concept favored the eventual triumph of the Christian forms of worship over the pagan rites that could be performed and witnessed by only a handful of courageous diehards. The split between the two competing rituals remained for some time, although the dual identities of the deity-saints provided a bridge, because the authorized Christian forms were not totally satisfactory either – socially or spiritually. The crisis in their world-maintenance activity could not be overcome entirely so long as the Christian forms remained alien rites that the Maya could not participate in actively and direct to their own purposes.

An early attempt to capture the apparatus of Christian worship was made in 1610 by two Indians who, proclaiming themselves "pope" and "bishop," proceeded to offer their own masses in the local church (with the addition of a few idols), to administer other Christian sacraments, and to ordain their own Maya clergy to assist them.[56] The political issue underlying the doctrinal split between Maya and Spaniard was especially clear here. The Spanish were determined to control all access to the sacred, and any appropriation of Christian symbols and liturgy represented as serious a challenge to their monopoly as pagan idolatries.[57] The clergy's indignation is thus explicable, but the fact remains that these and similar acts of appropriation represent in their own way an acceptance of Christianity. They find echoes in the Tzeltal Maya revolt of 1712 in Chiapas, in which native *fiscales* (the local equivalent of *maestros cantores*) simply constituted themselves as a Catholic priesthood in the service not of any overtly pagan deity, but of their own miraculous image of the Virgin.[58] In both cases the Indians were seeking to assert control over the new cult rather than reject it.

In Yucatan, Maya leaders less "audacious" than the self-proclaimed prelates were in the same period beginning to develop a more subtle and therefore more effective way of restoring unity to their collective religious enterprise. The purpose was the same, to Mayanize the Christian framework of public worship, but the means they chose were the officially sanctioned religious *cofradías* dedicated to the community saints.

ABBREVIATIONS

AA   Archivo del Arzobispado (Secretaría), Merida
AC   Archivo del Obispado, Campeche
AEY   Archivo del Estado de Yucatan, Merida
AGA   Archivo General del Arzobispado, Merida
AGI   Archivo General de Indias, Seville
AGN   Archivo General de la Nación, Mexico, D.F.
AHH   Archivo Histórico de Hacienda (in AGN)
ANM   Archivo de Notarías, Merida
BL   British Library, London
BN   Biblioteca Nacional, Mexico, D.F.
DHY   *Documentos para la historia de Yucatan*. 3 vols, France V.
        Scholes et al., eds. Merida: 1936–1938
IJ   Institute of Jamaica, Kingston
IY   Instituto Yucateco de Antropología e Historia, Merida
RY   "Relaciones de Yucatan." In *Colección de documentos
        inéditos relativos al descubrimiento, conquista y organización
        de las antiguas posesiones de Ultramar*. 25 vols, Madrid:
        1885–1932, vols 11 and 13
TUL   Tulane University Library, Latin American Library,
        New Orleans

NOTES

"The Cosmic Order in Crisis," reprinted from *Maya Society
under Colonial Rule* (Princeton, NJ, 1984). Copyright © 1984 by
Princeton University Press. Reprinted by permission of Princeton University Press (as indicated in the permission).

1 Michael Coe, "Iconology of Olmec Art," in *The Iconography of
  Middle American Sculpture*, by Ignacio Bernal, *et al.* (New York,
  NY, 1968), analyzes the "baby-faced jaguar" (or jaguar-faced baby)
  motif.
2 Visual images and written texts contain a vast amount of information about Mesoamerican "deities," but it is embedded in a
  symbolic system that may well be unsurpassed in its complexity
  and is probably no longer totally decodable. Within the limitations
  posed by the nature of the evidence and our own alien perceptions
  of it, several general studies stand out as especially illuminating
  as well as informative. J. Eric Thompson, *Maya History and Religion*
  (Norman, OK, 1970):159–373, is unequaled as a guide through the
  major domains of the lowland Maya's sacred system: ritual, gods,

myths; Arthur G. Miller's study of the sacred imagery of the east-coast Maya, *On the Edge of the Sea: Mural Painting at Tancah-Tulum, Quintana Roo, Mexico* (Washington DC, 1982): ch. 5, offers many insights of a more general nature as well. The rich conquest-period ethnographic material for the central highlands can be a helpful supplement to the scantier Yucatec data (bearing in mind regional differences), because of both the shared Mesoamerican substratum and the strong Mexican influence on Postclassic Maya "state" religion. On central Mexico, see Jacques Soustelle, *La pensée cosmologique des anciens Mexicains* (Paris, 1940) and Henry B. Nicholson, "Religion in Pre-Hispanic Central Mexico," in *Handbook of Middle American Indians* (Austin, TX, 1971) 10:395–466. Finally, Eva Hunt, *Transformation of the Hummingbird: Cultural Roots of a Zinacantecan Mythical Poem* (Ithaca, NY, 1977) is a *tour de force* of structural analysis of the "transformational system" of symbolic codes, linked to the major deity (or deity cluster) Tezcatlipoca (identified with the Maya Itzamna) and therefore a major key to the grammar of Mesoamerican cosmology.

3 Franciscan documents on their early missionary labors have disappeared (during the nineteenth-century secularizations, if not before). Extracts of some of the material on evangelization to 1600 were compiled by the order for a *pleito* with secular clergy, 1605–89: AGI, Escribanía 308-A, no. 1, piezas 1, 2, 9, and 10. This same material was used by the Franciscan chroniclers, Bernardo de Lizana, *Historia de Yucatan Devocionario de Nuestra Señora de Izmal y conquista espiritual* (Mexico, 1893), part 2, especially 42v–62, and Diego Cogolludo, Lib. 5, caps. 1, 5–9, 14. The firsthand account in Landa's, *Relación de la cosas de Yucatan*, trans. and ed. Alfred M. Tozzer (Cambridge: Peabody Museum of American Archaeology and Ethnology, 1941), 67–75, is extremely cursory.

4 The other, documented cases occurred in the southern zone of refuge.

5 See Arthur G. Miller, "The Iconography of the Painting in the Temple of the Diving God, Tulum, Quintana Roo, Mexico: The Twisted Cords," in Elizabeth P. Benson (ed.) *The Sea in the Pre-Columbian World* (Washington DC, 1977), on the *kusansum*, or *cuzanzum*, (living rope) symbolism.

6 For Spanish colonial accounts of these "superstitions," see Pedro Sánchez de Aguilar, *Informe contra idolorum cultores del obispado de Yucatan dirigo al Rey N. Señor en su Real Consejo de las Indias* (*c.* 1613) (Merida, 1937): 121–4; IY, Constituciones sinodales, 1722, Instrucciones a los curas de indios; AA, Visitas pastorales 3–6, Parish reports, Mani, Hopelchen, Teabo, Becal, and Bolonchenticul (1782), Chunhuhub, Tixcacalcupul, and Uayma (1784); AGI, Mexico 3168, Informe Bartolomé del Granado Baeza, 1 April 1813 (especially detailed). For ethnographic reports, see Daniel G. Brinton, "Folklore de Yucatan," and "Nagualism"; and Robert Redfield and Alfonso Villa Rojas, *Chan Kom: A Maya Village* (Washington DC, 1934), especially chs. 10 and 11.

7 The first report I have seen of this new association is AGI, Mexico 3168, Informe Bartolomé del Granado Baeza, 1 April 1813. On *pauahtuns*, see also Landa, *Relación*, 137–8, and notes 638–9; Roys, *Chumayel*, 110, and *Ritual of the Bacabs* (Norman, OK, 1965), especially 19. What the Spanish called *misas milperas* (also called *tich* or offering) are also reported in AA, Real cedulario 5, Royal cédula to Bishop, 11 March 1764 (extracting a letter from the governor); Papeles de los señores Gala, Guerra, Carrillo y Piña, Memorial Fr. Joseph Baraona, 21 May 1770; Visitas pastorales 3–6, Parish reports, Mani, Becal, Hopelchen, Teabo (1782), Chunhuhub, Tixcacalcupul, and Uayma (1784), with details very similar to the *uhanlicol* and other *milpa* ceremonies described and transcribed in Redfield and Villa Rojas, *Chan Kom*, 127–44, 339–56, and Villa Rojas, *The Maya of East Central Quintana Roo* (Washington DC, 1945), 111–17. Landa, *Relación*, scarcely mentions any aspect of private devotions; but see AGI, Justicia 249, Residencia D. Diego Quijada, 1565, cuad. 5, ff. 4,301–11, for a detailed description of what was clearly an *uhanlicol* for illness performed in the town of Chemax.

8 The distinction between Maya idolatry and superstition, although sharpening through the course of the colonial period, was already evident in the Ordenanzas of Tomás López, 1552 (Cogolludo, Lib. 5, caps. 16–19). For clerical attitudes toward Maya shamans in the late colonial period, see, in addition to sources cited in note 7, AA, Oficios y decretos 5, Expedte. sobre indios curanderos, 1806; and Cuentas de Fábrica 1, Chancenote, 1784–1816, Informe cura, 1813.

9 On personal or family idols or shrines, see RY 1: 52; Landa, *Relación*, 103, 110–11, 151, 154–6, 159–160. For views on the "abandonment of the temple cult" and the "atomization of religion," see Tozzer's discussion, in Landa, *Relación*, 103–9 note 496, and 152 note 756; and Harry E. D. Pollock, Ralph L. Roys, Tatiana Proskouriakoff and A. Ledyard Smith, *Mayapan, Yucatan, Mexico* (Washington DC, 1962):16, 136, 267, 428.

10 Aside from the public and private rituals, and combinations thereof, described in Landa, *Relación*, 138–66, 179–84, the distinction is brought out clearly in an idolatry case in Tixcacaltuyu, involving on the one hand family idols kept in homes, and on the other a large community idol, the object of collective devotions: AGI, Mexico 369, Bishop to Crown, 11 January 1686. Lizana, *Historia de Yucatan*, 56v–60v, describes a public sacrifice in Dzitas in 1551, aborted by Landa's timely (or untimely, depending on one's point of view) arrival to convert the populace.

11 Landa, *Relación*, 184: "Each town had the authority to sacrifice those whom the priest or *chilan* or lord thought best, and they had their public places in the temples for doing this, as if it were the most necessary thing in the world for the preservation of their public welfare."

12 The most detailed accounts of clandestine "idolatries" are the

135

records of investigations and trials conducted by Diego de Landa, 1562, contained in the *residencia* of Diego Quijada. Many of the accounts are published in France V. Scholes and Eleanor B. Adams (eds), *Don Diego Quijada Alcalde Mayor de Yucatán, 1561–1565*, 2 vols (Mexico, 1938) 1:24–343, but see also the unpublished records of investigations in the Valladolid area, 1558–62, in AGI, Justicia 249, Residencia Quijada, 1565, cuad. 5, and an excellent summary of the early idolatry material in France V. Scholes and Ralph L. Roys, "Fray Diego de Landa and the Problem of Idolatry in Yucatan," in *Co-operation in Research* (Washington DC, 1938). Many reports on idolatries from bishops and governors to the Crown, clustered in the late sixteenth and early seventeenth centuries, are contained in Mexico 359 and 369 (but see also Bishop to Crown, 24 February 1643, n.d. (c.1646) and 11 January 1686, in Mexico 369). The other major sources are RY, especially 2:147, 190, 213; and Sánchez de Aguilar, *Informe*, an extended account of idolatries from the 1580s to 1613, much of the evidence having been uncovered or processed by the author as curate of Chancenote and later as provisor of the diocese. On idolatries in the same period, see also Cogolludo, Lib. 11, cap. 4; and AGN, Inquisition 467, ff. 436–42, 1607, cited in Richard E. Greenleaf, "Inquisition and the Indians in New Spain: A Study in Jurisdictional Confusion," *The Americas* 22, (1965):143; and for further Inquisition records dealing peripherally with Indian idolatries, see note 25 below.

13 The tortures and their effects are described in Scholes and Adams, *Don Diego Quijada* 1:24–69, Declaraciones de algunos testigos, 1562. The stretching technique (*colgar*) that suspended the witness by his wrists (sometimes with weights attached to his feet) left a particularly strong impression on the Maya, who in the 1630s still referred to that period as "el tiempo de la cuelga" (Lizana, *Historia de Yucatan*, 9) and commemorated it in Ralph L. Roys, *The Book of Chilam Balam of Chumayel*, 2nd edn (Norman, OK, 1967):138, 152, 153. (Roys, by using the word "hang" instead of suspend, misses the connection the Maya made, p. 138, between the arrival of Bishop Toral and "when the hangings ceased." Toral put a stop to the trials.)

14 Sánchez de Aguilar, *Informe*, makes frequent reference to eastern Yucatan as more prone to idolatries, particularly the east coast and Cozumel, where the curate was supposedly drowned for his attempts to suppress pagan rites (pp. 120–1). See also, on cases of public idolatry in eastern Yucatan, AGI, Mexico 359, Governor to Crown, 11 March 1584.

15 Scholes and Adams, *Don Diego Quijada* 1: especially 41–128 (Procesos contra indios idólatras de Sotuta . . .), 135–62 (Información hecha en el pueblo de Homun . . .), and 162–9 (Testimonio de algunos españoles). See also, on *batabs* and *principales* in charge of the clandestine rites, Ordenanzas Tomás López, 1552, in Cogolludo, Lib. 5, caps. 16–19; Sánchez de Aguilar, *Informe*, 137–8 (on

D. Andrés Cocóm of Sotuta, 1583); AGI, Mexico 359, Governor to Crown, 11 March 1584; Mexico 3048, Governor to Crown, 16 April 1585; Mexico 369, Bishop to Crown, 24 February 1643; Cogolludo, Lib. 11, cap. 4 (c. 1630). On the role of *maestros cantores* and other church personnel, see RY 2:28, 190, 213.

16 First reported by Sánchez de Aguilar, *Informe*, 166, referring to the abandoned "cues" on the north coast around Río Lagartos. Cogolludo, Lib. 4, cap. 7, represents a later (1655) more relaxed attitude in reporting his discovery of offerings of cacao and copal in one of the "chapels" at the summit of the main pyramid at Uxmal as "some superstition or idolatry, recently committed, about which those of us there were unable to learn anything." AGI, Mexico 361, Ordenanzas Governor Esquivel, 1666, no. 6, still refers to "idolatrías . . . adorando y perfumando figuras falsas" but all relegated to "cuevas, milpas y lugares ocultos y retirados." With the exception of a case discovered in 1684 (AGI, Mexico 369, Bishop to Crown, 11 January 1686), these were highly furtive acts engaged in by small groups (with no further reference to idols), which the clergy could dismiss with more or less distaste as "superstitions," "memories of old errors," or not "formal idolatries": see IY, Constituciones sinodales, 1722, Instrucciones a los curas de indios; AGI, Mexico 3168, Bishop to Crown, 28 July 1737, who declared "formal idolatry" to be "entirely eradicated"; and the clerical accounts of *misas milperas* cited in note 7 above.

17 AGN, Inquisition 1256, no. 1, Proceso contra Pascual de los Santos Casanova, Hunucma, 1786–7 (summarized in Uchmany de la Peña, "Cuatro casos de idolatría," 279–89). Some of the *misas milperas* referred to in colonial documents could well be *cha-chaac* ceremonies rather than private *uhanlicol* rites. For a modern version of the *cha-chaac*, see Redfield and Villa Rojas, *Chan Kom*, 138–43.

18 Indians supposedly were not forced to accept baptism, but even by official policy they were to be punished if they resisted Christian instruction and persisted in pagan practices: Ordenanzas Tomás López, 1552 (Cogolludo, Lib. 5, caps. 16–19).

19 AGI, Mexico 3168, Bishop to Crown, 28 July 1737. For a range of clerical opinions, mostly, although not uniformly, pessimistic about the Indians' adherence to the faith, see AA, Visitas pastorales 3–6, Parish reports, 1782–4.

20 Robin Horton, "African Conversion," *Africa* 41 (1971):85–108 and "On the Rationality of Conversion," *Africa* 45 (1975):219–35, 373–99.

21 Also seen (again not necessarily inconsistently) as a dual, male–female creative power. J. Eric Thompson, *Maya History and Religion*, 200–6, 209–33, discusses the linguistic and iconographic evidence for Hunabku as supreme creator god among the Maya, personified in Itzamna, who incorporated in his many aspects "most" (perhaps all?) of the other major Maya gods. On the Aztec Ometeotl "as the personification of godhead in the abstract," subsumed in the Tezcatlipoca complex, see Henry B. Nicholson, "Religion in

Pre-Hispanic Central Mexico," in *Handbook of Middle American Indians* 10:395–466 (Austin, TX, 1971):411–12. For insights into the conception of the many as refractions of the one, I am indebted to E. E. Evans-Pritchard, *Nuer Religion*, (Oxford, 1956), chs. 2 and 3, and to Eva Hunt, *Transformation*, especially 55–6. See also Hunt's discussion of the fourfold (or eightfold) manifestations of Tezcatlipoca, seen as the highland equivalent of Itzamna (pp. 120–3).

22 See, for example, Lizana, *Historia de Yucatan*, 40–41v. Maya traditions in a sense encouraged this view by claiming that they had no idolatry or idols or sacrifices before the arrival of the Mexicans and Kukulcan (RY 1:52, 78–9, 121–2, 215, 225–6, 242–3, 254–5, 270–1), which I take to mean that, purged of Christian influences, the Mexicans introduced the proliferation of images and human sacrifice on a larger scale (and perhaps in new forms) in addition to new gods, such as Kukulcan; and that an esoteric cult of the high god and his major Maya manifestations lost some prominence – in other words, a shift in emphasis and ritual mode.

23 On the purist stance of the Erasmians, see Marcel Bataillon, *Erasmo y España* 2nd edn (Mexico: Fondo de Cultura Económica, 1966) and its appendix, "Erasmo en el Nuevo Mundo"; and William A. Christian Jr., *Local Religion in Sixteenth-Century Spain* (Princeton, NJ, 1980):158–65. The clergy themselves were divided (see, for example, the early conflict over the cult of the Virgin of Guadalupe, in Robert Ricard, *La conquista espiritual de Mexico*, translated by Angel María Garibay (Mexico, 1947):347–52); and in Yucatan, Franciscans and secular clergy alike promoted the cult of the saints and left enthusiastic reports of sweating and bleeding images, miraculous cures, and the other stimuli to popular devotion that the Erasmians deplored; see Sánchez de Aguilar, *Informe*, 113–14; Lizana, *Historia de Yucatan*, 17–33, 105–12; Cárdenas Valencia, *Relación historial*, 91–9, 100–1, 105–7; Cogolludo, Lib. 6, caps. 3 and 4, Lib. 9, caps. 17–21, Lib. 10, caps. 14–16, Lib. 11, caps. 1–3, 5, Lib. 12, caps. 9, 10, 12, 13, 19, 20. References to the devil (singular and plural) are legion.

24 See, for example, Sánchez de Aguilar, *Informe*, 114–18, on the famous "duende parlero" who terrorized Spaniards in the Valladolid region for decades; and the long treatise by Bartolomé de Las Casas, *Apologética historia de las Indias*, ed. Edmundo O'Gorman, 2 vols (Mexico, 1967) 1:449–522, on magic and the power of "demons." The rich Inquisition material for colonial Mexico has so far been quarried mainly for cases of heresy and "Judaizing," but see Gonzalo Aguirre Beltrán, *Medicina y magia: El proceso de aculturación en la estructura colonial* (Mexico, 1963); and on Spain in this period, Caro Baroja, *World of the Witches*. In Yucatan, witchcraft denunciations were directed primarily against mulattos and Indians (the latter handled in the diocesan courts), but the Spaniards reveal much of their own beliefs in their comments on and dealings with Indian magic.

25 See, for example, AGN, Inquisición 621, no. 1, Causa contra Luis

Ricardo and D. Alvaro de Osorio, 1672; no. 5, Denuncias sobre brujerías y ensalmos . . . Valladolid, 1672; Inquisición 908, no. 14, Causa contra Francisco Pantoja y cómplices, 1748; Inquisición 1140, no. 2, Denuncia sobre hechicerías . . . Campeche, 1797. See also AA, Oficios y decretos 5, Expedte. sobre indios curanderos, Campeche, 1806; Papeles de los señores Gala, Guerra, Carrillo y Piña, Informe Fr. Joseph de Baraona, 21 May 1770; Visitas pastorales 4, Parish report Teabo, 1782, on *vecino* beliefs that Indians were powerful sorcerers and on *vecino* participation in Maya rituals. Belief in the power of Indian magic did not necessarily involve sharing the Indians' belief system. For example, an African slave accused of participation in idolatries did not actually take part in the ritual or seem to have any clear idea of its particular significance to the Indians. He merely partook of some of the sacrificial food, which he regarded as having some kind of sacred power of possible benefit to him: see AGN, Inquisición 125, no. 69, Información contra Cristóbal, esclavo negro, 1582. See also Inquisición 213, no. 10, Causa contra Juan de Loria, 1467; and Inquisición 302, no. 17b, Proceso contra Juan Vela de Aguirre, encomendero, 1613–14. By contrast, another case concerned some *pardos* who participated fully in a *cha-chaac* ceremony (one of them was actually the leader), and who seem to have been culturally Maya (and no doubt close to pure Maya genetically): Inquisición 1177, no.7, Causa contra Apolonia Casanova, 1786; and Inquisición 1256, no. 1, Causa contra Pascual de los Santos Casanova, 1786–7.

26 AGN, Inquisición 516, no. 12, Causa contra Juan de Argaez, mulato, alias Montoya, 1673. For other cases of mulattos using Indian magic, 1612–72, see Inquisición 297, no. 5; 360, varios, 374, no. 10; 413, no. 8; 423, no. 20; 443, no. 6.

27 AGI, Mexico 3168. Informe Bartolomé del Grando Baeza, 1 April 1813.

28 On Brazil, see Roger Bastide, *The African Religions in Brazil*, translated by Helen Sebba (Baltimore, MD, 1978):131–3; Freyre, *Masters and Slaves*, 286–96.

29 For analyses of syncretism as an historical process (as opposed to descriptions of the product, which abound in the ethnographic literature), see William D. Madsden, "Religious Syncretism," in *Handbook of Middle American Indians* 6:369–492 (Austin, TX, 1967), and Wigberto Jiménez Moreno, "The Indians of America and Christianity," *The Americas* 14 (1958):411–31, on central and northern Mexico; Hugo G. Nutini and Betty Bell, *Ritual Kinship: The Structure and Historical Development of the Compadrazgo System in Rural Tlaxcala* (Princeton, NJ, 1980):287–304, on Tlaxcala; and on the Maya region, with emphasis on Yucatan, see Donald E. Thompson, "Maya Paganism and Christianity: A History of the Fusion of Two Religions," in *Middle American Research Institute Publication* (New Orleans, LA, 1954) 19:1–36.

30 Christian, *Local Religion*, discusses saints as highly localized corporate patrons and is in general a valuable guide to late sixteenth-

century Spanish forms of devotion (for instance, a shifting emphasis from saints' relics to images) that represent the root stock of colonial transplants.

31 I am suggesting only a difference in emphasis and not two separate belief systems for elite and masses; see, for comparison, Horton, "On the Rationality of Conversion" 1:226; 2:374–5.

32 Gordon Brotherston, "Continuity in Maya Writing: New Readings of Two Passages in the Book of Chilam Balam of Chumayel," in *Maya Archaeology and Ethnohistory*, edited by Norman Hammond and Gordon R. Willey (Austin, TX, 1979):249–56.

33 Lizana, *Historia de Yucatan*, 46v, 51, 55–6, mentions the lords of Campeche, Tixkumche, Uman, and Caucel and cooperation from Tutul Xiu, the lord of Mani.

34 Arthur G. Miller and Nancy M. Farriss, "Religious Syncretism in Colonial Yucatan: The Archaeological and Ethnohistorical Evidence from Tancah, Quintana Roo," in *Maya Archaeology and Ethnohistory*, 235–40, and Ralph L. Roys, France V. Scholes, and Eleanor B. Adams (eds), "Report and Census of the Indians of Cozumel, 1570," in *Contributions to American Anthropology and History* (Washington DC, 1940), 6:1–30, summarize much of the documentation on the desultory missionary activity on Cozumel and the east coast and Maya responses to Christianity. See especially AGI, Mexico 369, Relación de Fr. Gregorio de Fuenteovejuna y Fr. Hernando Sopuerta, 15 August 1573; Mexico 359, Governor to Crown, 11 March 1584; Mexico 3048, Governor to Crown, 16 April 1585; AA, Real cedulario 5, Representación . . . indios de Icab (Ecab), 6 April 1601, in Testimonio de la real ejecutoria, 22 October 1681.

35 Excavation data from the Tancah chapel are summarized in Miller and Farriss, "Religious Syncretism," 229–35.

36 Cogolludo, Lib. 4, cap. 9, discusses evidence for preconquest crosses on Cozumel and early Spanish ideas on the cross as evidence for Chilam Balam prophecies of the coming of Christianity (see also Lizana, *Historia de Yucatan*, 36v–39; Roys, *Chumayel*, 148, 167, 168; RY 1:44–5). But on the cross as the "first tree of the world," see Roys, *Chumayel*, 102, 168; Landa, *Relación*, 43, and notes 214 and 215; RY 1:45.

37 On east-coast cults, see Miller, *On the Edge of the Sea*, ch. 5. The sections of Roys, *Chumayel*, 164–9, which Roys entitles "Prophecies of a New Religion," seems to refer to, among a variety of by no means mutually exclusive interpretations, the return of Kukulcan and of Christ in an apocalyptic Last Judgment.

38 The ratio of *visita* towns to *cabeceras* was 8.3:1 among Franciscan *doctrinas* in 1580: DHY 2:48–50, Memoria Fr. Hernando de Sopuerta, 1580. According to the bishop's count, the ratio was 8.9:1 for all Indian parishes: DHY 2:55–65, Memoria de los conventos, vicarías y pueblos, 1582. On the use of *naguatlatos* and native catechists and the question of language competence among the Franciscans (a sensitive issue in their rivalry with the secular clergy), see AGI, Mexico 369, Avisos Bishop Toral, n.d. (c.1565),

and Bishop to Crown, n.d. (c.1599); DHY 2:48–50, Memoria Fr. Hernando de Sopuerta, 1580; DHY 2:70–94, Memorial Bishop to Crown, 6 January 1582; DHY 2:129–32, Bishop to Crown, 10 April 1601; "Visita García de Palacio, 1583"; Ciudad Real, *Relación* 2:472; Sánchez de Aguilar, *Informe*, 72–3, 135, 171; Lizana, *Historia de Yucatan*, 46–46v, 58.

39 Sánchez de Aguilar, *Informe*, 35, presents a long list of the "rudiments" of Christian doctrine, which he claimed "all the Indians from childhood learn and know completely." But see AGI, Mexico 369, Avisos Bishop Toral, n.d. (c.1565); and IY, Constituciones sinodales, 1722, Instrucciones a los curas de indios. For late colonial policy and practice in the teaching of doctrine and for assessments of the progress of Christianity among the Maya, see AGI, Mexico 3168, Bishop to Crown, 28 July 1737, and Informe Bartolomé del Granado Baeza, 1 April 1813; Papeles de los señores Gala, Guerra, Carillo y Piña, Memorial Fr. Joseph Baraona to Bishop, 21 May 1770; the section Visitas pastorales, most especially the detailed inspections and parish reports in legajos 3–6, 1782–4; and AGN, Historia 398, Exp. sobre establecimiento de escuelas en Yucatan, 1790–1805, Informes subdelegado Campeche, 1790.

40 Roys, *Chumayel*, 82 (and, less explicitly, 155). On the umbilical cord imagery, see Miller, "Iconography of the Painting." Brotherston, "Continuity in Maya Writing," 251–2, argues for a Maya response to Christian cosmology that was not only sophisticated but also well versed in medieval biblical scholarship.

41 AGI, Mexico 359, Governor to Crown, 11 March 1584. On Cozumel as a pre-Columbian pilgrimage centre, see RY 2:54–5; Landa, *Relación*, 109, 184; Cogolludo, Lib. 4, caps. 4 and 9.

42 Cogolludo, Lib. 4, caps. 19 and 20, lists the titular patrons of *cabeceras* and *visitas*. Out of 94 towns for which information is available on Marian advocation, the Immaculate Conception accounted for 54, the Assumption for 10, and Nativity, Dolores, Purification, Rosary, and Visitation were divided roughly equally among the rest (AGI, Mexico, 3066, Informaciones instruídas . . . cofradías, 1782, cuads. 5–10).

43 Aside from the physical evidence of extant images, which are hard to date, Cogolludo, Lib. 6, caps. 2 and 4, describes some of the Our Lady images.

44 *Diccionario de Motul maya-español, atribuido a Fray Antonio de Ciudad Real* (late 1550s), ed. Juan Martínez Hernández (Merida, 1929).

45 The Mesoamerican underworld was conceived as having 9 tiers, or stages, but heaven (not actually an antithesis but rather linked in the dualistic symbolism) may also have had 9 tiers rather than the generally believed 13: see Nicholson, "Religion in Pre-Hispanic Central Mexico," 407–8. See also J. Eric Thompson, *Maya History and Religion*, 280–2, on the 9 Maya Lords of the Underworld.

46 Spanish reports on the cult of the saints are rare, except for the hagiographical accounts by Lizana, Cárdenas Valencia, and Cogolludo of miracle-working images (see note 23 above), which tell

141

us more about Spanish than Indian expressions of piety. Not surprisingly, the clergy were more concerned with idolatries and other practices that they saw as pagan survivals than with more apparently orthodox forms of devotion. Nevertheless, much can be gleaned about Maya beliefs and practices from descriptions of and references to the annual round of church festivals as performed in the Indian parishes, including references to elements that the clergy perceived as idiosyncratically Maya but not necessarily objectionably pagan: see especially IY, Constituciones sinodales, 1722, Instrucciones a los curas de indios; and testimonies, parish reports and *autos de visita* in AA, Visitas pastorales 1 (1755–64), 3–6 (1782–4). More direct evidence of Maya attitudes and ideas about the saints can be obtained from scattered references in the Chilam Balam books, from testimony about the *cofradías* and their patrons in AGI, Mexico 3066, Informaciones instruídas . . . cofradías, 1782, cuads. 5–10; from the *libros de cofradía*; and from a variety of other Maya documents pertaining to the *cofradías*, ranging from deeds of endowment to the saints to petitions about the financing of fiestas, mainly in AA, Asuntos terminados and Asuntos pendientes.

47 This interpretation is not so much factually inaccurate as analytically misleading. The point is not whether Indians hid or hide images behind saints (see, for example, a report in AA, Visitas pastorales 5, Valladolid, 1784, that "idols of wax or clay" were found under the draperies of Christian saints in a local church), but whether the Indians addressed their devotions to the idols rather than to the saints. My contention is that the two were fused, with or without the material presence of the idols.

48 Anthony F. C. Wallace, *Culture and Personality* (New York, NY, 1961):202–6. See also Wallace, "Revitalization Movements," *American Anthropologist* 58 (1956):264–81; and Peter L. Berger, *The Sacred Canopy: Elements of a Sociological Theory of Religion* (Garden City, NY, 1969):45–6, 50, on the loss of "plausibility structure."

49 Scholes and Adams, *Don Diego Quijada* 1:78–9, 94, 124.

50 For material on idolatries, see notes 12, 14–16 above.

51 AGI, Mexico 359, Bishop to Audiencia, 2 May 1606.

52 Nutini and Bell, *Ritual Kinship*, 291–304, describe this process of fusion in colonial Tlaxcala, arguing that the friars were aware of and consciously fostered god–saint identifications, even choosing patron saints who would mesh well with local deities. The evidence for specific identifications between individual saints and deities is highly equivocal and the correlations are often strained. The Mesoamerican symbolic system was subtle, fluid, and rich enough to accommodate and reorder almost any set of superficial attributes contained in Christian hagiography and iconography. More important than any particular consonances is the merger at the more general level of collective advocates.

53 AGI, Mexico 3050, Autos criminales . . . pueblo de Cisteil, 1761.

54 AGI, Mexico 3050, Autos criminales . . . pueblo de Cisteil, 1761.

Although the Maya may have preferred not to have resident clergy, they seem to have valued Christian ritual. Similar, though nonviolent, complaints can be found in AA, Visitas pastorales and Arreglos parroquiales: see, especially, Arreglos parroquiales 1, Memoriales caciques and justicias of Xocen, Dzitnup, and Ebtun, 1782.

55 Eva Hunt, in her analysis of postconquest change in the Mesoamerican symbolic system (*Transformation of the Hummingbird*, ch. 9), suggests a somewhat more complex distinction among (1) messages, which change most rapidly; (2) codes (for example, spoken language); and (3) "armatures" or cultural configurations – roughly analogous to what I call ideational structure here – which are tied most closely to basic social organization (including man's link with the physical environment) and therefore, within Mesoamerican Indian society, have been the most stable part of the system.

56 Sánchez de Aguilar, *Informe*, 153–4, 170. The apostate Maya in the Tipu region taunted visiting friars with claims that they had their own priests to celebrate mass, using tortillas and *pozole* (Cogolludo, Lib. 11, cap. 14).

57 As early as 1552, Maya lords and *principales* were enjoined not to "dare to establish on their own any church or oratory or chapel" (Ordenanzas Tomás López, in Cogolludo, Lib. 5, caps. 16–19). See also clerical reactions to the audacity of giving saints' names to idols and claiming to speak to the Holy Spirit (AGI, Mexico 359, Bishop to Audiencia, 2 May 1606; Sánchez de Aguilar, *Informe*, 138), in the same way as in Europe the church has consistently incorporated or proscribed any relics, images, apparitions (or their sites), and other independent manifestations of the sacred.

58 Herbert S. Klein, "Peasant Communities in Revolt: The Tzeltal Republic of 1712" *Pacific Historical Review* 35 (1966):247–64, and, for more recent studies, Robert Wasserstrom, *Ethnic Relations in Central Chiapas 1528–1975* (Berkeley, CA, 1983), ch. 4, and Kevin Gosner, "Soldiers of the Virgin: An Ethnohistorical Analysis of the Tzeltal Revolt of 1712 in Highland Chiapas," Ph.D. dissertation, University of Pennsylvania, 1983.

6

SLAVE RESISTANCE IN COLONIAL SOUTH CAROLINA

Peter Wood

South Carolina was the only colony in mainland North America in which Blacks outnumbered Whites, which led Peter Wood to title his pioneering work Black Majority *(1974). This excerpt, concentrating on the Stono Rebellion of 1739, concerns the resistance of slaves to the plantation system. Naturally resistance was no easy thing in the plantation world, and slaves had every reason to think twice before putting themselves at risk. Indeed the relationship between master and slave, and between White and Black, in South Carolina was complex on every level: political, social, psychological. Wood's research indicates a wide range of acts of resistance (including remarks on poisoning and arson which we have had to leave out), and provides a glimpse at the inner workings and the social dynamics of slave resistance and slave revolt.*

By 1739 the slave system of South Carolina had existed for almost 3 generations. The techniques of planter domination were well tested and refined. Slave responses evolved into patterns of conduct that usually combined outward accommodation to the slave system with inward resistance (work-slowdowns, clever insolence, intentional carelessness). Outward, public, declared resistance amounted to revolt, and prompted often deadly retaliation, as in the Stono Rebellion. Hence, as the colony matured resistance became more subtle, especially among those born into slavery. Survival in this and other slave societies required high skill in the art of seeming to the masters what one was not, yet making one's true sentiments clear to one's fellows. Colonial situations in general develop this skill in the oppressed; mature colonialism cultivates the skill to exalted degrees (recall the Yucatec Maya of Nancy Farriss).

* * *

Increasingly overt white controls met with increasingly forceful black resistance. The stakes for Negroes were simply rising higher and the choices becoming more hopelessly difficult. As the individual and collective tensions felt by black slaves mounted, they continued to confront the immediate daily questions of whether to accept or deny, submit or resist, remain or flee. Given their diversity of background and experience, it is not surprising that slaves responded to these pressures in a wide variety of ways. To separate their reactions into docility on the one hand and rebellion on the other, as has occasionally been done, is to underestimate the complex nature of the contradictions each Negro felt in the face of new provocations and new penalties. It is more realistic to think in terms of a spectrum of response, ranging from complete submission to total resistance, along which any given individual could be located at a given time.

As in any situation overladen with contradictory pulls, there were those few persons who could not be located on such a spectrum at all; that is, their personalities "dis-integrated" in the face of conflicting pressures – internal and external – and their responses became unpredictable even to themselves. The Negro Act of 1751 made provision for local parishes to relieve poorer masters of the cost of confining and maintaining "slaves that may become lunatic."[1] This category of individuals is not easy to define, for mental illness, like physical illness, became an element in the incessant game of deception developing between masters and slaves; Negroes pretended outright insanity upon occasion, and owners readily called such bluffs, perhaps more frequently than they occurred.[2] Deception aside, it is no easy matter to define rational behavior within an arbitrary social system. Certain acts of resistance, such as appropriating goods and running away, usually involved prior calculation by their very nature, as did poisoning, arson, and conspiracy. Many other actions represented impromptu responses to trying situations, but even reactions which seemed most irrational in terms of straightforward appearances and consequences rested upon a rational appraisal of the slave environment.[3]

At one end of the spectrum of individual resistance were the extreme incidents of physical violence. There are examples of slaves who, out of desperation, fury, or premeditation, lashed out against a White despite the consequences. Jemmy, a slave of Captain Elias Ball, was sentenced to death in 1724 "for striking and wounding one Andrew Songster."[4] The master salvaged the slave's life and his own investment by promising to deport Jemmy forever within two months. For others who vented individual aggression there was no such reprieve. In August 1733 the *Gazette** reported tersely: "a Negro Man belonging to Thomas Fleming of Charlestown, took an Opportunity, and kill'd the Overseer with an Axe. He was hang'd for the same yesterday." An issue during 1742 noted: "Thursday last a Negro Fellow belonging to Mr. Cheesman, was brought to Town, tried, condemn'd and hang'd, for attempting to murder a white lad."[5]

Such explosions of rage were almost always suicidal, and the mass of the Negro population cultivated strict internal constraints as a means of preservation against external white controls. (The fact that Whites accepted so thoroughly the image of a carefree and heedless black personality is in part a testimony to the degree to which black slaves learned the necessity of holding other emotional responses in outward check.) This essential lesson of control, passed on from one generation to the next, was learned by early immigrants through a painful process of trial and error. Those newcomers whose resistance was most overt were perceived to be the least likely to survive, so there ensued a process of conscious or unconscious experimentation (called "seasoning" or "breaking" by the Whites), in which Africans calculated the forms and degrees of resistance which were most possible.[6]

Under constant testing, patterns of slave resistance evolved rapidly, and many of the most effective means were found to fall at the low (or invisible) end of the spectrum. For example, for those who spoke English, in whatever dialect, verbal insolence became a consistent means of resistance. Cleverly handled, it allowed slaves a way to assert themselves and downgrade their masters without committing a crime. All parties were aware of the subversive potential of words (along with styles of dress and bearing), as the thrust of the traditional term "uppity" implies, and it may be that both the black use of this approach and the white perception of it increased as tensions grew. In 1737 the Assembly debated whether the

* This refers to the *South Carolina Gazette*, published in Charlestown.

patrols should have the right "to kill any resisting or saucy Slave,"[7] and in 1741 the Clerk of the Market proposed that "if any Slave should in Time of Market behave him or herself in any insolent abusive Manner, he or she should be sent to the Work-house, and there suffer corporal Punishment."[8]

At the same time traits of slowness, carelessness, and literal-mindedness were artfully cultivated, helping to disguise countless acts of willful subterfuge as inadvertent mistakes.[9] To the benefit of the slave and the frustration of the historian, such subversion was always difficult to assess, yet considerable thought has now been given to these subtle forms of opposition.[10] Three other patterns of resistance – poisoning, arson, and conspiracy – were less subtle and more damaging, and each tactic aroused white fears which sometimes far exceeded the actual threat. All three are recognized as having been methods of protest familiar in other slave colonies as well, and each is sufficiently apparent in the South Carolina sources to justify separate consideration.

While poisoning and arson rarely involved more than one or two compatriots, organized forms of resistance, which involved greater numbers (and therefore higher risks), were not unknown in the royal colony. In fact uprisings appear to have been attempted or planned repeatedly by slaves. For obvious reasons, published sources are irregular on these matters – the *South Carolina Gazette* refrained from mentioning the Stono incident, which occurred within 20 miles of Charlestown – but a number of conspiracies were recorded. In these instances it is sometimes difficult to categorize the objectives of the insurgents, since often a will to overpower the Europeans and a desire to escape from the colony were intertwined in the same plot.[11] The province's first major conspiracy, uncovered in 1720, provides a case in point. "I am now to acquaint you," wrote a Carolina correspondent to the colony's London agent in June, "that very lately we have had a very wicked and barbarous plott of the designe of the negroes rising with a designe to destroy all the white people in the country and then to take the town in full body." He continued that through God's will "it was discovered and many of them taken prisoners and some burnt some hang'd and some banish'd." At least some participants in the scheme "thought to gett to Augustine" if they could convince a member of the Creek tribe to guide them, "but the Savanna garrison tooke the negroes up half starved and the Creeke Indians would not join them or be their pylott." A party of Whites and Indians had been dispatched to "Savanna Towne," where fourteen captives were being held, and it was planned that these rebels would "be executed as soon as they came down."[12]

This incident, or perhaps another similar one, was mentioned in an official representation sent to the king late in 1721. His majesty was informed that the "black slaves . . . have lately attempted and were very near succeeding in a new revolution, which would probably have been attended by the utter extirpation of all your Majesty's subjects in this province."[13] Not surprisingly, the Negro Act of the following year spelled out more fully than ever the punishments to be inflicted on any slaves attempting to rebel or conspiring together or gathering up "arms, powder, bullets, or offensive weapons in order to carry on such mutiny or insurrection."[14] A minister's letter from Goose Creek Parish in 1724 ascribed "secret poisonings and bloody insurrection" to certain Christian slaves.[15]

Another scantily documented incident occurred in mid-August 1730. A letter written five days after the episode and published in Boston conveyed the initial shock and fatalism felt by many Whites. It mentioned the prominent causes of failure in such attempts – divided leadership, insufficient recruitment, and premature discovery:

> I shall give an Account [the correspondent wrote from Charlestown] of a bloody Tragedy which was to have been executed here last Saturday night (the 15th Inst.) by the Negroes, who had conspired to Rise and destroy us, and had almost bro't it to pass: but it pleased God to appear for us, and confound their Councils. For some of them propos'd that the Negroes of every Plantation should destroy their own Masters; but others were for Rising in a Body, and giving the blow at once on surprise; and thus they differ'd. They soon made a great Body at the back of the Town, and had a great Dance, and expected the Country Negroes to come & join them; and had not an overruling Providence discovered their

Intrigues, we had been all in Blood . . . The Chief of them, with some others, is apprehended and in Irons, in order to a Tryal, and we are in Hopes to find out the whole Affair.[16]

What few details came to light may have been embroidered with time, for it seems likely that this foiled rebellion provided the basis for the tale told during the Revolution concerning a narrowly averted "Sicilian Vespers."* Although the Hessian officer, named Hinrichs, who recorded the story mistakenly placed it in 1736, the scheme he described, like the one narrated in the Boston letter, unfolded in August and involved conflicting plans for plantation murders and an attack on Charlestown. Moreover, it took the form of a large gathering several miles outside the city two days before the intended coup and ended only "when fate was merciful and betrayed the horrible plot." Since all these details conform with the letter sent to Boston, there seems little doubt that Hinrichs was referring to the incident of 1730. There is probably substance to his concluding remark that "Through torture and punishment their leaders were found out . . . and . . . tortured to death, while many others were subjected to severe bodily punishment."[17]

Despite harsh reprisals, however, secret gatherings of slaves, sometimes exceeding one hundred people, were again reported within several years. In February 1733 the Assembly urged the slave patrols to special watchfulness and ordered a dozen slaves brought in for questioning, but there is no sign that any offence was uncovered.[18] Late in 1736 a white citizen appears to have sought a reward for uncovering a Negro plot. Early in the following year the provost marshal took up three Negroes "suspected to be concerned in some Conspiracy against the Peace of this Government," and although the Assembly cleared and released the most prominent suspect, it did not deny the existence of a plot.[19]

By September 1738 the government had completed "An Act for the further Security and better Defence of this Province" and given instructions that the two paragraphs relating to slaves were to be reprinted in the *Gazette*.[20] The paper complied

* The Sicilian Vespers: a revolt begun in Palermo in 1282 in which most of the French ruling class was massacred.

several days later by publishing the section which ordered that within a month every slave-owner in the colony was to turn in to the militia captain of his local precinct "a true and faithful List, in Writing, of all the Slaves of such Persons, or which are under their Care or Management, from the Age of 16 Years to the Age of Sixty Years." Each list was required to specify "the Names, Ages and Country of all such Slaves respectively, according to the best of the Knowledge and Belief of the Persons returning the same."[21]

The statute imposed a heavy fine of £100 upon any master who neglected or refused to comply, so that the required local lists (if collected and sent to the governor annually as authorized) must have constituted a thorough census of the colony's adult slaves. The unlikely reappearance of even a portion of these lists would be a remarkable boon to historians, in light of the unique request for the original country of all slaves. This detail appears to bear witness to the fact that masters were generally interested and informed as to the origins of the Negroes they owned. It may also reflect the belief, commonly accepted in the Carolinas as elsewhere, that new slaves from Africa posed the greatest threat to the security of the white settlers. John Brickell explained at this time: "The Negroes that most commonly rebel, are those brought from Guinea, and who have been inured to War and Hardship all their lives; few born here, or in the other Provinces have been guilty of these vile Practices." When country-born slaves did contemplate rebellion, Brickell claimed, it was because they were urged to it by newcomers "whose Designs they have sometimes discovered to the Christians" in order to be "rewarded with their Freedom for their good Services."[22]

The thought that newcomers from Africa were the slaves most likely to rebel does not appear to have been idle speculation, for the late 1730s, a time of conspicuous unrest, was also a time of massive importation. In fact, at no earlier or later date did recently arrived Africans (whom we might arbitrarily define as all those slave immigrants who had been in the colony less than a decade) comprise such a large proportion of South Carolina's Negro population. By 1740 the black inhabitants of the colony numbered roughly 39,000. During the preceding decade more than 20,000 slaves had been imported from Africa. Since there is little evidence that mortality was disproportionately high among newcomers, this means that by the end of the 1730s fully half of the colony's Negroes had lived in the New World less than ten years. This proportion had been growing steadily. In 1720 fewer than 5 per cent of black adults had been there less than a decade (and many of these had spent time in the West Indies); by 1730 roughly 40 per cent were such recent arrivals. Heavy importation and low natural increase sent the figure over 50 per cent by 1740, but it dropped sharply during the nearly total embargo on the next decade, and after that point the established black population was large enough so that the percentage of newcomers never rose so high again.

Each of the lowland parishes must have reflected this shift in the same way. In St Paul's, for example, where the Stono Uprising originated, there were only 1,634 slaves in 1720, the large majority of whom had been born in the province or brought there long before. By contrast, in 1742 the parish's new Anglican minister listed 3,829 "heathens and infidels" in his cure, well over 3,000 of whom must have been slaves. Of these, perhaps as many as 1,500 had been purchased in Charlestown since 1730.[23] A predominant number of the Africans reaching the colony between 1735 and 1739 have been shown to have come from Angola, so it is likely that at the time of the Stono Uprising there were close to 1,000 residents of St Paul's Parish who had lived in the Congo–Angola region of Africa less than ten years before. While this figure is only an estimate, it lends support to the assertion in one contemporary source that most of the conspirators in the 1739 incident were Angolans.[24] The suggestion seems not only plausible, but even probable.

European settlers contemplating the prospects of rebellion, however, seem to have been more concerned with contacts the slaves might establish in the future than with experience that came from their past. White colonists were already beginning to subscribe to the belief that most Negro unrest was necessarily traceable to outside agitators. Like most shibboleths of the slave culture, this idea contained a kernel of truth, and it is one of the difficult tasks in considering the records of the 1730s and 1740s to separate the unreasonable fears of white Carolinians from their very justifiable concerns.

Numerous anxieties were intertwined. It was all too clear, for example, that internal and external threats to white security were likely to coincide and reinforce each other, if for no other reason than that the militia, with its dual responsibilities for defense and for control, was divided and thereby weakened in times of trouble. Even if not linked beforehand, hostile elements inside and outside the colony could be expected to join forces during any alarm, so Europeans were as anxious about foreign infiltration as domestic conspiracy. For this reason Indians often appeared to be the slaves' likeliest allies. For example, suspicion of a Negro plot had scarcely died in 1733, when an Indian slave was brought before the Assembly. He testified "that an Indian Woman had told him that all the Indians on the Continent design'd to rise and make War, against the English."[25] Had such word contained any substance, it might have triggered slave impulses to rise against the English as well, but this particular rumor apparently lacked foundation, and the informant was dismissed.

The following spring the Assembly sent a memorial to the king, outlining the threats posed by the Indians, Spanish, and French and asking assistance in defense. This document from 1734 stressed that white colonists faced "many intestine Dangers from the great Number of Negroes" and went on to observe, "Insurrections against us have been often attempted, and would at any time prove very fatal if the French shoud instigate them by artfully giving them [the Negroes] an Expectation of Freedom."[26] The next ten years were filled with enough dangers – real and imagined – from these various quarters to keep the English in a constant state of agitation. In 1748 James Glen, thinking back to this period, summarized the sea of anxieties which had beset white Carolinians:

Sometime ago the People of this Province were Annually alarmed with accounts of intended Invasions, & even in time of profound Peace they were made believe that the Spaniards had prepared Embarkations for that purpose at St. Augustine & the Havanna, or that the French were marching by Land from Louisiana with more Men than ever were in that Country to drive us into the Sea. Sometimes the Negroes were to rise & cut their Masters

Throats at other times the Indians were confederating to destroy us.[27]

Of the various sources of outside agitation none seemed so continually threatening after 1720 as St Augustine, for the abduction and provocation of slaves by the Spanish were issues of constant concern. While London and Madrid were reaching a peace settlement in 1713, Charlestown and St Augustine had renewed their agreement concerning the mutual return of runaways, but Spanish depredations continued long after the conclusion of the Yamasee War.* During the 1720s Spanish ships, "stiling themselves Guarda-Costas on Pretence of searching," plundered or captured English vessels bound for southern ports.[28] Often Africans were aboard these boats, as in the case of the sloop *Ann*, seized in 1721 coming from Barbados to South Carolina with a cargo of sugar, rum, and Negroes.[29] The disappearance to the southward of slaves owned in South Carolina continued also. In December 1722 a committee of both Houses concerned with the return of slaves from St Augustine urged higher rewards for taking up runaways. To guard against infiltrators who might encourage such defections, the committee also suggested that "a Law be passed to Oblige all Persons possessing Spanish Indians and Negroes to transport them off the Country."[30] A mission sent to Florida in 1726 to confirm the agreement about returning fugitives seems to have accomplished little, for the Assembly soon received a petition from Thomas Elliott and several other planters near Stono seeking government action since they had "had fourteen Slaves Runaway to St. Augustine."[31]

In June 1728 Acting Governor Arthur Middleton sent a formal complaint to authorities in London that not only were the Spanish "receivieing and harbouring all our Runaway Negroes, but also they have found out a New way of sending our own slaves against us, to Rob and Plunder us; –They are continually fitting out Partys of Indians from St. Augustine to Murder our White People, Rob our Plantations and carry off our slaves," Middleton stated, "soe that We are not only at a vast expence in Guarding our Southern Frontiers, but the Inhabitants are continually Allarmed, and have noe leizure to

* The Yamasee War was fought between colonists and the Yamasee (Amerindians) in 1715–16.

looke after theire Crops." The irate leader added: "The Indians they send against us are sent out in small Partys . . . and sometimes joined wth Negroes, and all the Mischeife they doe, is on a sudden and by surprize."[32]

These petty incursions soon subsided. Nevertheless, rumors reached South Carolina in 1737 from the West Indies of a full-scale Spanish invasion intended, in the words of Lieutenant Govenor Thomas Broughton, to "unsettle the colony of Georgia, and to excite an Insurrection of the Negroes of this Province." He reported to the Lords of Trade that the militia had been alerted, "and as our Negroes are very numerous An Act of the General Assembly is passed, to establish Patrols throughout the Country to keep the Negroes in order."[33]

The threatened assault never materialized, but in the meantime a new element was added to the situation. Late in 1773, the Spanish king issued a royal *cédula* granting liberty to Negro fugitives reaching St Augustine from the English colonies.[34] The edict was not immediately put into effect, and incoming slaves continued to be sold,[35] but in March 1738 a group of these former runaways appealed to the new governor for their freedom and obtained it. Seignior Don Manuel de Montiano established them on land two and a half miles north of St Augustine at a site called the Pueblo de Gracia Real de Santa Terese de Mose, which soon became known as "Moosa." With the approval of the Council of the Indies, the governor undertook to provision this settlement of several dozen families until its first harvest and arranged for a Catholic priest to offer them instruction.[36] He may also have urged other slaves to join them, for the captain of an English coasting schooner returning to Beaufort the following month testified that "he heard a Proclamation made at St Augustine, that all Negroes, who did, or should hereafter, run away from the English, should be made free." As a result, according to the captain, "several Negroes who ran away thither, and were sold there, were thereupon made free, and the Purchasers lost their Money."[37]

In November 1738, nineteen slaves belonging to Captain Caleb Davis "and 50 other Slaves belonging to other Persons inhabiting about Port Royal ran away to the Castle of St. Augustine."[38] Those who made it joined the Negro settlement at Moosa. It was apparently at this time that the Catholic king's edict of 1733 was published (in the words of a South Carolina report)

> by Beat of Drum round the Town of St. Augustine (where many Negroes belonging to English Vessels that carried thither Supplies of Provisions &c. had the Opportunity of hearing it) promising Liberty and Protection to all Slaves that should desert thither from any of the English Colonies but more especially from this. And lest that should not prove sufficient of itself, secret Measures were taken to make it known to our Slaves in general. In Consequence of which Numbers of Slaves did from Time to Time by Land and Water desert to St. Augustine; and the better to facilitate their Escape carried off their Master's Horses, Boats &c., some of them first committing Murder; and were accordingly received and declared free.[39]

When Captain Davis went to St Augustine to recover his slaves, he was pointedly rebuffed, a sign for Carolina's legislature that this difficulty might grow worse in the coming year.[40] Any premonitions which colonial officials might have felt were to prove justifiable, for the year 1739 was a tumultuous and decisive one in the evolution of South Carolina. Only the merest twist of circumstances prevented it from being remembered as a fateful turning-point in the social history of the early South.

In September 1739, South Carolina was shaken by an incident which became known as the Stono Uprising. A group of slaves struck a violent but abortive blow for liberation which resulted in the deaths of more than sixty people. Fewer than twenty-five white lives were taken, and property damage was localized, but the episode represented a new dimension in overt resistance. Free colonists, whose anxieties about controlling slaves had been growing for some time, saw their fears of open violence realized, and this in turn generated new fears.

According to a report written several years later, the events at Stono "awakened the Attention of the most Unthinking" among the white minority: "Every one that had any Relation, any Tie of Nature; every one that had a Life to lose were in the most sensible Manner shocked at such Danger daily hanging over their Heads." The episode, if hardly major in its own right, seemed to symbolize the critical impasse in which Carolina's English colonists now found themselves. "With Regret we bewailed our peculiar Case," the same report continued, "that we could not enjoy the Benefits of Peace like the rest of Mankind and that our own Industry should be the Means of taking from us all the Sweets of Life and of rendering us Liable to the Loss of our Lives and Fortunes."[41]

The Stono Uprising can also be seen as a turning-point in the history of South Carolina's black population. This episode was preceded by a series of projected insurrections, any one of which could have assumed significant proportions. Taken together, all these incidents represent a brief but serious groundswell of resistance to slavery, which had diverse and lasting repercussions. The slave system in the British mainland colonies withstood this tremor, and never again faced a period of such serious unrest. For Negroes in South Carolina the era represented the first time in which steady resistance to the system showed a prospect of becoming something more than random hostility. But the odds against successful assertion were overwhelming; it was slightly too late, or far too soon, for realistic thoughts of freedom among black Americans.

The year 1739 did not begin auspiciously for the settlement. The smallpox epidemic which had plagued the town in the previous autumn was still lingering on when the council and commons convened in Charlestown in January. Therefore, Lieutenant Governor William Bull, in his opening remarks to the initial session, recommended that the legislature consider "only what is absolutely necessary to be dispatched for the Service of the Province."[42] The primary issue confronting them, Bull suggested, was the desertion of their slaves, who represented such a huge proportion of the investments of white colonists. The Assembly agreed that the matter was urgent,[43] and a committee was immediately established to consider what measures should be taken in response to "the Encouragement lately given by the Spaniards for the Desertion of Negroes from this Government to the Garrison of St Augustine."[44]

Even as the legislators deliberated, the indications of unrest multiplied. In Georgia, William Stephens, the secretary for the trustees of that colony, recorded on 8 February 1739: "what we heard told us by several newly come from Carolina, was not to be disregarded, viz. that a Conspiracy was formed by the Negroes in Carolina, to rise and forcibly make their Way out of the Province" in an effort to reach the protection of the Spanish. It had been learned, Stephens wrote in his journal, that this plot was first discovered in Winyaw in the northern part of the province, "from whence, as they were to bend their Course South, it argued, that the other Parts of the Province must be privy to it, and that the Rising was to be universal; whereupon the whole Province were all upon their Guard."[45] If there were rumblings in the northernmost counties, Granville County, on the southern edge of the province, probably faced a greater prospect of disorder. Stephens's journal for 20 February reports word of a conspiracy among the slaves on the Montaigut and de Beaufain plantations bordering on the Savannah River just below the town of Purrysburg.[46] Two days later the Upper House in Charlestown passed on to the Assembly a petition and several affidavits from "Inhabitants of Granville County relating to the Desertion of their Slaves to the Castle of St. Augustine."[47]

That same week the Commons expressed its distress over information that several runaways heading for St Augustine had been taken up but then suffered to go at large without questioning. An inquiry was ordered, but it was not until early April that the Assembly heard concrete recommendations upon the problem of desertions. The first suggestion was for a petition to the English king requesting relief and assistance in this matter. Second, since many felt that the dozens of slaves escaping in November had eluded authorities because of a lack of scout boats, it was voted to employ 2 boats of 8 men each in patrolling the southern coastal passages for the next 9 months. Finally, to cut off Negroes escaping by land, large bounties were recommended for slaves taken up in the all-white colony of Georgia. Men, women, and children under twelve were to bring £40, £25, and £10, respectively, if brought back from beyond the Savannah River, and each adult scalp "with the two Ears" would command £20.[48]

In the midst of these deliberations, four slaves, apparently good riders who knew the terrain through hunting stray cattle, stole some horses and headed for Florida, accompanied by an Irish Catholic servant. Since they killed one White and wounded another in making their escape, a large posse was organized which pursued them unsuccessfully. Indian allies succeeded in killing one of the runaways, but the rest reached St Augustine, where they were warmly received.*[49] Spurred by such an incident, the Assembly completed work on 11 April on legislation undertaken the previous month to prevent slave insurrections. The next day a public display was made of the punishment of two captured runaways convicted of attempting to leave the province in the company of several other Negroes. One man was whipped and the other, after a contrite speech before the assembled slaves, "was executed at the usual Place, and afterwards hung in Chains at Hangman's Point opposite to this Town, in sight of all Negroes passing and repassing by Water."[50]

The reactions of colonial officials mirrored the desperate feelings spreading among the white population. On 18 May the Reverend Lewis Jones observed in a letter that the desertion of more than a score of slaves from his parish of St Helena the previous fall, in response to the Spanish proclamation, seemed to "Considerably Encrease the Prejudice of Planters agst the Negroes, and Occasion a Strict hand, to be kept over them by their Several Owners, those that Deserted having been Much Indulg'd."[51] But concern continued among English colonists as to whether even the harshest reprisals could protect their investments and preserve their safety.

A letter the same month from Lieutenant Governor Bull to the Duke of Newcastle, summarizing the situation, reflected the anxiety of the white populace:

My Lord,
I beg leave to lay before Your Grace an Affair, which may greatly distress if not entirely ruin this His Majesty's Province of South Carolina.

His Catholick Majesty's Edict having been published at St. Augustine declaring Freedom to all Negroes, and other slaves, that shall Desert from the English Colonies, Has occasioned several Parties to desert from this Province both by Land and Water, which notwithstanding

---

* They were warmly received because in the summer of 1739 Spain and Britain were soon to be at war, and the Spanish governor of Florida promised safe haven to slaves escaping from British colonies.

They were pursued by the People of Carolina as well as the Indians, & People in Georgia, by General Oglethorpes Directions, have been able to make their escape.[52]

Bull repeated the blunt refusal which the Spanish governor had given to deputies visiting St Augustine to seek the return of fugitives, and he reported: "This Answer has occasioned great disatisfaction & Concern to the Inhabitants of this Province, to find their property now become so very precarious and uncertain." There was a growing awareness among Whites, Bull concluded, "that their Negroes which were their chief support may in little time become their Enemies, if not their Masters, and that this Government is unable to withstand or prevent it."

Developments during the summer months did little to lessen tensions. In July the *Gazette* printed an account from Jamaica of the truce which the English governor there had felt compelled to negotiate with an armed and independent force of runaways.[53] During the same month a Spanish Captain of the Horse from St Augustine named Don Piedro sailed into Charlestown in a launch with twenty or thirty men, supposedly to deliver a letter to General Oglethorpe. Since Oglethorpe was residing in Frederica far down the coast, the visit seemed suspicious, and it was later recalled, in the wake of the Stono incident, that there had been a Negro aboard who spoke excellent English and that the vessel had put into numerous inlets south of Charlestown while making its return. Whether men were sent ashore was unclear, but in September the Georgians took into custody a priest thought to be "employed by the Spaniards to procure a general Insurrection of the Negroes."[54]

Another enemy, yellow fever, reappeared in Charlestown during the late summer for the first time since 1732. The epidemic "destroyed many, who had got thro' the Small-pox" of the previous year, and as usual it was remarked to be ".very fatal to Strangers & Europeans especially."[55] September proved a particularly sultry month. A series of philosophical lectures was discontinued "by Reason of the Sickness and Heat"; a school to teach embroidery, lacework, and French to young ladies was closed down; and the *Gazette* ceased publication for a month when the printer fell sick.[56] Lieutenant Governor Bull, citing "the Sickness with which it hath pleased God to visit this Province," prorogued the Assembly which attempted to convene on 12 September. The session was postponed again on 18 October and did not get under way until 30 October.[57] By then cool weather had killed the mosquitos which carried the disease, and the contagion had subsided, but it had taken the lives of the chief justice, the judge of the Vice-Admiralty Court, the surveyor of customs, the clerk of the Assembly, and the clerk of the Court of Admiralty, along with scores of other residents.[58]

The confusion created by this sickness in Charlestown, where residents were dying at a rate of more than half a dozen per day, may have been a factor in the timing of the Stono Rebellion,[59] but calculations might also have been influenced by the newspaper publication, in mid-August, of the Security Act, which required all white men to carry firearms to church on Sunday or submit to a stiff fine, beginning on 29 September.[60] It had long been recognized that the free hours at the end of the week afforded the slaves their best opportunity for cabals, particularly when Whites were engaged in communal activities of their own. In 1724 Governor Nicholson had expressed to the Lords of Trade his hope that new legislation would "Cause people to Travel better Armed in Times of Publick meetings when Negroes might take the better opportunity against Great Numbers of Unarmed men."[61] Later the same year the Assembly had complained that the recent statute requiring white men "to ride Arm'd on every Sunday" had not been announced sufficiently to be effective, and in 1727 the Committee of Grievances had objected that "the Law wch obliged people to go arm'd to Church &^{ca} wants strengthening."[62] Ten years later the presentments of the Grand Jury in Charlestown stressed the fact that Negroes were still permitted to cabal together during the hours of divine service, "which if not timely prevented may be of fatal Consequence to this Province."[63] Since the Stono Uprising, which caught planters at church, occurred only weeks before the published statute of 1739 went into effect, slaves may have considered that within the near future their masters would be even more heavily armed on Sundays.[64]

One other factor seems to be more than coincidental to the timing of the insurrection. Official word of hostilities between

England and Spain, which both Whites and Blacks in the colony had been anticipating for some time, appears to have reached Charlestown the very weekend that the uprising began.[65] Such news would have been a logical trigger for rebellion. If it did furnish the sudden spark, this would help explain how the Stono scheme, unlike so many others, was put into immediate execution without hesitancy or betrayal, and why the rebels marched southward toward Spanish St Augustine with an air of particular confidence.

During the early hours of Sunday, 9 September 1739, some 20 slaves gathered near the western branch of Stono River in St Paul's Parish, within 20 miles of Charlestown. Many of the conspirators were Angolans, and their acknowledged leader was a slave named Jemmy.[66] The group proceeded to Stono Bridge and broke into Hutchenson's store, where small arms and powder were on sale. The storekeepers, Robert Bathurst and Mr Gibbs, were executed and their heads left upon the front steps.

Equipped with guns, the band moved on to the house of Mr Godfrey, which they plundered and burned, killing the owner and his son and daughter. They then turned southward along the main road to Georgia and St Augustine and reached Wallace's Tavern before dawn. The innkeeper was spared, "for he was a good man and kind to his slaves,"[67] but a neighbor, Mr Lemy, was killed with his wife and child and his house was sacked. "They burnt Colonel Hext's house and killed his Overseer and his Wife. They then burnt Mr Sprye's house, then Mr Sacheverell's, and then Mr Nash's house, all lying upon the Pons Pons Road, and killed all the white People they found in them."[68] A man named Bullock eluded the rebels, but they burned his house. When they advanced upon the home of Thomas Rose with the intention of killing him, several of his slaves succeeded in hiding him, for which they were later rewarded. But by now reluctant slaves were being forced to join the company to keep the alarm from being spread. Others were joining voluntarily, and as the numbers grew, confidence rose and discipline diminished. Two drums appeared; a standard was raised; and there were shouts of "Liberty!" from the marchers. The few Whites whom they encountered were pursued and killed.

By extreme coincidence, Lieutenant Governor Bull was returning northward from Granville County to Charlestown at this time for the beginning of the legislative session. At about 11:00 in the morning, riding in the company of four other men, Bull came directly in view of the rebel troop, which must have numbered more than fifty by then. Comprehending the situation, he wheeled about, "and with much difficulty escaped & raised the Countrey." The same account states that Bull "was pursued," and it seems clear that if the lieutenant governor had not been on horseback he might never have escaped alive. Bull's death or capture would have had incalculable psychological and tactical significance. As it was, the rebels probably never knew the identity of the fleeing horseman or sensed the crucial nature of this chance encounter. Instead they proceeded through the Ponpon district, terrorizing and recruiting. According to a contemporary account, their numbers were being "increased every minute by new Negroes coming to them, so that they were above Sixty, some say a hundred, on which they halted in a field and set to dancing, Singing and beating Drums to draw more Negroes to them."[69]

The decision to halt came late on Sunday afternoon. Having marched more than ten miles without opposition, the troop drew up in a field on the north side of the road, not far from the site of the Jacksonburough ferry. Some of the recruits were undoubtedly tired or uncertain; others were said to be intoxicated on stolen liquor. Many must have felt unduly confident over the fact that they had already struck a more successful overt blow for resistance than any previous group of slaves in the colony, and as their ranks grew, the likelihood of a successful exodus increased. It has been suggested that the additional confidence needed to make such a large group of slaves pause in an open field in broad daylight may have been derived from the colors which they displayed before them.[70] Whatever the validity of this suggestion, the main reason for not crossing the Edisto River was probably the realistic expectation that by remaining stationary after such an initial show of force, enough other slaves could join them to make their troop nearly invincible by morning.

But such was not to be the case, for by Sunday noon some of the nearest white colonists had been alerted. Whether Bull himself was the first to raise the alarm is unclear. According to one tradition, the Reverend Stobo's Presbyterian congregation at Wiltown on the east bank of the Edisto was summoned directly from church, and since this would have been the first community which Bull and his fellow riders could reach, the detail is probably valid.[71] By about 4:00 in the afternoon a contingent of armed and mounted planters, variously numbered from twenty to one hundred, moved in upon the rebels' location (long after known as "the battlefield"[72]).

Caught off-guard, the Negroes hesitated as to whether to attack or flee. Those with weapons fired 2 quick but ineffective rounds; they were described later in white reports as having "behaved boldly."[73] Seeing that some slaves were loading their guns and others were escaping, a number of Whites dismounted and fired a volley into the group, killing or wounding at least fourteen. Other rebels were surrounded, questioned briefly, and then shot.

White sources considered it notable that the planters "did not torture one Negroe, but only put them to an easy death," and several slaves who proved they had been forced to join the band were actually released.[74] Those who sought to return to their plantations, hoping they had not yet been missed, were seized and shot, and one account claimed that the planters "Cutt off their heads and set them up at every Mile Post they came to."[75] Whether the riders used drink to fortify their courage or to celebrate their victory, a bill of more than £90 was drawn up the next day for "Liquors &c" which had been consumed by the local militia company.[76]

Although secondary accounts have suggested that the Stono Uprising was suppressed by nightfall,[77] contemporary sources reveal a decidedly different story. By Sunday evening more than twenty white settlers had already been killed. Initial messages from the area put the number twice as high and reported "the Country thereabout was full of Flames."[78] The fact that black deaths scarcely exceeded white during the first twenty-four hours was not likely to reassure the planters or intimidate the slave majority. Moreover, at least thirty Negroes (or roughly one-third of the rebel force) were known to have escaped from Sunday's skirmish in several groups, and their presence in the countryside provided an invitation to wider rebellion. Roughly as many more had scattered individually, hoping to rejoin the rebels or return to their plantations as conditions dictated.

During the ensuing days, therefore, a desperate and intensive manhunt was staged. The entire white colony was ordered under arms, and guards were posted at key ferry passages. The Ashley River militia company, its ranks thinned by yellow fever, set out from Charlestown in pursuit. Some of the militia captains turned out Indian recruits as well, who, if paid in cash, were willing to serve as slave-catchers. A white resident wrote several weeks later that within the first two days these forces "kill'd twenty odd more, and took about 40; who were immediately some shot, some hang'd, and some Gibbeted alive. A Number came in and were seized and discharged."[79] Even if these executions were as numerous, rapid, and brutal as claimed, the prospect of a sustained insurrection continued. It was not until the following Saturday, almost a week after the initial violence, that a white militia company caught up with the largest remnant of the rebel force. This band, undoubtedly short on provisions and arms, had made its way thirty miles closer to the colony's southern border. A pitched battle ensued, and at length (according to a note sent the following January) "ye Rebels [were] So entirely defeated & dispersed y^t there never were Seen above 6 or 7 together Since."[80]

It was not until a full month later, however, that a correspondent in South Carolina could report that "the Rebellious Negros are quite stopt from doing any further Mischief, many of them having been put to the most cruel Death."[81] And even then, white fears were by no means allayed. The Purrysburg militia company had remained on guard at the southern edge of the colony, and in Georgia General Oglethorpe, upon receiving Lieutenant Governor Bull's report of the insurrection, had called out rangers and Indians and issued a proclamation, "cautioning all Persons in this Province, to have a watchful Eye upon any Negroes, who might attempt to set a Foot in it."[82] He had also garrisoned soldiers at Palachicolas, the abandoned fort which guarded the only point for almost 100 miles where horses could swim the Savannah River and where Negro fugitives had previously crossed.[83] Security in South Carolina itself was made tight enough, however, so that few if any rebels reached Georgia. But this only increased the anxiety of Whites in the neighborhood of the uprising.

In November, several planters around Stono deserted their homes and moved their wives and children in with other families, "at particular Places, for their better Security and Defence against those Negroes which were concerned in that Insurrection who were not yet taken."[84] And in January, the minister of St Paul's Parish protested that some of his leading parishioners, "being apprehensive of Danger from yᵉ Rebels Still outstanding," had "carried their Families to Town for Safety, & if yᵉ Humour of moving continues a little longer, I shall have but a Small Congregation at Church."[85] The Assembly placed a special patrol on duty along the Stono River and expended more than £1,500 on rewards for Negroes and Indians who had acted in the white interest during the insurrection. Outlying fugitives were still being brought in for execution the following spring,[86] and one ringleader remained at large for three full years. He was finally taken up in a swamp by two Negro runaways hopeful of a reward, tried by authorities at Stono, and immediately hanged.[87]

It is possible to emphasize the small scale and ultimate failure of the uprising at Stono or to stress, on the other hand, its large potential and near success. Either approach means little except in the wider context of slave resistance during these years. Certain elements of the insurrection – total surprise, ruthless killing, considerable property damage, armed engagements, protracted aftermath – are singular in South Carolina's early history. Yet it remains only one swell in the tide of rebellious schemes which characterize these years. In retrospect, its initial success appears a high-water mark, and its ruthless suppression represents a significant turning of the tide. But the troubled waters of resistance did not subside any more abruptly than they had risen. For several years after the outbreak in St Paul's Parish, the safety of the white minority, and the viability of their entire plantation system, hung in serious doubt for the first time since the Yamasee War.

ABBREVIATIONS

BPRO	Trans.: Records in the British Public Record Office relating to South Carolina, 1663–1782. These 36 handwritten volumes were compiled in 1895 under the direction of W. Noel Sainsbury and are known as the Sainsbury Transcripts; they are available in the South Carolina Department of Archives and History. The first 5 volumes have been published in facsimile form (Atlanta, Ga, and Columbia, SC, 1928–47)
CRSG	Allan D. Candler and Lucien L. Knight, eds, *The Colonial Records of the State of Georgia*, 26 vols (Atlanta, Ga, 1904–16)
DRNY	E. B. O'Callaghan, *et al.*, eds, *Documents Relative to the Colonial History of the State of New York*, 15 vols (Albany, NY, 1855–83)
JNH	*Journal of Negro History*
JSH	*Journal of Southern History*
Parish Trans.:	Parish Transcripts, NYHS. (Mr Parish and his colleagues transcribed all they could find in the British Public Records which pertained to Negroes and slaves in the North American colonies.)
Pringle Letterbook:	The Letterbook of Robert Pringle, 1737–45, SCHS. Walter B. Edgar has edited a 2-volume set of this letterbook (Columbia, SC, 1972)
SCCHJ	South Carolina Commons House Journals: Alexander S. Salley, ed., *Journal of the Commons House of Assembly*, 21 vols (Columbia, SC, 1907–46); and J. H. Easterby and Ruth S. Green, eds, *The Colonial Records of South Carolina*, 1st ser.: *The Journal of the Commons House of Assembly, 1736–1750*, 9 vols (Columbia, SC, 1951–62)
SCDAH	South Carolina Department of Archives and History, Columbia, SC
SCG	*South Carolina Gazette*
SCHGM	*South Carolina Historical and Genealogical Magazine* (called the *South Carolina Historical Magazine* since 1952, but cited here as *SCHGM* throughout)
SCUHJ	Journals of the South Carolina Upper House in the SCDAH

Statutes   Thomas Cooper and David J. McCord, eds, *The
            Statutes at Large of South Carolina*, 10 vols (Columbia,
            SC, 1836–41)
SPG   Society for the Propagation of the Gospel

NOTES

This chapter consists of selections from *Black Majority* (New
York, 1976) reprinted by permission of Alfred W. Knopf.

1 *Statutes*, 7:424.
2 Inventories from the colonial period note an occasional slave who
  "pretends to be mad." Cf. "Charles Cotesworth Pinckney's Plantation Diary, April 6–Dec. 15, 1818," SCHGM 41 (1940):139.
  Among those "not working" at his Crescent Plantation, Pinckney
  cites "Old Sambo (pretends to be crazy)."
3 See Winthrop Jordan, *White Over Black* (Chapel Hill, NC, 1968)
  393.
4 Parish Trans., SC, Box I, folder 4, pp. 3a–4 (copied from SCCHJ,
  24 January 1724).
5 SCG, 25 August 1733; 28 June 1742.
6 An Englishman, after observing the relations of masters to slaves
  along the American coast, commented: "as to their general Usage
  of them, 'tis monstrous, and shocking. To be sure, a *new Negro*,
  if he must be broke, either from Obstinacy, or, which I am more
  apt to suppose, from Greatness of Soul, will require more hard
  Discipline than a young Spaniel: You would really be surpiz'd at
  their Perseverance; let an hundred Men shew him how to hoe, or
  drive a Wheelbarrow, he'll still take the one by the Bottom, and
  the other by the Wheel; and they often die before they can be
  conquer'd:" "Itinerant Observations in America" (Anonymous),
  printed in the *London Magazine* (1745–6) and rep. in Ga. Hist. Soc.,
  Collections, 4 (1878):38.
7 SCCHJ, 1736–9, 221.
8 Memorial of William MacKay, 21 May 1741, SCCHJ 1741–2, 16–17.
  MacKay explained that his proposal arose "from the disorderly
  Behaviour of several of the Butchers and their Attendants, which
  indeed was a Reproach to any Christian well governed Country,
  and which they had been then so long used to that they were
  become quite ungovernable, and abusive to the Town's People
  who went to buy, and to the Country People that came to Sell
  Provisions at Market."
9 Consider the following passage by a Virginia tobacco planter:
  "There is nothing so absurd as the generality of negroes are. If in
  the beginning of cutting tob°, without watching they will cut all
  before them, and now when there is danger of losing tob° by the
  frost should it happen, they will not cut pl[an]ts really ripe because

they may be the thicker, just as if there was time to let it stand longer:" "Extracts from the Diary of Colonel Landon Carter," *William and Mary Quarterly* 13 (1905):223.

10 Historians have only recently begun to appreciate again the degree to which work slowdowns, the destruction of tools, and general malingering evolved into semi-conscious tactics of agricultural sabotage. William W. Freehling, *Prelude to Civil War* (New York, 1965), 66, alludes to the stock image which grew up among South Carolina planters of "the seemingly innocent but cunning laborer who could misunderstand adroitly, loiter diligently, or destroy guilefully." "Culpable carelessness" was the vivid phrase coined by one nineteenth-century editor and cited in Herbert Aptheker's brief review of the subject: "Slave Resistance in the United States," in Nathan Huggins, Martin Kilson, and Daniel Fox, eds, *Key Issues in the Afro-American Experience* (New York, NY, 1971) 1:163–73. (Historians of American labor have made less progress in documenting and explaining the similar covert and pervasive tactics used by European immigrant workers to contain managerial drives for industrial efficiency in more recent times.)

Among the most interesting discussions of this entire topic is George M. Frederickson and Christopher Lasch, "Resistance to Slavery," *Civil War History* 13 (1967):315–29. However, while their article lends considerable refinement to the theoretical discussion of resistance, it relies like so many previous studies upon only a small number of original sources, drawn entirely from the nineteenth century. Indeed, it is regrettable that so central an article belabors the misleading viewpoint (p. 324; cf. p. 319) that for considering Negro dissatisfactions "adequate records of personal slave response simply do not exist." Eugene D. Genovese, who has made important conceptual contributions in this area, rightly points out in private correspondence (6 February 1973) that interpretations of slave work habits must go beyond questions of inadequate incentives and modes of resistance to relate pre-industrial work patterns among Afro-Americans to those analyzed by E. P. Thompson and others among Europeans.

11 For a useful study which seeks to categorize numerous revolts, see Marion D. DeB. Kilson, "Towards Freedom: An Analysis of Slave Revolts in the United States," *Phylon* 25 (1964):175–87. The tendency of white sources to either minimize or exaggerate Negro conspiracies is discussed in Herbert Aptheker, *American Negro Slave Revolts* (New York, 1969), ch. 7.

12 Letter to Mr Boone, 24 June 1720, BPRO Trans., 8:24–7. The same letter appears in British Public Record Office, *Calendar of State Papers Colonial Series, American and West Indies, 1720–1721* (London, 1916), 57. One portion reads: "I think it proper for you to tell Mr. Percivall at home that his slaves was the principal rogues and 'tis my opinion his only way will be to sell them out singly or else I am doubtful his interest in slaves will come to little for want of strict management. Work does not agree with them."

13 Representation of the Lords Commissioners for Trade and Plantations, to the King, 8 September 1721, in *DRNY*, 5:610.

14 *Statutes*, 7:375. Since the financial loss from executing slaves was being borne locally at this time, which may have prompted those deciding such cases to restrict capital punishment, the act ordered that whenever the convicting judges sentenced some slaves to "suffer death as exemplary, and the rest to be returned to the owners," those owners were to share the cost of the executed slaves. (*Statutes*, 7:375).

15 Richard Ludlam to David Humphreys, 2 July 1724, cited in Frank J. Klingberg, *An Appraisal of the Negro in Colonial South Carolina* (Washington DC, 1941), 46.

16 *Boston Weekly News-Letter*, 22 October 1730. The letter from Charlestown is dated 20 August 1730.

17 "The Diary of Captain Johann Hinrichs," in Bernard Alexander Uhlendorf (ed. and trans.), *The Siege of Charleston, with an Account of the Province of South Carolina: diaries and letters of Hessian officers from the von Jungkenn papers in the William L. Clements Library* (Ann Arbor, Mich., 1938):323. Hinrichs's journal is generally careful, and it is far more probable that he received the wrong year and certain traditional trimmings from his informant than that he recorded a totally fictitious event, as suggested by Jordan, *White Over Black*, 153 and Aptheker, *American Negro Slave Revolts*, 184.

18 SCCHJ, 26 February 1733, cited in Aptheker, *American Negro Slave Revolts*, 183.

19 SCCHJ, 1736–9, 23, 28, 29, 245, 264.

20 SCCHJ, 1736–9, 586.

21 SCG, 21 September 1738. The statute continued: "And to the End that the Number of able Slaves may be constantly known, the said Lists shall be renewed . . . once in every Year, on the first Muster Day after the 25th of March. And such Lists shall be return'd by the respective Captains to the Governor, Lieutenant Governor or President, within one Month after the same shall be given to the said Captains respectively."

22 John Brickell, *The Natural History of North Carolina* (Dublin, 1737), 274. (Compare this with nineteenth-century industrial lore concerning recent immigrants as the frequent originators of labor unrest.)

23 William Orr, 30 September 1742, cited in Klingberg, *Appraisal*, 81.

24 "Account of the Negroe Insurrection," 233. The hypothesis that recently imported Blacks were frequently troublesome owing to group resistance based on a common African background was raised in Eugene D. Genovese, "Slave Revolts in the New World: A Comparative Analysis" (paper presented to the Southern Historical Association, 1968).

25 SCUHJ, 30 May 1733, Parish Trans., SC, Box I, folder 4, p. 32a.

26 9 April 1734, BPRO Trans, 16:398–9.

27 3 February 1748, BPRO Trans, 23:71.

28 SCCHJ, 1 July 1741, p. 82, SCDAH.

29 BPRO Trans, 10:38.

30 SCUHJ, 12 December 1722, mfm BMP/D 487, SCDAH. For other references to slaves escaping to St Augustine at this time, see the same source, 22, 23 June and 6, 14 December 1722.

31 SCCHJ, 10 February 1728, Parish Trans., SC, Box I, folder 4, p. 20a.

32 13 June 1728, BPRO Trans. 13:61–7. Middleton reported that 4 Negroes carried off from an estate on the Combahee River near Port Royal in 1726 were later seen in St Augustine and that the following summer 2 white captives were present when the Spanish governor sent out 4 dozen Yamasees, promising 30 pieces of eight for every English scalp and 100 pieces "for every live Negro they should bring." The party murdered several border scouts and penetrated to a plantation within 10 miles of Ponpon, where they took the scalps of 2 more Whites named Micheau and Wood. A band of 15 planters pursued them and recovered the 10 slaves they were carrying away, but more successful raids followed. Middleton wrote that in September 1727, 2 pettiaugers [boats] "Manned with Six of our Runaway Slaves and the rest Indians" took 8 white captives from French's Island. "The Indians would have murthered them all for the sake of their Scalps, but this time the Negroes would not agree to it." This was probably the same raid described to Carolina authorities by John Pearson, an English mariner (20 October 1727, BPRO Trans. 19:127–8). He reported that while he was in St Augustine that month, "Two Canoes, one with Indians, and the other with Negroes returned from Hilton head," carrying 8 English prisoners, one Negro Man, and a mulatto boy. He observed that there were "about Ten Negroes and fourteen Indians Commanded by those of their own Colour, without any Spaniards in Company with them." While Pearson was testifying in late October, a schooner manned by Spaniards and South Carolina runaways was preparing for a further raid. The vessel entered the North Edisto River, where its crew plundered the David Ferguson plantation and carried away 7 Negroes. "It seems," concluded Middleton, "the Governor of Augustine Makes Merchandize of all our slaves, and ships them off to Havanah for his own Profit, as we are told by the Spaniards themselves at St. Augustine."

33 6 February 1737, BPRO Trans. 18:170.

34 Wilber H. Siebert, "Slavery and White Servitude in East Florida, 1726–1776" *Florida Historical Society Quarterly* 10 (1931):3–4.

35 SCCHJ, 1 July 1741, 83, SCDAH.

36 Siebert, "Slavery and White Servitude in East Florida, 1726–1776," 3–4. See also I. A. Wright, "Dispatches of Spanish Officials bearing on the Free Negro Settlement of Gracia Real de Santa Teresa de Mose, Florida," *JNH* 9 (1924):144–95.

37 21 April 1738, BPRO Trans. 19:76.

38 SCCHJ, 19 January 1739, 596.

39 SCCHJ, 1 July 1741, 83.

40 SCCHJ, 19 January 1739, 596. Davis, a sugar trader familiar with the coast, reported to a Georgian (15 December 1738) that he had seen his slaves in St Augustine and they had laughed at him: "The Journal of William Stephens," CRSG 4:247–8.

41 SCCHJ, 1 July 1741, 84.

42 SCCHJ, 17 January 1739, 590. Bull continued: "The Desertion of our Slaves is a Matter of so much Importance to this Province that I doubt not but you will readily concur in Opinion with me that the most effectual Means ought to be used to discourage and prevent it for the Future, and to render as secure as possible so valuable a Part of the Estates and Properties of his Majesty's Subjects."

43 SCG, 25 January 1739. Charles Pinckney, the Speaker of the Assembly, was reported as saying: "We consider the Desertion of our Slaves as a Matter of very ill Consequence to the Estates and Properties of the People of this Province; and if some speedy and effectual Care is not taken to prevent it before it becomes more general, it may in time prove of the utmost Disadvantage."

44 SCCHJ, 19 January 1739, 595–6.

45 "The Journal of William Stephens," 275.

46 "The Journal of William Stephens," 283–4.

47 SCCHJ, 1736–9, 631–2.

48 SCCHJ, 1736–9, 628, 680, 681; cf. 707.

49 "An Account of the Negroe Insurrection in South Carolina," (undated, c.1740), in CSRG, 232–3. According to the account of this March escape, "four or five who were Cattel-Hunters, and knew the Woods, some of whom belonged to Captain Macpherson, ran away with His Horses, wounded his Son and killed another Man . . . They reached Augustine, one only being killed and another wounded by the Indians in their flight. They were received there with great honours, one of them had a Commission given to him, and a Coat faced with Velvet." See also SCCHJ, 1739–41, 229–30; 23 February 1743, 235.

50 SCG, 12 April 1739.

51 Quoted in Klingberg, Appraisal, 68. Klingberg mistakes this incident for the Stono Rebellion later in the year. He also appears to have mistaken the date of the letter, which was 18 May. See SPG Transcripts in the Library of Congress, series B, vol. 7, part 1, p. 233.

52 BPRO Trans. 20:40–1.

53 SCG, 28 July 1739.

54 SCCHJ, 1 July 1741, 83–4.

55 James Killpatrick, An Essay on Inoculation occasioned by the Small Pox being Brought Into South Carolina in the Year 1738 (London, 1743), 56; letter of 16 October 1739, Pringle Letterbook.

56 SCG, 13 October, 1 December 1739.

57 SCG, 15 September, 20 October 1739.

58 Yates Snowden, History of South Carolina, 5 vols (Chicago and New York, 1920) 1:231.

59 A letter from South Carolina, dated 28 September, was reprinted in the *Boston Weekly Newsletter*, 8 November 1739: "A terrible Sickness has rag'd here, which the Doctors call a yellow billious Fever, of which we bury 8 or 10 in a Day; the like never known among us; but seems to abate as the cold Weather advances."

60 SCG, 18 August 1739.

61 5 May 1724, BPRO Trans. 10:111.

62 SCCHJ, 4 June 1724, 7, 9; 13 January 1727, 69.

63 SCG, 26 March 1737. It is significant that the next set of presentments dealt with the other side of the coin. It was objected in October that the Sabbath laws were being violated "in several Parts of the Country by laying Negroes under a Necessity of Labouring on that Day, contrary to the Laws of God and Man:" SCG, 5 November 1737. Whether Sunday labor reduced or enhanced the prospects of rebellion would be debated repeatedly by Whites in the next several years.

64 A similar law, which made clearer provisions for the security of Charlestown, was passed in 1743: *Statutes*, 7:417–19.

65 "The Journal of William Stephens," 412. A confirmation that war had been declared and the first news of an insurrection at Stono reached Georgia before noon, 13 September, via the same "express" from Charlestown.

66 U. B. Phillips, *American Negro Slavery* (Baton Rouge, La, 1966), 473, gives the leader's name as Jonny. Aptheker points out in *Slave Revolts*, 187n, that Dr Ramsey called the leader Cato and used the date 1740. (He could have been referring to a later incident mentioned below.) To avoid such confusions, I have bypassed derivative secondary sources and pieced together the following description of the Stono Uprising from the contemporary materials which survive.

67 "Account of the Negroe Insurrection," 234. This would suggest that even in the midst of the most desperate revolt, slave violence was by no means haphazard. Such an instance of discretion was not unique. During Tacky's Rebellion in Jamaica in 1760, for example, slaves chose to spare one Abraham Fletcher while killing more than three dozen other whites: Robert Renny, *An History of Jamaica* (London, 1807), 66.

68 "Account of the Negroe Insurrection," 234.

69 "Account of the Negroe Insurrection," 234.

70 Fisher, *Negro Slave Songs in the United States* (New York, 1969), 70, points out that members of secret West African cults often claimed to derive invincible powers from the presence of a special banner (much as Roman legions or American marines have historically drawn inspiration from the sight of certain standards): "Negro cultists in many instances acted as though they were invulnerable. A picture of one of their banners in Africa, drawn by a slave trader of the eighteenth century, shows the cultist carrying a large grigri bag. In it were charms to preserve one from hurt or harm . . . Jemmy's insurrectionists in South Carolina in the eight-

eenth century and the Vesey plotters of that same area in the nineteenth century were reckless because of dependence upon their banners." Cf. William C. Suttles, Jr, "African Religious Survivals as Factors in American Slave Revolts," *JNH* (1971), 97–104.

71 Alexander Hewatt, *An Historical Account of the Rise and Progress of the Colonies of South Carolina and Georgia*, 2 vols (London, 1779), repr. in Carroll, ed., *Historical Collections of South Carolina* 1:332. The account in Edward McCrady, *South Carolina under the Royal Government*, which follows Hewatt, suggests that Bull went to Charlestown via John's Island while a companion named Golightly rode the 8 miles to Wiltown church.

72 *SCHGM* 10 (1909):28.

73 "Account of the Negroe Insurrection," 235. One slave was said to have answered his owner's query as to whether he truly wished to kill his master by pulling the trigger on his pistol only to have the weapon misfire, at which the planter shot him through the head: "A Ranger's Report of Travels with General Oglethorpe, 1739–1742," in N. D. Mereness, ed., *Travels in the American Colonies* (New York, 1916), 223.

74 "Account of the Negroe Insurrection," 235.

75 "A Ranger's Report," 223.

76 SCCHJ, 1739–1741, 158.

77 This version is repeated in Sirmans, *Colonial South Carolina*, 207–8, and it has recently been echoed in Richard Hofstadter, *America at 1750: A Social Portrait* (New York, 1971), 129.

78 "The Journal of William Stephens," p. 412; cf. "A Ranger's Report," p. 222, which says "about forty White People" died.

79 *Boston Weekly News-Letter*, 8 November 1739, extract of a letter from South Carolina dated 28 September.

80 Andrew Leslie to Philip Bearcroft, St Paul's Parish, SC, 7 January 1740, quoted in Klingberg, *Appraisal*, 80.

81 *Boston Weekly News-Letter*, 30 November 1739. Although the printer put 18 August, the date on the letter from South Carolina must have been 18 October or thereabouts. The correspondent added: "The Yellow Fever is abated, but has been very mortal."

82 "The Journal of William Stephens," 427; cf. "A Ranger's Report," 222.

83 "Account of the Negroe Insurrection," 236.

84 SCCHJ, 21 November 1739, 37.

85 Letter of Andrew Leslie to Philip Bearcroft, St Paul's Parish, SC, 7 January 1740, quoted in Klingberg, *Appraisal*, 80.

86 SCCHJ, 1739–41, 341, 528–9.

87 SCG, 27 December 1742; SCCHJ, 1742–4, 263.

7

PORTS OF COLONIAL BRAZIL

A. J. R. Russell-Wood

Examining places like Jamestown helps us learn about European implantation in the Americas; examining port cities helps us understand better the economic operation and social organization of mature colonial societies. A. J. R. Russell-Wood, in this essay on Brazilian ports, illustrates the variety of functions which ports served. On one level, they acted as points of contact between Europe and its colonies. In mature societies, the Europeans first entered the Americas through these ports. As the implanted societies and economies stabilized, the ports increasingly developed and interacted with colonial and imperial hinterlands. Urban populations diversified in order to fulfill better the market economic (and, in the case of Brazil, political) functions which cities assumed. Moreover, at least in colonial Brazil, the ports' populations came to resemble those in Atlantic European cities; class and racial stratification increased.

Ports served as the funnels through which imports and exports found their markets. Crops – in Brazil's case mostly sugar – arrived from the hinterland en route to Portugal or other Atlantic societies. In return, Europeans sent consumer goods for planter consumption. Ports thus linked several regions and populations. The changing composition of the population (as well as its social and spatial organization) is perhaps a reflection of the colonial and imperial economy's development and sophistication.

* * *

Brazil is endowed with 4,603 miles of coastline bordering the Atlantic and with river systems giving access to the interior. The Bay of All Saints and the Bay of Guanabara are joined by numerous and less famous, but no less protected and extensive, havens for ocean-going vessels, ranging from the Lagoa dos Patos in the south to the Bay of Marajó in the north. The

174

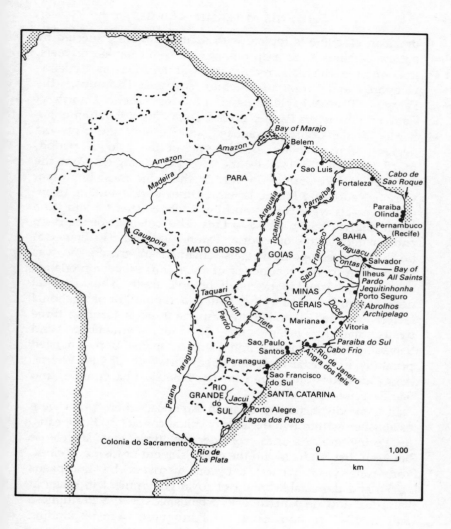

Bay of Marajo

Belem

Sao Luis

Amazon

Amazon

Madeira

PARA

Parnaiba

Fortaleza

*Cabo de
Sao Roque*

Paraiba
Olinda

Pernambuco
(Recife)

Gauapore

MATO GROSSO

Araguaia

Tocantins

GOIAS

BAHIA

Paraguacu

Sao Francisco

Contas

Salvador

*Bay of
All Saints*

Ilheus

*Pardo
Jequitinhonha*

Porto Seguro

*Abrolhos
Archipelago*

Taquari

Coxim

MINAS
GERAIS

Doce

Pardo

Tiete

Mariana

Vitoria

Paraguay

Sao Paulo

Santos

*Paraiba do Sul
Cabo Frio*

Angra dos Reis

Rio de Janeiro

Parana

Paranagua

Sao Francisco
do Sul

RIO
GRANDE
do
SUL

Jacui

SANTA CATARINA

Porto Alegre

Lagoa dos Patos

Colonia do Sacramento

*Rio de
La Plata*

0   1,000

km

Brazilian coastline is replete with secure harbors protected by natural features such as promontories, sand banks, or reefs. In addition to the major river systems of the Amazon–Madeira–Guaporé and tributaries, the Araguaia–Tocantins, the Paraguay–Paraná–La Plata, and the São Francisco, north of Cabo Frio the rivers Paraíba do Sul, Jacuí, Doce, Jequitinhonha, Pardo, Rio das Contas, Paraguaçú, and Parnaíba afford varying degrees of navigability. By the end of the colonial period, Brazil counted the establishment of ports ranging from the Amazon to Rio Grande do Sul. Of these the most important were Salvador and Rio de Janeiro. Other ports handling deep-water vessels were Santos and Pernambuco (Recife) and, to a lesser degree, Belém and São Luís. The potential of the deep and sheltered bays of Vitória, Paranaguá, and São Francisco do Sul for ocean-going vessels remained underused and was attributable to the economies of their immediate hinterlands and to established patterns of oceanic trade. The historical development of Brazil, rather than geographical or navigational factors, resulted in the more important ports forming three dyads: namely, Belém and São Luís, Pernambuco and Salvador, Rio de Janeiro and Santos. Smaller ports engaged primarily in coastal trade included Fortaleza, Ilhéus, Vitória, Angra dos Reis and Paratí on the Baía da Ilha Grande, and São Francisco do Sul.

In contradistinction to Spanish America, where ports were established within two decades of initial contact by Europeans, in Portuguese America considerable time was to elapse between first landfalls and the establishment of towns or cities. Forty-nine years passed between discovery by Europeans (1500) and the establishment of royal government in Brazil at Salvador. Rio de Janeiro was established by the Portuguese only in 1565. In both cases the Portuguese were responding to external forces: in the former, realization that the failure of the donatory system would be seen by foreign powers as an Achilles' heel to be exploited unless a Portuguese presence were established; in the latter, the presence in the Bay of Guanabara of the French who were ousted from their settlement by Estácio de Sá in 1567. Salvador and Rio shared at least two characteristics. Their initial importance was commercially and geopolitically strategic as part of the Portuguese world system; neither topography nor selection of site was to prove ideally suited for the establishment of an urban center. In Portuguese America it was commonplace (as in Salvador, Rio de Janeiro, and Vitória) for ports to be established some degree removed – usually further within a bay – from the site of initial settlement. Recife came into being because of its sheltered port and because Olinda lacked access to the sea. By contrast, Salvador, Rio de Janeiro, Santos, and Pernambuco were multifunctional (with administration, commerce, and defense) from their inception; São Luís and Belém had been established as fortified outposts of empire and only gradually were to assume administrative roles and become commercial entrepôts. Other ports came into existence as part of a natural response to commercial needs but, for the most part, were slow to gain prominence, and only a few were to achieve the status of city, *cidade*, in the colonial period.

The remarkable aspect of Portuguese America was that, except for São Paulo (founded 1535?) and mining townships which came into being in the eighteenth century, ports were the only urban centers in the colony. In a legal sense the only true cities (*cidades*) in the colony, prior to the elevation of São Paulo (1712) and Mariana (1745) to the status of cities, were the cities of the Atlantic seaboard: Olinda (1537), Salvador (1549), and Rio de Janeiro (1565). Towns (*vilas*) were: Santos (1532), Vitória (1535, later named Vila Nova do Espírito Santo and moved in 1551, becoming a city in 1823), São Luís (1612 foundation by French, taken by Portuguese 1615), Belém (1616), Paraíba (16??), Paranaguá (1646–9?), Fortaleza (1699, city 1823), Recife (1710, city 1823), and Porto Alegre (1810). For much of Brazilian history, *vila* or *cidade* was synonymous with *port*.

In this chapter I consider four broad issues: first, the symbiosis between ports and the sea, and its implications; second, relationships between ports and their immediate geographical environs, the Brazilian hinterland, and the wider world; third, the multifunctional roles of ports;* fourth, Salvador as a case study with particular attention to demography, social composition, and sectoral distribution.[1]

---

* In this selection, we have eliminated Russell-Wood's section on the multifunctional role of ports.

PORTS AND THE SEA

Geographic, oceanographic, and navigational factors determined the relative importance of Brazilian ports. That all the ports shared access to the Atlantic did not mean that all derived equal benefits from their location. Coastal shipping confronted several difficulties. On the southeastern coast the Abrolhos Archipelago was an obstacle to shipping between Salvador and Rio de Janeiro, and Cabo de São Roque and offshore reefs made the northeastern coast hazardous. The Atlantic wind and current system also placed constraints on Brazilian ports. The north Atlantic gyre runs clockwise, whereas the south Atlantic gyre is counterclockwise. There is intertropical convergence on the Equator. Northeast trades took Portuguese vessels down to the northeast coast of Brazil, but passage southward beyond São Roque would be impeded by the head-on southeast trades. For coastal shipping, the northeast monsoon (October to April) permitted sailing from Pernambuco to Bahia in four to five days, and the southeast monsoon (April to October) would permit passage from Bahia to Pernambuco. To run north along the southeast coast of Brazil would be to run against the prevailing Brazil current.[2]

Physical hazards and the combination of winds and tides were to have important implications for the colony itself, for the manner in which it was regarded by Portugal, and for its relations with a wider world. At the local level, the prospect of establishing linkages between ports on the northeast coast of Brazil with those on the southeast coast was virtually eliminated. The potential for development for regular, year-round, two-way contacts between ports on the southeast coast was diminished. Effectively, trade and communications, passage of persons, or the transportation of military matériel between ports on the northeastern and southeastern coasts of Brazil was hazardous and rare. Even between ports on the southeastern coast, passage was determined by the monsoon seasons. Travel between Pernambuco and Salvador was best accomplished between the beginning of October and the end of April with the northeast monsoon. The southeast winds most favored navigation from Salvador to Pernambuco between the end of April and the beginning of October. The impact was also apparent in the scheme of imperial control.

Recognizing the virtual impossibility of maritime communications between ports on the northeast coast of Brazil with those on the southeast, most particularly the capital cities of Salvador (1549–1763) and Rio de Janeiro (1763–), the Portuguese Crown was led to establish the separate administrative entity of the Estado do Maranhão distinct from the Estado do Brasil. This was tacit acknowledgment that communications between Lisbon and São Luís or Belém were easier than between these ports and Pernambuco, Salvador, or Rio de Janeiro and that it was not feasible for viceroys or governors-general in Salvador or Rio to dispatch orders to ports on the northeastern coast.[3] With the development and widespread use of the chronometer in the nineteenth century, communications were improved but only by dint of sweeping northeastward out to sea before turning south-southwest to round the cape. The advent of steam would alleviate the problem in the nineteenth century.

Wind systems and currents, together with navigational limitations that prevailed during the colonial period, had an impact on the schedule of vessels engaged in the *carreira do Brasil*, although to a lesser degree than those of the more rigorous and less forgiving *carreira da India*. Opportunism, rather than numerous attempts by the Portuguese Crown to set sailing times and control the anarchy of individual captains, prevailed. But there was the inescapable fact that what usually was an uneventful run could turn unpleasant for vessels that chose to ignore the seasons and were becalmed in the Equatorial zone outward-bound or were beset by late autumnal or early winter gales in the latitude of the Azores homeward-bound.

According to one eighteenth-century seadog, vessels should leave Lisbon between 15 and 25 October to arrive in Pernambuco before 15 December; from there to Salvador was less than a week's sailing, and favorable winds would bring one to Rio de Janeiro before year's end. A royal order of 11 August 1632 ruled that vessels outward-bound for Brazil leave Lisbon between 1 October and the end of February. A royal decree in 1690 ruled that vessels leave Portugal between 15 December and 20 January and depart Brazilian ports for Portugal between the end of May and 20 July. In fact, in the eighteenth century, most fleets from Lisbon destined for Salvador or Pernambuco left Lisbon in April; those for Rio de Janeiro most frequently left Lisbon in March, April, and May.

As regards the homeward-bound leg, there was greater irregularity. October was the month of the greatest number of arrivals in Lisbon of vessels from Salvador; however, with the exception of June, vessels from Salvador put into the Tagus every month of the year. July was the month of the greatest number of arrivals from Pernambuco. This monthly variation in the greatest numbers of arrivals of vessels from Salvador and Pernambuco – the two major export ports for sugar – meant that the Lisbon market would not be glutted and that the price of the commodity would be maintained. As for vessels homeward-bound from Rio, the greatest number arrived in the Tagus in August and October. Vessels from Maranhão arrived in Lisbon in December and January and, as was not the case with other ports of origin, no vessel from Maranhão arrived in Lisbon between July and September. Overall, 31 per cent of vessels leaving Lisbon for Brazil did so in April (thereafter, in decreasing order, December, January, February, March, and May). As for arrival in Lisbon from Brazil, the most favored months (in decreasing order) were October, August, December, and January.[4]

Vessels of the *carreira do Brasil* were not the only oceanic vessels to put into Brazilian ports. Rarely did Indiamen from Lisbon put into Brazilian ports outward-bound. If they did, the schedule would be to leave Lisbon in February, March, or April to cross the Equator before June, arrive at Salvador in May or June, and depart only in November to catch favorable winds. But, after the discovery of gold and diamonds in the late seventeenth and early eighteenth centuries, this became more common under one pretext or another for homeward-bound Indiamen. Ideally such vessels should have left Cochin or Goa with the northeast monsoon in late December or January, arriving in Brazilian ports in March, April, or May, and leaving for Portugal in May, June, or July. Late departures from India in February or March meant that the *náos* hit heavy weather off the Cape of Good Hope in May and June and often put into Brazilian ports with vessel and crew in distress.[5]

If wind and current primarily determined both the sailing schedules and the presence in Brazilian ports of vessels of the *carreira da India* or the *carreira do Brasil*, then commercial and administrative factors not only contributed to the number and nature of such vessels but determined those ports on which their presence would be most felt. During the sixteenth and early seventeenth centuries, individual captains took their caravels to and from Brazil at will, often sustaining heavy losses first at the hands of pirates and later during the Dutch war. Despite its shortcomings, the Brazil Company (founded 1649, incorporated by the Crown 1664) had promoted the concepts of armed convoys and the bringing together of individual vessels into fleets. A royal order of 24 July 1660 prohibited individual voyages.[6] The results had been so favorable as to lead to the continuation of both the fleet system and the presence of accompanying war ships after the abolition of the company in 1720. The Portuguese Crown rang the changes on the convoy system in the course of the eighteenth century, terminating it in 1765, reinstating the practice from 1797 to 1801, and finally abolishing it. Fleets from Brazil to Europe counted as many as one hundred sails in the late seventeenth and eighteenth centuries, which made them the largest fleets in the world at that time.[7] In addition to the vessels of the *carreira do Brasil*, rarely did a year pass without a homeward-bound Indiaman putting into a Brazilian port. Furthermore, there were vessels engaged directly in trade between Brazilian ports and West Africa. Intensive but irregular in nature, between 1743 and 1756 the numbers of such vessels were established at twenty-four per annum for the round trip.

The impact of this oceanic and transoceanic trade was not the same on all ports of Brazil and it varied over time. Voyage time from Lisbon to Recife was about 60 days, to Salvador 70–80, and 80–90 to Rio de Janeiro. Homeward-bound, the corresponding times were 75, 84, and 97 days for fleets and some two weeks less for single vessels. From Angola, sailing times were 35 days to Pernambuco, 40 to Salvador, and 50 to Rio de Janeiro.[8] In general, Salvador was especially favored both as regards the European and African trades and because its port facilities and shipyard made it a welcome haven for homeward-bound Indiamen. For the Brazil Company, the terminal ports had been Salvador, Rio de Janeiro, and Recife; this same trinity was to be favored in the eighteenth century with the organization of the Brazil fleets into three distinct convoys. The establishment of chartered trading companies by the

Marquis of Pombal* promoted trade to the Amazon region (Maranhão–Pará) and to northeast Brazil (Pernambuco–Paraíba) for some twenty years but, by the latter part of the eighteenth century, Salvador and Rio de Janeiro had firmly established their preeminence as the prime port cities of Portuguese America.

As ports, Salvador and Rio de Janeiro in particular, and others to a lesser degree commensurate with their relative importance and intensity of oceanic trade, were subjected to social tensions, administrative and financial pressures, and demands on public and private facilities unknown to townships in the interior. During those months when fleets were in port, such pressures and tensions could reach crisis proportions, paralyze local government, exhaust municipal coffers, stretch the royal treasury to the limits, and imbue port cities with a frenetic quality that was psychologically and socially disruptive. Although crews of vessels engaged in the *carreira do Brasil* were smaller than the Indiamen, in both cases the sheer volume of sailors coming ashore was disruptive. Sometimes the arrival of an Indiaman would coincide with the presence in port of the Brazil fleet. We may examine the impact of this influx under three heads: crime, bio-medical repercussions, and provisioning.

Despite Portuguese maritime achievements, mariners as a group were relegated to the lower strata of society and referred to by one commentator as *fex maris*. A royal edict of 1749 prohibited the use of swords and certain other weapons to mariners and "people of equal or inferior standing." When they came ashore in Brazilian ports, sailors fully lived up to this unsavory reputation. Rampant prostitution, widespread immorality, drunkenness, street fights, and an increased incidence of robberies characterized those months when a fleet was in port. Civil and ecclesiastical authorities expressed concern, with limited effect. The populace of Salvador so resented the outrageous behavior of sailors that there was a large-scale fight in 1557. Seamen deserted, and convicts – either forcibly pressed into service in Lisbon or *en route* to exile in Brazil or Angola – availed themselves of the first landfall to escape.

---

* The Marquis of Pombal (Sebastião José de Carvalho e Mello, 1699–1789) served as Prime Minister of Portugal from 1756 to 1777.

Another expression of crime was the widespread contraband in gold, diamonds, oriental cloths, and silks in Brazilian ports.

Even on the limited crossing from Lisbon or Oporto, illness attributable to malnutrition, exposure, accidents, and disease occurred. Rare was the Indiaman homeward-bound that did not put into Salvador or Rio de Janeiro with a substantial part of the ship's complement incapacitated, often to the point of having to be hospitalized in a Brazilian port.[9] Medical supplies, pharmaceutical items, medical assistance, and hospital accommodation were strained to the utmost. The quality of care varied. Fortunate was the captain or officer who found lodging in a private house, whereas sailors or grummets (apprentice seamen) were condemned to the hospital of Misericórdia. Appalling conditions in hospitals were evidenced by an observation at the end of the eighteenth century that mariners, despairing of being cured, discharged themselves voluntarily and resorted to begging before finding relief in death brought on by excessive drinking.[10] Furthermore, sick mariners transmitted diseases to the local people. Often those who did arrive healthy contracted malaria or yellow fever. In addition to diseases transmitted by sailors of the *carreira do Brasil* and the *carreira da India*, there were those transmitted by slaves brought from Africa. Transmittable diseases ascribed to African origin included leprosy, chicken pox, and yellow fever. Slaves were victims of "dropsy" or edema, yaws, scabies, intestinal parasites, dysenteries, and the dreaded *mal do bicho*. On more than one occasion inspecting medical teams complained of the fetid stench in the holds of slave ships. Transmission of disease was not attributable solely to blue-water vessels arriving in Brazilian ports. The transmission of yellow fever to Salvador in 1686 was commonly attributed to sailors from Pernambuco who had gone to a brothel in the lower city of Salvador, whence the disease had spread to the city and Recôncavo.[11]

Provisioning of vessels also placed a heavy onus on the local populace, especially in smaller ports. Meat, salt, and water were three basic commodities. But even for Salvador and Rio de Janeiro, which depended on neighboring rural communities for foodstuffs, supply networks were so precarious and the reserves so limited that viceroys or governors had to intervene personally to ensure that vessels received adequate supplies for their ongoing voyages. Pressures and priorities could shift between ports at different periods. With the advent of the Pombaline trading companies supplying slaves to Pernambuco and further north, vessels headed south and provisioned in Rio de Janeiro before returning to West Africa.[12] Such an onus was not limited to foodstuffs but included heavy demands for rope, sails, rigging, and supplies from ships' chandlers, as well as the skills of carpenters, caulkers, blacksmiths, and coopers. Sickness or death among ships' complements meant that replacements had to be found from among the local population of Brazilian port cities. Volunteers were few. Viceroys or governors-general resorted to scouring prisons; at other times, able-bodied men or vagrants were press-ganged into service. More serious, and more disruptive to port cities, was the "recruitment" of artisans whose land-based skills were transferable to a maritime environment, namely carpenters, caulkers, and coopers, as well as ferryboat personnel.

Local officials attempted to respond to these challenges unique to port cities. A "captain of the people of the sea" was appointed specifically to have jurisdiction over sailors of the Indiamen while in port, but it appears that his presence may have exacerbated rather than relieved tensions. Municipal and gubernatorial legislation was promulgated to limit severely the carrying of sidearms or concealed weapons by sailors. More stringent vigilance was exercised over deportees, convicts, and other undesirables *en route* to exile in the colonies or to man garrisons of empire. There was greater security for churches, which seem to have been favored targets for criminal impulses (not limited to seamen). Efforts made to curb contraband were onshore investigations, inventories of cargo and personal belongings, and onboard searches and inspections prior to disembarkation. Medical assistance fell victim to the division of responsibilities between the Crown, municipal authorities, the Santa Casa da Misericórdia, and charitable individuals. In Salvador, dissatisfaction with the Misericórdia hospital – which had been allocated the royal concession of tithes to offset heavy expenses incurred in treating mariners – led deepwater captains to propose the creation of a sailors' hospital. The viceroy approved this in principle in 1715 only for the motion to be defeated by self-interested opposition from brothers of the Misericórdia and councillors of the city council.

Although there may have been an increase in pharmacies in

the eighteenth century (the religious orders played a major role in the import of supplies for pharmacies housed in monasteries), pharmacies associated with the Misericórdias appear to have been the major source for supplies. As regards transmission of contagious diseases, as early as 1626 the Council of Salvador had initiated quarantine, and the vessels were quarantined at the *ponta do curral* and the Ilha dos Frades in the seventeenth and eighteenth centuries. The Crown, at the request of the city council of Salvador in 1694, approved the appointment of an officer of health whose duties included onboard medical inspections of all vessels arriving in Brazilian ports from Africa.[13] Although the Misericórdias were not above criticism, the truth of the matter was that royal and municipal authorities were totally dependent on branches of the charitable brotherhood for medical services in the colony. Prior to 1700, such medical assistance was available only (with the possible exception of São Paulo in 1599) in ports: Santos (1543), Salvador (1550?), Espírito Santo (later Vitória, pre-1551), Olinda and Ilhéus (pre-1560s), Rio de Janeiro (1560–70s?), Porto Seguro (pre-1600), Paraíba (1604), Itamaracá (1611), Belém (1619), São Luís (pre-1653). As for a more regular system of provisioning foodstuffs, officials were at the mercy of local producers, who raised prices arbitrarily or delayed supplies. In short, efforts by the authorities were of limited effect, and problems continued throughout the colonial period in all the major ports of Brazil. The amelioration that occurred was attributable less to official efforts on these many fronts than to the critical reduction of the average period when vessels were in Brazilian ports – from two or three months in the seventeenth and eighteenth centuries to some fifteen days in the nineteenth century.

The maritime presence was an essential part of the social fabric of ports, and two aspects of this presence merit further discussion. Against the depressing picture of a social milieu characterized by turbulence, tension, and lack of self-control, there was one positive feature. This was the creation of chapels, churches, and brotherhoods by men of the sea in port cities. As early as 1542 master mariners of the *carreira da India* had established the church of Chagas in Lisbon, and this example was to be emulated in ports of Brazil. Such brotherhoods celebrated masses and the festival of the patron saint and, within financial constraints, provided members with medical assistance, rations, clothing, and a Christian burial. The sailors' brotherhood of São Pedro Gonçalves in Rio de Janeiro sought royal permission in the early eighteenth century to possess a bier for the funerals of its members.[14] Such entities played an important, albeit low-profile, role in their communities. Sources suggest that membership in such brotherhoods was not limited to "men of the sea," although evidence of active maritime service may well have been a criterion for eligibility for election to the governing body. For the sailors these brotherhoods represented a spiritual and possibly an emotional investment in a shore community, as well as providing assistance. For civil authorities and landsmen, such brotherhoods were evidence of participation by mariners in the civil, social, and spiritual life of their communities and may have offset criticism of the more abhorrent behavior of some sailors on shore.

The second aspect concerned the social and economic vitality of the ports, especially their occupational structure. The diversity of shipping in Brazilian ports is amazing, ranging from canoes, large rowboats or galleys, and launches to brigantines, sloops, caravels, and carracks. Vessels not only had to be built, they had to be repaired, and dockyards of varying degrees of sophistication came into being to fulfill this dual function. The construction of ocean-going vessels in Brazil was usually through official initiative rather than being in private hands. Not only was the capital investment beyond the means of most individuals, but, by its very nature, shipping was of strategic as well as commercial importance. As such, it was an industry over which the Crown was well advised to exercise close control. In all ports there were small shipyards from the outset, but naval yards (*arsenais*) were fewer and were established later. The first shipyard was established in 1550, on royal order, by Tomé de Sousa in Salvador. Initially, smaller vessels such as *bergantins* (two-masted barks) and caravels had been built primarily for use in the Bay of All Saints and coastal shipping; in the seventeenth century, this activity was expanded to include galleons and carracks. In 1790 an Arsenal da Marinha was created in Salvador, modeled on that of Lisbon. It has been estimated that during the colonial period some 45 vessels were built on the Ribeira de Náus in Bahia: 8 carracks, 8 frigates, 1 corvette, 13 schooners, 12 artillery boats, and 3 messenger boats (*correios*).[15] In this activity Salvador was preeminent in a network of local yards. Bahia was not alone. A royal order of 2 January 1666 created a yard for building armed frigates in Rio de Janeiro. The second half of the eighteenth century witnessed an increase in productivity. The creation of the Arsenal de Marinha (1763) gave fresh impetus, but only one carrack (Náo São Sebastião) was built in Rio before the arrival of the court in 1808, when there was a further surge in construction.[16] On the northeast coast, São Luís was an excellent location for shipyards because of the high tides. The Companhia Geral do Grão Pará ordered the building in Belém of three long-distance vessels for trade to Europe. In Pará, the Casa das Canoas was replaced in 1761 by a shipyard (*estaleiro*) which was very productive at the end of the eighteenth century. The Crown encouraged the building of larger vessels by tax exemptions and privileges for individuals or by investing funds derived from the royal fifths and the *donativo real* (as occurred in 1738). In 1651 the crown ordered the annual building in a Brazilian port of a galleon of 700–800 tons – an expression of intent – although it is unlikely this was fully implemented. A royal order of 1757 ordered that preference in the transportation of merchandise be given to vessels built in Brazil.[17]

Salvador and Belém had certain natural advantages over Rio de Janeiro and Pernambuco. They were ideally located as regards raw materials, especially with ready access to a variety of woods. In the case of Salvador, wood was brought preferably from Alagoas and Cairú or regions beyond the immediate sugar-plantation zone because of friction with sugar-plantation and mill owners who also had heavy demands for wood for their mills. This was but one major resource. Cotton produced a sail that was both durable and light. The bark of annonaceous trees and fibers from the embira and the piassava palm were ideal for cordage and caulking. Resin from the camaçari plant was excellent for tarring. During his viceroyalty, the Marquis of Lavradio encouraged the Dutchman João Hopman in Rio de Janeiro to manufacture guaxima commercially for cordage, shrouds, and stays.[18]

The industry of building, repairing, and careening vessels had four features that gave a special character to the workforce in Salvador. First, the industry was a stimulant for ancillary activities and industries. These included transportation, gathering natural fibers for cordage, selecting and cutting timber, weaving cotton for sails, making cordage, and a wide range of artisan trades. In the case of Salvador, there was a connection between the whaling station on the island of Itaparica and the dockyard because some of the products of the whaling factory were used in the preparation of pitch. In the mid-eighteenth century the factory had a workforce of 421 (272 slaves, 71 free blacks, 56 mulattos, 20 whites, and 2 Indians).[19] Second, a dockyard was labor-intensive. Third, it required a labor force that ranged across the spectrum from skilled to unskilled. In Salvador there was a hierarchy of skills: the masters in charge of less skilled artisans, namely the master of the yard (*patrão mor*), the master cooper, master stonemason, master caulker, master flagmaker, master tinsmith, master saddler, master pulleymaker, master ironsmith, master sailmaker, and master of carts. These managed a workforce that included white artisans, freedmen, and slaves who had acquired specialist skills. There may have been as many as 600 slaves sawing wood or carpentering. In Salvador, white women were employed as seamstresses. In Belém, Indians worked in the dockyard and proved adept at some specialist tasks such as making cordage from vegetable fibers – a cultural legacy they passed on to the Portuguese. Fourth, the workforce comprised artisans from a wide range of occupations. These included: loggers, ox-cart drivers, boatsmen, carpenters and joiners, makers of pitch, weavers of cotton, sailmakers, seamstresses, stonemasons and makers of lime (for the slipway), caulkers, coopers, painters, ropemakers, tinsmiths, saddlers, flagmakers, and cabinet makers. One group that may not have been as well represented was smiths because, wherever possible, iron items were salvaged from other vessels or were sent from Portugal (and were often of foreign origin).

It is difficult to assess the skills and quality of the labor force. The building or rebuilding of the three-decked Indiaman Nossa Senhora da Caridade, São Francisco de Paula e Santo António took two years (1755–7) and cost 105,746$525 *réis*. John Byron, the English admiral who put into Rio de Janeiro in 1764, hired Portuguese caulkers "at which work they were employed for some time." In view of the low rates paid in the dockyards, it may well have been that they could not attract better-qualified artisans who could find more gainful employment on a plantation or in the city. Where specialist skills were required, artisans were imported from Portugal and designs for vessels were made in the mother country and sent to Brazil accompanied by orders to alter the original as little as possible.[20]

PORTS, HINTERLANDS, AND THE WIDER WORLD

Port cities did not exist in a vacuum but in relationship to their immediate geographical hinterlands, Brazil, and the wider world. Before considering particularities, it might be well to dwell on what comprises a hinterland.

The designation "hinterland" carries certain connotations: that it is a single area with territorial integrity; that there is a static quality to the boundaries of such a territory; that there is no gradation between hinterlands; that there is a continual territorial nexus between a city and its hinterland. In my view, "hinterland" can transcend the narrowly geographical to connote several evolving connections – personal, familial, psychological, social, cultural, administrative, and commercial, among others. Finally, the notion of what comprises a hinterland is highly subjective and may depend on the status and perceptions of an individual or a group.

The Brazilian case introduces perspectives that may contribute to the discussion. So close were human, political, commercial, and cultural ties between Salvador and Dahomey and the Bight of Benin – certainly as close as those between Salvador and Jacobina, let alone Fortaleza – that West Africa might be regarded as part of the hinterland of Salvador.[21] To turn to the more conventional notion of a territorial nexus between a port and its hinterland, for Brazil this hinterland was frequently less characterized by territorial integrity than by an archipelagic quality. Spheres of influence, each with one or more nuclei, might exist in virtual isolation from each other or might intersect in a random irregular manner. Such configurations were highly fluid and susceptible to change. The critical component in such reorientations was the commercial profitability and strength of the market. In the 1740s Mato Grosso afforded such an opportunity, and fluvial links were established to São Paulo (via the Tietê, Pardo, Coxím, Taquarí, Paraguay) and

Grão Pará (via the Amazon–Madeira–Guaporé and the Araguaia–Tocantins).

The geographical entity that might be taken to comprise the hinterland of Rio de Janeiro in 1650 had altered radically by 1750. Illustrative of such a change was Goiás, which comprised the hinterland of Rio de Janeiro or Santos, but which, with the opening of the road from Belém to Cuiabá in 1742, also became the hinterland for Belém. Conversely, royal concern with contraband led to the closing of some roads from Bahia and Pernambuco to the mining areas, thereby attenuating ties between northeast ports and Minas Gerais and underlining the already apparent move for Minas Gerais to be considered instead as a part of the hinterland of Rio de Janeiro. A single territorial entity could come to comprise the hinterland of more than one port city.[22]

Certainly, whereas the councillors of Recife or Salvador might look on the Várzea or the Recôncavo as being the hinterland of their respective ports, it was less likely that – despite common ties to the *sertão* of the São Francisco River – the latter region would have been looked on in the same way. In fact there were primary, secondary, and even tertiary hinterlands. The attribution or allocation of one or the other region to one of the above theoretical divisions depended as much on perception as on the relative intensity of commercial, political, or social links, or even on purely geographical proximity. In some cases there was a one-way dependence of the hinterland on the port; in other instances there was reciprocal interdependence, as in the case of Paranaguá–Curitiba or Santos–São Paulo. For Brazil the concept of a primary hinterland was applicable to Salvador, Rio de Janeiro, and Recife within the first century of colonization because of the role of these ports as centers for the export of agricultural commodities and hides to Europe and because of their dominant role in the coastal trade.

And yet even here there were differences in the nature of the hinterlands. The Recôncavo of Bahia was more densely populated and had more plantations despite soil and rainfall conditions similar to the Várzea of Pernambuco. Population density and size, topography, soil, and rainfall differentiated both the Várzea and the Recôncavo from the hinterland of Rio de Janeiro with its backdrop of the Great Escarpment. Secondary and tertiary hinterlands were to take on importance only in the seventeenth and eighteenth centuries, in part because of the development of a more diversified economy but primarily because of mineral discoveries. For the most part, linkages between ports and the interior were least apparent and least effective in the administrative sector and were most in evidence in commercial exchanges and movement of people.

The development of the hinterlands of Salvador and Rio de Janeiro demonstrated how historical developments altered relationships between port cities and their hinterlands. Salvador was the major port for the northeast whereas Rio de Janeiro was unchallenged as the major port of southeastern Brazil. There were major differences between the two hinterlands. Agriculture determined settlement patterns and commercial development in the Bahian hinterland, whereas for Rio the driving force was mining. Both hinterlands came to develop diversified economies, but in the northeast sugar and tobacco predominated. The most compelling differences were the sudden territorial expansion, the increase in administrative importance, the demographic growth, and the forward economic leap of the hinterland of Rio de Janeiro – all within less than thirty years. The move to the west gathered momentum in the first half of the eighteenth century and had its most dramatic effect on the central southern region, namely the hinterland of Rio de Janeiro.

From the 1690s on, there was an ever-increasing flow of people to the mining areas and, subsequently, an ebb and flow of hopefuls between the mining zones. New captaincies were created in Minas Gerais, São Paulo, Mato Grosso, and Goiás. Townships came into being, in turn forming their own immediate hinterlands. Royal government – governors, personnel, civil servants, and treasury officials – made its presence felt in the newly developing areas far more than had been, or was to be, the case in the *sertão* of the northeast. The ports of Salvador, Recife, São Luís, and Belém were all to be affected in varying degrees by this relocation of the commercial epicenter of Brazil. The mining regions became points of articulation between the north, northeast, southeast, and south of Brazil. But it was Rio de Janeiro that was most affected by these developments and was under pressure as the prime port of imports and exports for the mining areas as the eighteenth century progressed.

The major port cities of Brazil were components – and more active participants than their Caribbean and Atlantic counterparts in the Spanish empire – in the broader framework of a Portuguese seaborne empire reaching from the Maghreb to the Moluccas. Such a framework included maritime ties not merely to Portugal (usually Lisbon and Oporto but, to a lesser degree, Faro and Setúbal) and to West Africa, but also to East Africa, Cochin and Goa, Macao, and Nagasaki. There was a constant ebb and flow of commodities and people throughout this system of empire. If Bahia was famed for its tobacco in the palaces of West African kings and at the court of the Manchu emperor in Peking, so too did oriental pepper, nutmeg, clove, cinnamon, ginger, spices, trees, silks, and porcelain find ready acceptance in Brazil. Blacks from Angola served on vessels in the South China Sea, and Javanese on homeward-bound Indiamen. Jesuits moved freely between the different provinces of the Society of Jesus, as did other missionaries. Soldiers saw service in garrisons in Brazil, Africa, India, Malacca, and beyond. Several viceroys of Brazil (most notably Vasco Fernandes César de Meneses, count of Sabugosa) had held high office in India, as had other senior administrators. In domestic, church, and military architecture there were characteristics common to all points of empire. Even words of oriental provenance found their way to Brazil, along with customs such as the use of the *palanquin* or sedan chair. Ports of Brazil were also the foci for contraband trade with the Caribbean, North America, Northern Europe, and West Africa. The majority of goods exported from Portugal to other European nations were of Brazilian origin and, in turn, Brazil received commodities made in England, Hamburg, and France. In short, East met West in the ports of colonial Brazil, imbuing these ports with a uniquely international quality that even Lisbon did not possess.[23]

Port cities and towns – by virtue of their location on the Atlantic coast and because of topographical features and diplomatic agreements precluding access from the north or the west – were the sole gateways to Portuguese America. To be sure, access from Upper Peru and overland from the Río de la Plata did occur, but only rarely and usually by individuals. The same circumstances dictated that ports were the major points of egress from the colony. Customs houses were established in ports for this precise reason. In short, ports played an essential function as points to which commodities and persons would be drawn, if they were to have access to Brazil, and the same principle held true for commodities and persons leaving Portuguese America. Salvador and Recife fulfilled this function for the northeast, as did Rio de Janeiro for the central and southern regions.

The ports of Brazil do not appear to have exerted, in their own right, a strong centripetal force. Immigrants aspiring to pass to the interior and commodities landing on the wharves had destinations other than the ports themselves. This traffic, be it of commodities, of free men and women, or of slaves, reached its greatest intensity in the eighteenth century, when the lure of easy wealth and burgeoning markets in the mining zones came to exert an undeniable centripetal force, syphoning human and other resources from the littoral, from West Africa, and from other parts of the Portuguese world – including the metropolis. The reverse lay in the exodus of gold and persons from the mining areas with final destinations beyond Brazilian ports.

SALVADOR AND RIO DE JANEIRO

Salvador and Rio de Janeiro are unique in that both were (and are) major ports and both were capitals of Brazil, raising the question of whether their importance as ports can be separated from their role as capitals. In the Brazilian case, the two become intertwined.

Salvador was the first seat of crown government in Brazil and the place of residence of governors-general and viceroys. The first bishopric of Brazil was established there in 1551, and in 1676 this was raised to the rank of metropolitanate, the sole metropolitanate of colonial Brazil. The highest court of appeals (Relação) of Portuguese America was established in 1609, suppressed during the Dutch invasion, and restored in 1652. This remained the only high court of appeals in the colony for over a century, until the establishment of a parallel court in Rio de Janeiro in 1751. The treasurer-general of Brazil resided and worked in Salvador. The first permanent mint was established in 1694. It was not all work and no play. The count of Sabugosa (viceroy, 1720–35) stimulated the arts, encouraged a comedy theater, and saw the creation of a literary academy known as the Academy of the Forgotten. The Jesuit College put on sacred operas and tragicomedies on saints' and holy days.

By contrast, the city of Rio de Janeiro was only established by the Portuguese in 1565, and the governor was subordinate to the governor-general or viceroy in Salvador. Initially the governor exercised jurisdiction over an enormous area, but this was to be whittled down with the establishment of the new captaincies of São Paulo e Minas de Ouro (1709) and further subdivision into Minas Gerais (1720) and São Paulo (1720). A bishopric was only established in 1676. In the eighteenth century its area of jurisdiction was to be trimmed by the establishment of bishoprics in Mariana and São Paulo. A Relação was established in 1751, largely in response to appeals from the burgeoning population of Minas Gerais, whose access to justice was thwarted by the tyranny of distance in reaching Salvador. Rio de Janeiro counted a mint and a network of strong defensive forts and redoubts. In the first half of the eighteenth century, Rio assumed increasing importance for economic reasons: decline in sugar prices, which struck the northeast hard, and burgeoning mineral strikes in the central southern region.

Changing political, diplomatic, and military considerations gave Rio considerable strategic importance because of its proximity to the gold and diamond mines of Minas Gerais. The long and successful governorship of Gomes Freire de Andrade (1733–63) enhanced not only his personal reputation but that of Rio de Janeiro. After 1748, subordinate to him were the captaincies of Rio de Janeiro, Minas Gerais, São Paulo, Goiás, Mato Grosso, Santa Catarina, Rio Grande do Sul, and Colônia do Sacramento on the Rio de la Plata. In short, Freire de Andrade exercised jurisdiction over a greater area of Brazil than did the viceroy in Salvador. This swing in importance from the northeast to the southeastern and central southern region of Brazil was finally consecrated with the official transfer of the capital in 1763.

The builders of Salvador and Rio de Janeiro lacked the advice and guidelines that, for their counterparts in Spanish America, were to be codified in the *Ordenanzas de Descubrimiento e Pobla-*

ción. But they adopted many of the same criteria: namely, safe anchorage, elevated location, healthy environment, defensible position, and access to land for agriculture and for building materials. Nor did the Portuguese place as much priority on regulating the positions of major buildings, on locating squares, and on the layout of streets – although they were not as insensitive to the geometrical tendencies of sixteenth-century Europe as is sometimes maintained. The site chosen by Tomé de Sousa had been on the southeastern shore just within the Bay of All Saints. Uneven ground a kilometer long and 350 meters wide at its widest point, at the top of steep cliffs some 60 meters high, presented a suitable location. At the foot of the escarpment was a narrow strip of beach. This in itself divided the city naturally into two parts. By the end of the sixteenth century the wattle-and-daub buildings of the primitive settlement had given way to fine stone buildings. Salvador had a walled upper city and counted a governor-general's palace; a Jesuit college (1549); Carmelite (1580), Benedictine (1581), and Franciscan (1594) monasteries; a cathedral; a bishop's palace, many churches, a Santa Casa de Misericórdia, and the city residences of sugar planters and the more prominent civil servants. The lower city was the commercial zone, with cellars, warehouses, loading-wharves, and a customs house.

On his visit in 1610 Pyrard de Laval noted that "for more than a quarter of a league, are well-built houses on both hands, forming a long and handsome street, well crowded with all manner of merchants, craftsmen and artisans." Movement between the port area and the upper city was by four steep *ladeiras*, difficult at the best of times and especially hazardous in wet weather. All heavy merchandise had to be hauled up by a windlass operated on a counterpoise system. This picture of the city in the early seventeenth century underwent only minor alterations during the colonial period. There was greater settlement in the upper city around the Desterro and the monasteries of the Carmelites and Benedictines. Convents of Santa Clara do Desterro (1677), Nossa Senhora da Lapa (1744), and of the Mercês (1745) were built. By the 1750s the city counted three hundred churches or chapels. One outcome of this expansion was that, whatever plan there might have been originally for formal layout got lost in the multiplication of narrow streets and twisting alleys. As for the lower city, there was great commercial expansion. In 1623 this lower city became a parish. Finally, while still treacherous, communications between the upper and lower cities were improved. A defensive network of fortresses, forts, and redoubts had been established from the fortress of Santo António de Barra to the fort at Itapagipe and across to the fortress of São Lourenço on Itaparica.[24]

If it is difficult to reach any secure figures for the overall population, a breakdown by race is virtually impossible before the eighteenth century. The Jesuit Fernão Cardim referred in 1584 to 3,000 Portuguese, 8,000 Indians converted to Christianity, and between 3,000 and 4,000 slaves of Guiné. In the major Brazilian port cities, persons of African descent were in the majority. In Salvador in 1714 the French engineer Frézier estimated that, for every score of people on the streets, 19 were slaves. In 1759, Caldas estimated that every second person in Salvador was a slave. Manuel da Cunha Menezes's census for Salvador in 1775 carried the observation that "the majority are black and *pardo* slaves, however the majority of the hearths (*fogos*) are of whites."[25] The "Mappa Geral" of 20 June 1775 which listed 7,345 hearths and 33,635 souls, included racial data: Whites, 10,720 (plus 277 clergy); free *pardos*, 4,213; free *prêtos*, 3,730; and slaves, 14,695. Whites were outnumbered 2 to 1 by persons of African descent and comprised 32.7 per cent of the population. A further breakdown reveals that 43.7 per cent of the population were slaves and that 23.6 per cent were freedmen (*pardos*, 12.52 per cent; *prêtos*, 11.08 per cent). Although there were substantial numbers of free persons of African descent in the city, this document does not provide any data on the incidence of manumission.[26]

The 1775 "Mappa Geral" also provides a breakdown by civil status, as shown in table 1, but with apparent anomalies in the figures presented. Given the multiracial nature of Bahian society, it is nothing short of extraordinary that 100 per cent of marriages by white males should have been with white females and that this was also the case of freedmen of African descent. Travelers and Portuguese officials commented on the proclivity – and even preference – shown by Portuguese males for *mamelucas* (females of mixed European and Indian origin) and mulatto women, which makes the data all the more unusual. The document goes on to note that the number of males totals 8,403 and of females 10,537. Once ecclesiastics, married men, and widowers were eliminated (the latter 2 categories on the grounds that they were "paes de familia"), 3,140 white bachelors were left for military service.

Table 1 Civil status of Whites and free Blacks in Salvador, 1775

Marital status	Whites		Free Blacks (forros)	
	Male	Female	Male	Female
Married	1,697	1,697	440	440
Widowed	184	237	37	156
Single	3,140	1,803	963	1,694
TOTALS	5,021	3,737	1,440	2,290

Source: "Mappa Geral no qual se vêem todas as moradas de cases que ha na Cidade do Bahia . . . ," Bahia, 20 June 1775. *Apud* Edmondo de Castro e Almeida, *Inventário dos documentos relativos ao Brasil existentes no Archivo de Marinha e Ultramar de Lisboa* (Rio de Janeiro, 1914) 2: no. 8813.

Deficiencies in the data notwithstanding, let us turn to the composition of the society of colonial Salvador and attempt a preliminary sectoral analysis. Brazilian port cities and towns shared characteristics with the metropolis and other colonies – namely social, racial, and economic stratification, together with a keen sense of hierarchy. Although the medieval European notion of "estates" was blurred in the colonies, it was not entirely absent. The urban elite of Salvador was usually of Portuguese descent and comprised owners of plantations, sugar mills, and cattle ranches who also owned city residences and – increasingly in the eighteenth century – spent more time in the port cities than in the countryside. They exercised financial power and enjoyed political authority. For such persons, ports were essential for overseas exports of major commodities (sugar, tobacco, hides) and as local markets for their crops. In exchange, they contributed to local commerce by purchasing manufactured imports, to the protobanking system by taking loans from monastic and conventual institutions and brotherhoods, and to the life of the community by making social and financial investments in brotherhoods and civil life. Members of this elite formed part of a kinship and commercial network in the city and Recôncavo. They had access to the highest dignitaries of Church and state in the colony and even to the king and his ministers at court. In Salvador, planters dominated the Senado da Câmara in the seventeenth century and shared political authority with a merchant class in the eighteenth century, when there appears to have been an alliance between landed capital holdings and commercial wealth.[27]

Intense rivalry between merchants and planters, such as occurred in Pernambuco and gave rise to the War of the Peddlers (1711), was not present in Salvador. That an enterprising individual could bridge both worlds was demonstrated by Francisco Fernandes do Sim (1593–1664). He was a merchant in Salvador engaging in the wine and sugar trades who married the daughter of a sugar-mill owner and died a wealthy man (owner of three plantations, one mill, and ten city houses) and a philanthropist.[28]

There was a hierarchy within the merchant community. At the upper end was a basic distinction made by José Caldas in his 1759 survey of the merchant community of Salvador. This was between (to use his words) those "que frequentão o comércio" and "homens de negócio." The former were merchants or *comerciantes* and ranged from those engaged in long-distance trading by land or sea in the import–export business to those dealing more locally and more modestly. "Businessmen" served essentially as bankers (in the absence of banks in the colony), advancing credit, making loans, and underwriting insurance costs. One such in Salvador was João de Mattos de Aguiar (d. 1700), of whom it was said by a contemporary: "All his wealth (with the exception of two houses and a few cattle corrals) was placed on loan and so great were the returns that not even he himself knew the exact amount of his fortune."[29] At the upper end of the financial scale, the distinction became blurred by merchants who were sufficiently wealthy to assume the role of merchant bankers. Also associated with the business community were commission agents (*comissários*), who took goods on consignment.

One basic question was whether the merchant community of Salvador served merely as agents for metropolitan interests and merchant houses, or came to form a recognizably colonial collective mentality. While there was certainly dependence on Portugal for financing and commercial connections, and many were partners or agents of Portuguese merchants, my feeling is that, by the mid-eighteenth century, one can talk confidently about the Brazilianization of commerce.

Financing was being obtained in the colony and commercial houses were established in the ports by persons either of long-standing residency in the colony or with strong kinship ties to relatives (usually brothers) in Portugal or even West Africa. These were not major shareholding operations but enterprises with a strong family component. At the end of the colonial period, Rio de Janeiro could count more *casas de negócios* (126) than Salvador (75). Corporate bodies did not come into full force until the establishment of chambers of commerce in the early nineteenth century. But a palliative to the merchant communities had been the establishment in 1751 by the Crown in the ports of Rio de Janeiro, Salvador, Recife, and São Luís of Mesas de Inspeção. Multifunctional, such boards of inspection heard commercial litigation and vetted commercial petitions before forwarding them to Lisbon.[30]

At a more modest level were shopkeepers (*mercadores de loja*), tavern keepers, and even street vendors. Such were essentially dealing in the retail trade, and in 1705 Dom Pedro II defined "merchant" as being "applicable only to persons in an open shop who are actually engaged in measuring, weighing, and selling any kind of merchandise to the people." Artisans fell into this social group, and every port could count a Street of the Coopers, Street of the Shoemakers, or Street of the Tinsmiths. This corporate solidarity was also manifested in the brotherhoods in Salvador, Rio de Janeiro, and Recife, whose membership was exclusively artisans. Such brotherhoods brought together artisans in related areas: for example, São José in Rio de Janeiro and Salvador for the building trades (predominantly stonemasons, carpenters), and workers in wood (cabinet makers, coopers). The brotherhood of São Jorge in Rio included locksmiths, blacksmiths, cutlers, gunsmiths, tinsmiths, gilders, and swordmakers.

William Dampier, a visitor to Salvador in 1699, noted the prosperity of artisans, especially those who could afford a slave. Perhaps unwittingly, Dampier was emphasizing the substantial stratification among artisans. A master mason or master carpenter with his own yard, or atelier, was in a very different position from a regular mason or carpenter who did not have a shop, or those persons (often of African descent)

who had the requisite skills but remained essentially journey-
men. There was a stratification within the trades: an ironsmith
was of higher status than a barber–surgeon.

Trades were not limited to white males but were practiced
by persons of African descent. "Barbers" (*barbeiros*) were virtually all of African descent (both slave and free). Spix and
Martius in Pernambuco and Henry Koster in Rio de Janeiro all
agreed that mulattos showed the greatest aptitude for the
trades. Although not formed into corporations, others also
plied their skills. Especially apparent in Recife, Salvador, and
Rio de Janeiro were ferrymen and boatmen, many of African
descent, both slave and free – who provided essential transportation of people and specie between city centers and suburbs
and between the suburbs.[31] Participation in such trades was
not limited to males or to persons of African or European
descent. White and Indian women wove cotton and sewed
sails in the dockyards of port cities. Finally, there was the
active participation in the retail trade of women of African
descent who acted as intermediaries (*ganhadeiras*) in the purchase and resale of meat and fish and who dominated the
domestic market scene in Salvador, much to the disgust of
Santos Vilhena.[32]

Salvador had a large administrative presence, both civil and
ecclesiastical. The civil bureaucracy included the viceroy, the
secretary of state, justices of the high court, and the treasurer-
general. Lower-ranking functionaries were the innumerable
secretaries, scribes, bailiffs, porters, assistants, and guards who
made up the civil bureaucracy of empire. The ecclesiastical
bureaucracy included the archbishop, vicars-general, deans,
canons and chaplains, and menials such as sacristans, choirboys, bellringers, and porters. The third branch of government
was the military, with regiments of artillerymen and infantry.
Two other prominent sectors were the regular and secular
clergy and members of liberal professions (lawyers, doctors,
surgeons). At the lowest end of society were slaves, the poor,
and the destitute.

The ecclesiastical bureaucracy of Salvador in 1756 may be
defined as those whose salaries were paid by the Crown.
Under the leadership of the archbishop, the senior dignitaries
included the vicar-general, 3 judges of the ecclesiastical court,
a dean, 9 canons, and lower-ranking churchmen. The above,

numbering 39, were directly associated with the cathedral. In addition, there were 9 parish priests and their 18 assistants. The clergy totaled 66. Assisting these men of the cloth were laymen. Sixteen were associated with the cathedral directly and included a master of ceremonies, a sacristan, 6 choirboys, a bell ringer, 2 organists, and a porter. The ecclesiastical court required a staff of 7. In each of 9 parishes there was a lay sacristan. In all, the lay staff paid from the royal treasury numbered 32.

Those on the royal payroll were not the only persons in holy orders in Salvador. Among their college, novice house, and 2 seminaries, the Jesuits numbered 201. In addition, there were 80 still in training. Members of the other orders included 96 Carmelites, 70 Benedictines, 45 Franciscans, 28 Italian Capuchins, 24 of St Theresa, and 6 Augustinians for a total of 269. In addition there were the nuns of Santa Clara do Destero (65) and of Nossa Senhor a da Lapa (20), and the Ursulines (50), numbering 135 in all. Members, male and female, of the regular orders, and of the Society of Jesus in the city, totaled 605.

Table 2 Civil servants and support staff, Salvador, 1759

Government office	Employees
High court	19
Chancellery	3
Customs	24
Treasury	26
Royal arsenal	22
Board of Inspection	19
Criminal/civil courts (*ouvidorias*)	12
Juizo de fora	5
Juizo de ausentes	5
Juizo do orfãos	12
Juizo dos cativos	4
Mint	25
Provedoria de comarca	6
Secretariat of State	7
Viceroy and guards	7
Senado da Cámara	6
TOTAL	202

Source: José Antonio Caldas, *Notícia geral de toda esta Capitania da Bahia desde o seu descobrimento até o presente ano de 1759* (Salvador: Tip. Beneditina, 1951) 73–88, 205–15.

In the captaincy of Bahia 2,000 persons were estimated to be in holy orders.[33]

The administrative aspect of government ranged from the viceroy down to the lowliest porter or bailiff. Table 2 shows the distribution of civil servants and support staff. Of these, 58 were described as scribes, 14 as bailiffs, and 14 as porters.[34]

The military contingent broke down into two regiments of infantry numbering 1,200 soldiers and one artillery batallion of 300, making a total of 1,500 paid soldiers. The auxiliaries (non-paid) numbered 5,312 and included 397 of the Henriques, composed of Blacks.[35]

The mobility of the commercial community would make any sectoral analysis difficult. However, a listing of 197 persons engaged in trade can be divided into five categories, listed in table 3.

Table 3 The commercial and business sector, Salvador, 1759: a contemporary classification

"People who engage in commerce and who are considered to have enough wealth to be able to continue"	14
"People who engage in commerce and who manage their business with adequate reserves and high potential and who have wealth"	21
"Persons who have established business houses"	19
"Those businessmen who are considered well versed in mercantile precepts and with the capacity to engage in commerce"	22
"Businessmen, merchants, traders, who live from some form of business"	121
TOTAL	197

Source: José Antonio Caldas, *Notícia geral de toda esta Capitania da Bahia*, 525–33.

There are additional data on the business activities of persons falling into the last and most general category, "businessmen, merchants, traders, who live from some form of commerce." Information on the geographical patterns of trade and on the predominant business activities still exists. The regions shown in table 4 are those to which these merchants of Salvador traded. No less interesting are the descriptions of the predominant business activities, which may or may not overlap with commerce shown in table 5.

Table 4   Trading activities, by region, of Bahian merchants, 1759

Region	Number of merchants
Portugal	43
Portugal and Mina only	10
Costa da Mina only	8
Portugal and Minas Gerais	4
Angola only	4
Angola and Mina	2
Portugal, Mina, and Minas Gerais	1
Portugal and Angola	1
Portugal, Mina, Angola	1
Colônia do Sacramento	1
Unspecified, "various regions"	7

Source: José Antonio Caldas, Notícia geral de toda esta Capitania de Bahia, 525–33.

In considering this mercantile community, it is well to bear in mind that this refers only to the mercantile elite of Salvador. Evidently, at least by general perception, the truly wealthy were few; and even those who merited entry as successful businessmen formed a very small part of the population of Salvador.[36]

There is little information on the other sectors of the commercial community of Salvador, which would have included shopkeepers, tavern owners, street vendors, and artisans. Taking a document signed by 76 vendeiros in 1718 as a base, Rae Flory has suggested that the number of vendors with their own places of business may have numbered some 200.[37] This would have been on the low side by midcentury and would not take into account the very active street training and sales of foods by regateiras and go-betweens, often women of African descent. Nor does it include the artisans of Salvador, the oficiaes mecânicos, who were so prominent in the life of the port. While neither notarial records, the registers of licenses recorded with the Senado da Câmara, nor brotherhood memberships can provide even a rough estimate of the numbers of artisans in Salvador, information from a variety of sources can throw light on the more prominent trades and the relative standing numerically of the trades vis-à-vis each other.

Table 5 Identification of commercial sector by activity, Salvador, 1759

Commission agents	24
Advancing money	9
Shop only	8
Commission and with own *fazenda*	6
Commission and with a shop	5
Merchant (*mercador*)	4
Administration of contracts	3
Collecting debts	1

Source: José Antonio Caldas, *Notícia geral de toda esta Capitania de Bahia,* 525–33.

CONCLUSION

In this paper I have tried to answer one basic question: what made ports unique? It is evident that their importance could fluctuate, perhaps because of European rather than American factors. Political events in Europe led to the Dutch invasion of the northeast, to the French capture of Rio de Janeiro, and to the events in southern Brazil in the "debatable lands." The Napoleonic invasion of the Iberian Peninsula heralded the arrival of the royal court in Rio de Janeiro (in 1808) and the opening of the ports, and moreover contributed to the Balkanization of the northeast. Policy changes in Portugal contributed to the ebb and flow in the fortunes of individual ports. The Pombaline initiatives in establishing trading companies to the northeast coast of Brazil enhanced the importance of São Luís and Belém. Economic developments within the colony had an impact on the ports. The discovery of gold and diamonds was the single most critical factor, but the cultivation of cotton in the late eighteenth century was to enhance the reputation of the Maranhão and the northern part of Brazil. To some degree the fortunes of the colony (and of the mother country) were subject to the whim of demand cycles in Europe and to competition from other areas of major commodities (for example, sugar from the West Indies).

Events within the colony also contributed to the ebb and flow in the importance of respective ports. And yet the picture may not have been as gloomy as the immediate participants imagined. Certainly the gold strikes did disrupt the supply of labor, commerce, and society of the northeast, but – fulminations of city councillors in Salvador notwithstanding – the impact was short-term, and Salvador was eventually able to recover its commercial preeminence. In the long term the experience was energizing: introducing new players into the commercial arena, forcing a rethinking of commercial practices, and opening up windows of commercial opportunity.

There was also the cruel irony that, because of their locations, ports were not only the first to receive new ideas but also the most vulnerable to foreign influences, foreign commercial overtures, and the winds of change in Europe and in North America regarding relations between a metropolis and its colonies. In the Brazilian case, it was precisely in the eighteenth century that the true riches of Brazil were finally revealed – in the reigns of Dom João V (1706–50) and Dom José I (1750–77) – leading the Crown to develop even greater feelings of paranoia and fear of foreign invasion. Pombal strove (fruitlessly, as it turned out) to nationalize the Luso-Brazilian economy. Within the colony were conflicts and conspiracies, and the impact of the Enlightenment was making itself felt. Was it not likely that books and ideas from Europe and the United States would receive greater diffusion in the ports? Or perhaps ports, in and of themselves, generate a more independent way of life and freedom of thought – or at least openness to new ideas.

The study of ports in colonial Brazil contributes to our understanding of the culture, economies, and societies of individual ports and may raise more questions than can be answered. To what extent were ports agents for change, catalysts for economic, social, and political aspirations? Did their status as ports have an impact on their administration and society, making these more conservative or more open to innovation? Above all, did the phenomenon of being ports differentiate them from other towns and cities? In the case of Brazil, the major ports were multifunctional as centers of commercial exchange and of administration (both civil and ecclesiastical) as well as garrison posts for defense, and represented the major demographic nuclei of the colony. A study of these ports, of their relationships to their hinterlands and to the wider world, provides the starting-point for an analytical framework that may be applied to comparative history. Salvador and Rio de Janeiro, because of their status as capitals as well as ports, invite broader comparisons both to ports of the Atlantic basin and to capital cities elsewhere. To what extent were these ports constrained by forming part of a network of imperial control? Were they on occasion able to act independently of imperial dictates? This raises the broader question of relations between Portuguese America and the metropolis and invites comparisons to the great seaborne empires of Spain, England, and the United Provinces. What were the priorities of the metropolitan powers? How did these priorities change, and did these priorities coincide with or conflict with colonial priorities and aspirations? Did colonial interests truly represent a sum of the parts, or were regional and sectoral interests so strong as to preclude a colonial position? This may stimulate discussion of what constituted and distinguished power and authority, and who exercised power or authority. Traditional points of comparison, for example between Portuguese and Spanish America, may need to be rethought. Our study of ports of Portuguese America underlines their individuality as active participants in a broader network of economic, social, and cultural relations that were transoceanic, extending to Europe, Africa, and Asia, as well as to North and South America.

NOTES

1 An agenda for urban research has been provided in numerous articles by Richard M. Morse, "Recent Research on Latin American Urbanization: A Select Survey with Commentary," *Latin American Research Review* (hereafter *LARR*) 1, no. 1 (Fall 1965):35–74; "Trends and Patterns of Latin American Urbanization, 1750–1930," *Comparative Studies in Society and History* 16, no. 4 (September 1974):416–47; "Some Characteristics of Latin American Urban History," *American Historical Review* 67, no. 2 (January 1962):317–38; "Recent Research: Trends and Issues in Latin American Urban Research, 1965–1970," *LARR* 6, no. 1 (1971):3–52, and 6, no. 2 (1971):19–75; "A Prolegomenon to Latin American Urban History," *Hispanic American Historical Review* (hereafter *HAHR*) 52, no. 3

(August 1972):359–94. For colonial urban history, see Susan M. Socolow and Lyman L. Johnson, "Urbanization in Colonial Latin America," *Journal of Urban History* 8, no. 1 (November 1981):27–59; Woodrow Borah, "Trends in Recent Studies of Colonial Latin American Cities," *HAHR* 64, no. 3 (August 1984):535–54; Richard M. Morse, "The Urban Development of Colonial Spanish America," *The Cambridge History of Latin America* (Cambridge: Cambridge University Press, 1984), 2:67–104 and 814–24. For colonial Brazil, see Morse, "Brazil's Urban Development: Colony and Empire," in *From Colony to Nation: Essays on the Independence of Brazil*, ed. A. J. R. Russell-Wood (Baltimore, Md: Johns Hopkins University Press, 1975), 155–81; Stuart B. Schwartz, "Cities of Empire: Mexico and Bahia in the Sixteenth Century," *Journal of Inter-American Studies and World Affairs* 2 (1969):616–37; and the studies of Roberta Marx Delson, "Planners and Reformers: Urban Architects of Late Eighteenth-Century Brazil," *Eighteenth Century Studies* 10 (Fall 1976):40–51; "Land and Urban Planning: Aspects of Modernization in Early Nineteenth-Century Brazil," *Luso-Brazilian Review* 16 (Winter 1979):191–214; *New Towns for Colonial Brazil* (Ann Arbor, Mich.: University Microfilms International, 1979); and, with John P. Dickenson, "Perspectives on Landscape Change in Brazil," *Journal of Latin American Studies* 16, no. 1 (May 1984):101–25.

2 Frédéric Mauro, *Le Portugal et l'Atlantique au XVIIe siècle (1570–1670): Etude économique* (Paris: SEVPEN, 1960), 13–27.

3 This prevented the meticulous José Antonio Caldas from including information on Maranhão in his otherwise comprehensive *Notícia geral de toda esta Capitania da Bahia desde o seu descobrimento até o pezente anno de 1759*, facsimile edn (Salvador: Tip. Beneditina, 1951), 10, 236. For firsthand seventeenth-century pilot accounts of the sea routes from Rio Grande to Maranhão and Pernambuco to Maranhão, see Frédéric Mauro, *Le Brésil au XVIIe siècle: Documents inédits relatifs à l'Atlantique portugais* (Coimbra, 1961), 79–87, 113–20.

4 Mauro, *Le Portugal et l'Atlantique*, 70–1; Virgílio Noya Pinto, *O ouro brasileiro e o comércio anglo-português*, 2d edn (São Paulo: Editoria Nacional, 1979), 133–85.

5 A general survey of the Brazil and India fleets is C. R. Boxer, *The Portuguese Seaborne Empire, 1415–1825* (London: Hutchinson, 1969), 205–27. On Brazilian ports as way stations, see C. R. Boxer, "The Principal Ports of Call in the Carreira da India," *Luso-Brazilian Review* 8, no. 1 (June 1971):3–29; Alexander Marchant, "Colonial Brazil as a Waystation for the Portuguese India Fleets," *Geographical Review* 31 (1941):454–65; José Roberto do Amaral Lapa, *A Bahia e a carreira da India* (São Paulo: Editora Nacional, 1968).

6 K. R. Andrews, *Elizabethan Privateering: English Privateering during the Spanish War, 1585–1603* (Cambridge: Cambridge University Press, 1964), 133, 200–21; C. R. Boxer, "English Shipping in the Brazil Trade, 1640–1665," *The Mariner's Mirror* 37 (July 1951):197–230. C. R. Boxer, "Padre António Vieira, SJ, and the Institution of the Brazil Company in 1649," *HAHR* 29, no. 4

(November 1949):474–97; C. R. Boxer, "Blake and the Brazil Fleets in 1650," *The Mariner's Mirror* 36 (July 1950):202–28.

7 Boxer, *Portuguese Seaborne Empire*, 224.

8 Mauro, *Le Portugal et l'Atlantique*, 25–7, 71–4, 171; Noya Pinto, *O ouro brasileiro*, 135–6.

9 For a 1639 account by Luís Lopes, SJ, of a crossing from the Azores to Salvador, see Mauro, *Le Brésil au XVIIe siècle*, 17–68. Conditions on East Indiamen are in C. R. Boxer, ed., *The Tragic History of the Sea, 1589–1622* (Cambridge: Hakluyt Society, 1959), and *Further Selections from "The Tragic History of the Sea, 1559–1565"* (Cambridge; Hakluyt Society, 1968); see also A. Marques Espardeiro, "A higiene nas náus de viagem em meados do século XVIII," *Boletim da Sociedade de Geografia de Lisboa* (October–December 1958):279–96.

10 Luiz dos Santos Vilhena, *Recopilação de notícias soteropolitanas*, 2 vols (Bahia: Imprensa Official, 1922), 1:134.

11 On slave ailments and mortality, see Thales de Azevedo, *Povoamento da Cidade do Salvador*, 2nd edn (São Paulo: Companhia Editora Nacional, 1955), 218, no. 245; Mauro, *Le Portugal et l'Atlantique*, 169–72; Herbert S. Klein, *The Middle Passage: Comparative Studies in the Atlantic Slave Trade* (Princeton, NJ: Princeton University Press, 1978), 51–72; Philip D. Curtin, "Epidemiology and the Slave Trade," *Political Science Quarterly* 83, no. 2 (June 1968):190–216; Joseph C. Miller, *Way of Death: Merchant Capitalism and the Angolan Slave Trade, 1730–1830* (Madison: University of Wisconsin Press, 1988), 382–4, 411–13, 424–32.

12 António Carreira, *As companhias pombalinas de navegação, comércio, e tráfico de escravos entre a costa africana e o nordeste brasileiro* (Oporto: Imprensa Portuguesa, 1969).

13 For a general survey of hospital conditions in Salvador, see A. J. R. Russell-Wood, *Fidalgos and Philanthropists: The Santa Casa da Misericórdia of Bahia, 1550–1755* (Berkeley: University of California Press, 1968), especially 266–71. For a comparison, see Laima Mesgravis, *A Santa Casa de Misericórdia de São Paulo, 1599?–1884* (São Paulo, 1977).

14 Arquivo Nacional, Rio de Janeiro, codice 952, vol. 22 (1st part), f.52. See also Vivaldo Couracy, *O Rio de Janeiro no século dezessete* (Rio de Janeiro: Livraria José Olympio Editora, 1965), 208.

15 Heitor Ferreira Lima, *História político-econômica e industrial do Brasil* (São Paulo: Editora Nacional, 1976), 71, corrects José Gabriel de Lemos Brito, *Pontos de partida para a história econômica do Brasil*, 3d edn (São Paulo: Companhia Editora Nacional, 1980), 253. See also José Roberto do Amaral Lapa, *A Bahia e a carreira da India* (São Paulo: Editora Nacional, 1968), 51–81, and his "História de um navio" in *Economia colonial* (São Paulo, 1973), 231–78; Luís Monteiro da Costa, *Construções navais da Bahia no século XVII: O galeão "Nossa Senhora do Pópulo"* (Salvador, 1952); J. F. de Almeida Prado, *A Bahia e as capitanias do centro do Brasil (1530–1626)*, 3 vols (São Paulo: Editora Nacional, 1945–50).

16 Juvenal Greenhalgh, *O arsenal de marinha do Rio de Janeiro na história (1763–1822)* (Rio de Janeiro, 1951).

17 Lemos Brito, *Pontos de partida*, 245–59; Ferreira Lima, *História politico-económica*, 67–80; Almirante Antonio Alves Camara, *Ensaio sobre as construções navais indígenas do Brasil* (São Paulo, 1937); Sousa Viterbo, *Trabalhos nauticos dos portugueses nos séculos XVI e XVII*. Pt 2, *Construtores navaes*, 2 vols (Lisbon, 1898–1900).

18 Gabriel Soares de Sousa, *Tratado descritivo do Brasil em 1587* (São Paulo: Editora Nacional, 1938), 422; Amaral Lapa, *Bahia e a carreira da India*, 83–107; Dauril Alden, *Royal Government in Colonial Brazil* (Berkeley: University of California Press, 1968), 369–72.

19 Ferreira Lima, *Formação industrial*, 86–8.

20 Amaral Lapa, "História de um navio," 269; Robert E. Gallagher, ed., *Byron's Journal of his Circumnavigation, 1764–1766* (Cambridge: Hakluyt Society, 1964), 24–5. See also Amaral Lapa, *A Bahia*, 109–38; Caldas, *Notícia geral*, 214–15.

21 For such connections, see the numerous studies by Pierre Verger, *Note sur le culte des Orisha et Vodoun à Bahia, la Baie de tous les saints au Brésil et l'ancienne Côte des Esclaves en Afrique* (Amsterdam: Swets and Zeitlinger, 1970); *Flux et reflux de la traite des nègres entre le golfe de Bénin et Bahia de Todos os Santos du dix-septième au dix-neuvième siècle* (Paris: Mouton and Co., 1968), with special attention to the photographs; *Bahia and the West Coast Trade, 1549–1851* (Ibadan: Ibadan University Press, 1964); "Role joué par le tabac de Bahia dans la traite des esclaves au Golfe de Bénin," *Cahiers d'études africaines* 4, no. 15 (1964):349–69.

22 David M. Davidson, "How the Brazilian West was Won: Freelance and State on the Matto Grosso Frontier, 1737–1752," in *Colonial Roots of Modern Brazil*, ed. Dauril Alden (Berkeley: University of California Press, 1973), 61–106; Amaral Lapa, "Do comércio em area de mineração," in *Economia colonial*, 15–110; Sérgio Buarque de Hollanda, *Monções* (Rio de Janeiro: Casa do Estudante do Brasil, 1945), and *Caminhos a fronteiras* (Rio de Janeiro: Livraria José Olympio Editora, 1957); Russell-Wood, "Colonial Brazil: The Gold Cycle, ca. 1690–1750," in *Cambridge History of Latin America*, ed. Leslie Bethell (Cambridge: Cambridge University Press, 1984), 2:547–59.

23 André João Antonil, *Cultura e opulencia do Brasil*, ed. Andrée Mansuy (Paris: Institut des hautes études de l'Amérique latine, 1968), pt. 2, chs 1 and 2; Amaral Lapa, "O Brasil e as drogas do oriente," *Studia* 18 (August 1966):7–40; José Jobson de A. Arruda, *O Brasil no comércio colonial* (São Paulo: Atica, 1980), 279–92, 321–3.

24 The foundation of Salvador is described in Pedro Calmon, *História da fundação da Bahia* (Bahia: Publicações de Museu do Estado, 1949), and Theodoro de Sampaio, *História da Fundação da Cidade do Salvador* (Bahia: Tip. Beneditina Ltda, 1949). Descriptions of the city at various times are: Gabriel Soares de Sousa, *Notícia do Brasil*, commentary and notes by Pirajá da Silva, 2 vols, 8th edn (São Paulo: Editora Nacional, 1949), 1:256–7; *The Voyage of François*

Pyrard de Laval to the East Indies, the Maldives, the Moluccas, and Brazil, trans. Albert Gray, 2 vols (London, 1887–90); 2:310–11; William Dampier, *A Voyage to New Holland &c. in the Year 1699; Wherein are Described the Canary-Islands, the Isles of Mayo and St. Jago, the Bay of All Saints, with the Forts and Town of Bahia in Brazil* (London, 1703), 51–6; Johann Baptist von Spix and Carl Friedrich Philip von Martius, *Reise in Brasilien in den Jahren 1817–1820*, 3 vols (Stuttgart, 1966), 2:630–73. Caldas, *Notícia geral*, is an indispensable source of information. See also Thales de Azevedo, *Povoamento da Cidade do Salvador*; Katia M. de Queirós Mattoso, *Bahia: A Cidade do Salvador e seu mercado no século XIX* (Salvador, 1978), 83–105.

25 Fernão Cardim, *Tratados da terra e gente do Brasil* (Rio de Janeiro: J. Leite e cia, 1925), 288; Amédée François Frézier, *Relation du voyage de la mer du sud aux côtes du Chily et du Pérou, fait pendant les années 1712, 1713 & 1714* (Paris, 1716: new ed. Caracas: Biblioteca Ayachuco, 1982), 275; "Mappa de todas as freguezias," in Castro e Almeida, *Inventário* 2, no. 8750.

26 Castro e Almeida, *Inventário* 2, no. 8813. This can be compared to Rio de Janeiro in 1799: total population, 43,376; Whites, 19,578; free *pardos*, 4,227; Blacks, 4,585; slaves, 14,986: Mary Karasch, "Suppliers, Sellers, Servants, and Slaves," in *Cities and Society in Colonial Latin America*, ed. Louisa Schell Hoberman and Susan Migden Socolow (Albuquerque: University of New Mexico Press, 1986), 254.

27 Stuart B. Schwartz, *Sugar Plantations in the Formation of Brazilian Society: Bahia, 1550–1835* (Cambridge: Cambridge University Press, 1985), 264–94; Russell-Wood, *Fidalgos and Philanthropists*, 118–24; Rae Flory and David Grant Smith, "Bahian Merchants and Planters in the Seventeenth and Early Eighteenth Centuries," *HAHR* 58, no. 4 (November 1978):571–94; John N. Kennedy, "Bahian Elites, 1750–1822," *HAHR* 53, no. 3 (August 1973):415–39; for merchant representation on the Senado from 1680 to 1729, see Rae Jean Dell Flory, "Bahian Society in the Mid-Colonial Period: The Sugar Planters, Tobacco Growers, Merchants, and Artisans of Salvador and the Recôncavo" (Ph.D. diss., University of Texas at Austin, 1978), 264–5; Lugar, "Merchants," in Hoberman and Socolow, *Cities and Society*, 64–5.

28 Lugar, "Merchants," 58; Russell-Wood, *Fidalgos and Philanthropists*, 118, 186, 191, and illustration between pp. 206 and 207. Dwight E. Petersen, "Sweet Success: Some Notes on the Founding of a Brazilian Sugar Dynasty, the Pais Barreto Family of Pernambuco," *The Americas* 40, no. 3 (1984):325–48.

29 Caldas, *Notícia geral*, 525–6; Rocha Pitta, *História da America portugueza*, livro x, 17.

30 Lemos Britto, *Pontos de partida*, 275; Lugar, "The Merchant Community," 259–66; Russell-Wood, "As frotas de ouro do Brasil, 1710–50," *Estudos econômicos* 13 (1983): especially 707–13.

31 Mary Karasch, "From Porterage to Proprietorship: African Occupations in Rio de Janeiro, 1808–1850," in *Race and Slavery in the*

Western Hemisphere: Quantitative Studies, ed. Stanley L. Engerman and Eugene Genovese (Princeton, NJ: Princeton University Press, 1975), 379.

32 Santos Vilhena, *Recopilação de notícias*, 1:127–32.
33 Caldas, *Notícia geral*, 11–23, 71, 453.
34 Caldas, *Notícia geral*, 73–88, 205–15.
35 Caldas, *Notícia geral*, 217–18, 222–5, 331–43.
36 Caldas, *Notícia geral*, 525–33.
37 Flory, "Bahian Society," 225.

8

THE FUR TRADE AND EIGHTEENTH-CENTURY IMPERIALISM

W. J. Eccles

*The fur trade was one of the major extractive enterprises in mainland North America. Beaver pelts in particular brought high prices in Europe, especially in the era when the beaver hat was the height of fashion. The best pelts came from the colder reaches, where beavers needed the most insulation. Beavers were trapped and hunted to the point of extinction in New England and easternmost Canada in the seventeenth century, prompting both the French and the English to enlist the aid of Amerindians to bring in pelts from the interior of North America. By the mid-eighteenth century the fur trade in North America had a history that spanned 150 years. It had developed into a sophisticated business, with efficient markets and a highly articulated division of labor. Amerindians trapped and skinned the beaver; cour-*eurs de bois *traded for the pelts; Montreal and Albany merchants managed the export to Europe. It showed all the hallmarks of a mature colonial enterprise.*

In this article William J. Eccles explains how the commerce in pelts in northern North America was an instrument of foreign policy for the French, the British, and the Iroquois. The close interconnection between trade and imperial strategy, implying a measure of coordination among commercial and political elites, is also indicative of the mature development of the British and French North American empires of 1750.

The fur trade involved several Amerindian peoples in the Atlantic economy, but without forced labor of the sort commonplace in the haciendas and mines of early Latin America. Instead, the Huron, Algonquian, Iroquois and others sold pelts in order to get European trade goods, manufactures, and, conspicuously, liquor. Caribbean rum helped to lubricate the North American fur trade. With astonishingly few men, the French, based in Montreal, managed to extend their

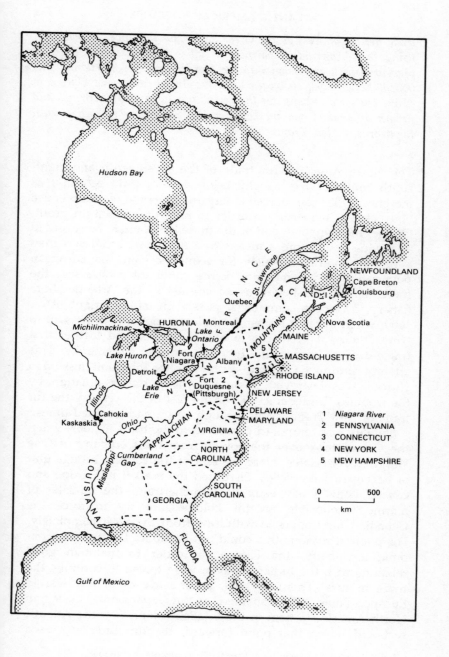

Hudson Bay

NEWFOUNDLAND
Cape Breton
Louisbourg

F R A N C E

St. Lawrence

A C A D I A

Quebec

Montreal

Nova Scotia

HURONIA

Michilimackinac

Lake Ontario

MAINE

Fort Niagara

Lake Huron

1 N

Albany

5

MOUNTAINS

MASSACHUSETTS

Detroit

Lake Erie

E

Fort 2
Duquesne
(Pittsburgh)

3

RHODE ISLAND

NEW JERSEY

Illinois

Cahokia

DELAWARE

1   *Niagara River*

Kaskaskia

Ohio

APPALACHIAN

MARYLAND

2   PENNSYLVANIA

VIRGINIA

3   CONNECTICUT

L O U I S I A N A

Cumberland
Gap

NORTH
CAROLINA

4   NEW YORK

5   NEW HAMPSHIRE

Mississippi

SOUTH
CAROLINA

0   500

GEORGIA

km

FLORIDA

Gulf of Mexico

trade net as far west as the Great Lakes and the upper Mississippi, using their Amerindian partners as allies in a successful effort to prevent British expansion into the North American heartland. This policy, Eccles says, succeeded until the British conquered Quebec in 1759. The Amerindians, for their part, sought to play the British and French off against one another, a policy which worked well – until the demise of New France.

* * *

The North American fur trade of the seventeenth and eighteenth centuries has usually been viewed, until recently, as merely another commercial enterprise governed by the premise "buy cheap, sell dear" in order to reap the maximum profit. Of late, the Canadian end of the trade has come to be regarded as having been more a means to a non-commercial end than a pursuit conducted solely for economic gain. As European penetration and dominance of the continent progressed, the trade, which had begun as an adjunct of the Atlantic shore fishery, became a commercial pursuit in its own right. After 1600, when the first Roman Catholic missionaries were sent to New France, it became a means to finance and further that tragic drive to convert the Indian nations to Christianity. This attempt continued until mid-century, when the Jesuit mission in Huronia was destroyed, along with the Hurons as a nation, by the Iroquois Confederacy.[*1] For the rest of the century the fur trade of New France went through vexed and troubled times.[2]

Stability was temporarily restored to the trade in 1663, when the Crown took over the colony from the Company of One Hundred Associates. Near the end of the century a huge glut of beaver fur completely disrupted the market in Europe and caused Louis Phélypeaux de Pontchartrain, the minister of marine responsible for the colonies, to try to force the Canadian fur traders to withdraw from the west completely. For political reasons this could not be done. Despite its economic unviability, the French, in order to maintain good relations with the Indian nations, were forced to continue the trade in furs. Then, in 1700, on the eve of a new war in Europe, Louis XIV embarked on an expansionist policy in North America to hem in the English colonies on the Atlantic seaboard. From that point forward, the fur trade was used

* Bruce Beresford's movie *Black Robe* (1991) confronts this theme.

mainly as a political instrument to further the imperial aims of France.

In the 1650s, after the Iroquois had virtually destroyed the Huron nation and scattered the Algonquian nations allied with it far to the west, French traders began to push into the interior of the continent, where they established direct trade relations with the hunting nations that had previously supplied furs to the Huron middlemen. These traders, a mere handful at first, voyaged through the Great Lakes and beyond, then down into the Mississippi Valley. This French thrust into the west occurred just as the Five Nations Iroquois Confederacy, having subdued the tribes surrounding them and being well supplied with firearms by the Dutch and English merchants of Albany, embarked on an imperialistic drive to conquer and control the Ohio Valley, a region almost as vast as the kingdom of France.[3] Their first incursion into the region in 1678 was repelled by the Illinois nation. The following year Robert Cavelier de La Salle began establishing fur-trade posts on the Illinois River and thereby claimed suzerainty for the French Crown over the lands of both the Illinois and the Miami nations.[4]

In 1680 the inevitable clash came between these rival imperial powers. La Salle's lieutenant, Henri de Tonty, attempted to mediate when an Iroquois army invaded the Illinois country. He received a nasty wound for his pains but managed to escape to Michilimackinac* with his men.[5] The French presence in the west was now seriously threatened. An attempt to cow the Iroquois by military force failed miserably. Instead, the Iroquois dictated humiliating peace terms to the governor-general of New France, Le Febvre de La Barre, and stated their determination to destroy the Illinois, whom the French claimed to be under the protection of Louis XIV. When La Barre protested this arrogant Iroquois declaration, the great Onondaga chief and orator Hotreouati brusquely retorted: "They deserve to die, they have shed our blood."[6] To that La Barre could make no response. He was, when Louis XIV was informed of what had transpired, summarily dismissed from his post and recalled to France in disgrace.[7]

The long-range aim of the Confederacy appears to have been to bring under subjection all the Indian nations south of the

---

* This is the strait that connects Lake Michigan and Lake Huron.

Great Lakes as far as the Mississippi, and at the same time to divert the western fur trade from Montreal to Albany with the Confederacy controlling it. Because the Iroquois failed to provide a written record of their aims, their motives cannot be determined with certainty; yet their actions and the policies they pursued during the ensuing decades indicate clearly enough that what they sought was power – dominance over this vast region – rather than mere commercial advantage.

A few years after this Franco-Iroquois struggle in the interior of North America was joined, events occurred in Europe that were to affect it profoundly. The Revolution of 1689 ousted James II and brought William of Orange, bitter enemy of Louis XIV, to the throne of England. This ushered in hostilities between England and France that were to occupy nineteen of the ensuing twenty-four years. The Iroquois, now confident of English military aid, pressed their attacks against the French in the west and at their settlements in the St Lawrence Valley, inflicting heavy casualties. The settlers, aided by some 1,500 Troupes de la Marine, regular troops sent from France, managed to beat back these attacks and in the process became, of necessity, highly skilled at guerrilla warfare. The alliance with the Indian nations, who had long feared the Iroquois was strengthened, and the war carried to the enemy. Iroquois casualties mounted, and the frontier settlements of their ineffectual English allies were ravaged by Canadian war parties. Both the Iroquois and the English colonials were relieved when, in 1697, the war ended in Europe. The Iroquois, now bereft of English logistical support, their fighting strength reduced by casualties and disease to half what it had been, were forced to sue for peace.[8]

This proud people had, however, not been brought so low that they would accept any terms that the French cared to impose. Consequently, the negotiations dragged on for four years. Moreover, the twenty-eight tribes allied with the French had to be party to the peace treaty that was eventually drawn up at Montreal in 1701. The principal factor that now made possible an enduring peace between the French and the Iroquois, thereby ending a war that had lasted for nearly a century, was that the French negotiators recognized the Iroquois presence to be an essential buffer between their Indian allies in the northwest and the English colonies. Moreover, the

Iroquois had learned to their cost that they could not rely on the English for military support. Rather, they perceived that the English had always sought to make use of them merely to serve English ends. There was no longer any question of the French seeking to destroy the Iroquois; in fact, just the reverse had become the case. The Iroquois had now to abandon all hope of ever driving the French out of Canada or from the posts in the west. The French presence had become essential to them to balance that of the English and to allow them to play one off against the other. Thus the French negotiators were able to insert a clause into the peace treaty declaring that in any future war between England and France the Iroquois would remain neutral. At one stroke the greatest military threat to New France and the main defense of New York had been eliminated; and this occurred just as England and France were preparing for a renewal of hostilities that were to last for more than a decade.[9]

On the French side, the preceding wars had been fought for a specific Canadian aim, control of the western fur trade, and France had provided the military aid needed to achieve that end. The ensuing wars were to be fought solely for French imperial aims. In 1701, with the War of the Spanish Succession about to erupt, Louis XIV declared that the English colonies must be hemmed in between the Atlantic and the Appalachians. On no account were the English to be allowed to flood over that mountain range to occupy the region between it and the Mississippi. Were they to do so, Louis feared, their numbers would swell immeasurably and England's wealth and power would increase proportionately. In all likelihood they would then push southwest to conquer Mexico with its silver mines. With Louis XIV's grandson now on the throne of Spain, France had to defend the Spanish colonies as though they were her own.[10] Louis XIV feared that English domination of North America would upset the balance of power in Europe. The French in America, with their Indian allies, were to be the means of containing the English colonies.[11] In the implementation of this imperial policy the fur trade had a vital role to play, of an importance far in excess of its economic value.

In 1701 Louis XIV gave orders for the creation of the new colony of Louisiana, in the Mississippi Valley, to forestall the English, who, it was reported, planned to establish a settlement at the mouth of that great river.[12] Another French settlement was ordered to be placed at the narrows between Lake Erie and Lake Huron. This new colony, to be named Detroit, was intended to bar English access to the northwest and maintain French control of the western Great Lakes.[13] It is not without significance that the Canadian merchants and the royal officials at Quebec were bitterly opposed to both these settlements, declaring that they would be the ruin of Canada – Detroit because it would bring the Indian nations allied with the French into close proximity to the Iroquois, who might grant them access to the Albany traders, Louisiana because the fur traders who obtained their trade goods on credit from the Montreal merchants would be tempted to defraud their creditors by shipping their furs to France from the port to be established on the Gulf of Mexico.[14]

French imperial policy now required that the Indian nations of the west and of Acadia be welded into a close commercial alliance and that all contact between them and the English colonists be prevented by one means or another. The main instruments of this policy, it was envisaged, would be missionaries and fur traders. The great age of French proselytization that had produced the Jesuit martyrs was, however, a thing of the past. The clergy were eager enough to serve, but some of them were ill-suited for the task and too often their efforts were hampered by squabbling among rival groups, secular priests with Jesuits, Capuchins with both. For several years the bishop of New France was an absentee, unable to restore order and discipline from his residence in Paris.[15] Thus the implementation of this new policy was left to two groups: the Canadian fur traders; and the officers and men of the colonial regulars, the Troupes de la Marine, who garrisoned the reestablished posts.

The fur trade was now definitely subordinated to a political end. It was required to pay a large share of the costs of maintaining a French presence in the interior to bar the English from it. The west was divided into regions, each with a central post commanded by an officer of the colonial regulars. For some years these officers were not permitted to engage in the trade, the sole right to which in each region was auctioned off to merchants on a three-year lease.[16] When it was found that this led to exploitation of the Indians by merchants whose only aim was to make as great a profit as possible during their lease, the trade was turned over to the commandants, who could, it was thought, be kept under tighter control by the senior officials at Quebec.[17] Complaints against them by the Indians could bring instant recall and might jeopardize promotion or the granting of commissions to sons.

The post commandants usually formed companies in partnership with Montreal merchants who provided the trade goods, hired the *voyageurs*, and marketed the furs, and professional traders who took charge of the actual trading with the Indians. The *modus operandi* was thus very simple: the companies usually comprised 3 men for a 3-year term, at the end of which the merchant who had supplied the goods withdrew their cost, and whatever profit or loss remained was shared by the partners.[18] At the main bases of Michilimackinac and Detroit the trade was open to all who obtained a permit from the governor-general and paid the base commandant his 500 *livre* fee. From these fees the commandants had to pay the costs of maintaining the posts, thereby sparing the Crown the expense.[19]

Louix XIV, in order to end the war that was reducing his government to bankruptcy, agreed to make sweeping concessions on the Atlantic frontier of New France to avoid having to make them in Europe. He therefore agreed to cede Newfoundland and Acadia, the latter "within its ancient limits," to England. A joint commission was appointed to determine those limits, but, predictably, no agreement could be reached and France retained Cape Breton, where it proceeded to construct the fortress of Louisbourg as a naval base for the protection of French maritime interests in the North Atlantic. The British continued to claim title to all the land up to the St Lawrence River, and it was upon the Indian nations of the region – the Abenakis, Micmacs, and Malecites – that the French relied to hold the English back from the vital St Lawrence waterway.[20] The governor-general at Quebec made sure that those nations were well supplied with all the European goods they needed and that a continual state of hostility existed between them and the expanding population of New England.[21]

In the implementation of this policy the French received unwitting aid from the New England settlers. What the latter coveted most was land for settlement, the very land that the Indians required to maintain their hunting economy and that they believed had been granted them by God for that purpose. The Indians denied that they were or ever had been subjects of either the French or the English Crown. They asserted vehemently that the French could not have ceded their land by treaty as the Massachusetts authorities claimed, since no one could cede what had never been his.[22] Although the French, with their meager population, did not covet any of that land, they were determined to deny it to the English. In 1727 the king stated in a *mémoire* to the governor-general and intendant at Quebec that he had learned with pleasure that the Abenakis of Saint-François and Bécancourt intended to continue the war against the English and not to entertain any proposals for peace until the English had razed the forts they had built on Abenaki lands. "This is so important for Canada," the *mémoire* went on, "that the Sieur de Beauharnois could not take measures more just than such as would foment that war and prevent any accommodation."[23]

To the north, where France had relinquished its claims to Hudson Bay, a dispute arose over the interpretation of the covering clause in the Treaty of Utrecht. The British claimed that they had thereby gained title to all the lands whose waters drained into Hudson Bay – almost one-quarter of the continent. They themselves, however, negated their claim by insisting that the operative clause in the treaty state that France *restored* rather than *ceded* to Great Britain the lands claimed by the latter – this in order to establish that Britain had always had the prior claim. France agreed but riposted by declaring that only the lands that Britain had formerly occupied could be restored to her: by definition, restoration could not be made of lands that had never been conquered, purchased, or occupied.[24] In fact, merely an infinitesimal fraction of that vast territory had ever even been seen by a British subject. The argument was really an academic one, since the Hudson's Bay Company made no attempt to challenge French control of the interior. As long as enough furs reached its posts to produce a dividend for its shareholders, the company's servants were content to remain in a "sleep by the frozen sea."[25]

The French now established fur-trade posts on the rivers that ran down to the bay and thereby controlled the flow of furs to the English. They kept the choicest furs for themselves and allowed the Indians to trade only their poorer-quality pelts at the Bay Company's posts.[26] Had it not been that the Indians were astute enough to maintain trade relations with both the English and the Canadians in order to reap the advantages of competition, Britain's hold on Hudson Bay would early have been severed.[27]

From the signing of the Treaty of Utrecht in 1713 to the conquest of New France,* the French maintained their presence among the nations of the west, penetrating steadily farther into the interior until they eventually reached the barrier of the Rocky Mountains.[28] Only at Detroit, Kaskaskia, and Cahokia in the Illinois country, and on the lower Mississippi, were they able to establish small agricultural settlements.[29] Elsewhere they merely maintained fur-trade posts consisting of three or four log buildings surrounded by a palisade. Always these posts were placed in an area that no Indian nation claimed as its own – Detroit, for example – or were established with the express permission of the dominant nation of the region. Some of the posts had been maintained during the Iroquois war, ostensibly as bases and places of refuge for the nations allied with the French against the Iroquois Confederacy. Experience had proved that posts on the fringe of Iroquois-controlled territory were more prisons than forts. Their garrisons did not dare venture beyond musket-range of the palisades, and too many of the men, deprived of fresh meat or fish, reduced to hard rations of stale salt pork and sea biscuit, succumbed to scurvy.[30]

After the Iroquois wars of the seventeenth century, and with the proclamation of Louis XIV's containment policy in North America, fur-trade posts had to be sustained among all the nations that could conceivably have contact, direct or indirect, with the English colonials or the Hudson's Bay Company. With the exception of the Sioux, who always kept the French at arm's length, most of the nations were glad to have these posts on their territory. Although the French maintained that the posts gave them title to the land, their claims were made to exclude the English, not to deny the Indians' title, something they did not dare do. The French were certainly not

* In 1759.

221

sovereign in the west, for sovereignty implies the right to impose and collect taxes, and to enforce laws – and they were never able to do either. The Indians never considered themselves to be French subjects, and the French were never able to treat them as such.[31] Moreover, the Canadian *voyageurs* who transported trade goods and supplies to the western posts and took the furs back to Montreal always had to travel in convoy for protection against the Indians through whose lands they passed. One or two canoes alone were an invitation to extortionate demands or outright pillage.[32] The Indians allowed the French only the right of passage to the posts, since this assured them a ready supply of European goods close at hand. The land on which the trading posts stood they considered still to be theirs, the French occupants being mere tenants during the Indians' pleasure.

Another significant factor in this imperial rivalry was the superiority of most French trade goods. In only one item, woolen cloth, did the English have an advantage, and even this is open to question. The factors at the Hudson's Bay Company's posts were continually pleading with their superiors in London to provide them with goods of the same quality as those traded by the French.[33] In one of the more important trade items, liquor, the French had a distinct advantage. Showing commendable good taste, the Indians greatly preferred French brandy to the rot-gut rum and gin supplied by the British and Americans. The Hudson's Bay Company produced imitation brandy made from cheap gin with alarming additives to give it the color and something resembling the taste of cognac, but it never replaced the real thing in the Indians' opinion.[34] Alcohol was crucial in the fur trade for two reasons. First, the Indians craved it more than anything else; even though they knew that it could destroy them, they could not resist it, and they would go to any lengths to obtain all that was available.[35] Second, from the purely economic aspect of the trade, alcohol was the ideal exchange item. Of other goods – cloth, wearing apparel, pots, knives, axes, muskets – the Indians had a limited need. It is now coming to be recognized that they were by no means as dependent on European goods as has been claimed.[36] A musket would last many years, as would other metal goods. A few items of clothing each year per family did not result in large entries in the Montreal merchants' ledgers. An Indian hunter could garner enough pelts in a couple of months' good hunting to provide for his family's needs, but the appetite for *eau de vie* was virtually insatiable, driving the Indians to produce furs in ever larger quantities. In the 1790s a Nor'wester, Duncan McGillivray, remarked: "When a nation becomes addicted to drinking it affords a strong presumption that they will soon become excellent hunters."[37]

The French traders who lived among the Indians were only too well aware of the terrible effects that liquor had on their customers. Frequently they paid for it with their lives when Indians, in their cups, went berserk and set about them with knife or *casse-tête*.[38] Some of the senior French officials who were involved in the fur trade for personal gain tried to make light of these dread effects. Governor-general Louis de Buade, comte de Frontenac, for example, contended vociferously that the Indians did not get any more drunk, or behave any worse when in their cups, than did the average Englishman or Netherlander.[39] The French missionaries, in particular the Jesuits who resided in the Indian villages, knew better. They fought to have liquor barred completely from the trade and threatened excommunication for any traders who persisted in its use.[40] Governor-general Philippe de Rigaud de Vaudreuil and his successor, Charles de la Boische, marquis de Beauharnois, both recognized the horrors caused by the liquor trade, but for political reasons they had to condone it, while at the same time striving to restrict its use to prevent the worst abuses. As they and others pointed out to Jean-Frédéric Phélypeaux, comte de Maurepas, appointed minister of marine in 1723, were they to refuse to trade alcohol, the Indians would go to the Anglo-American traders, who had no scruples whatsoever, despite frequent pleas from tribal chieftains to keep the rum peddlers out of their villages.[41] Thus in the imperial contest liquor was a powerful but pernicious weapon.

Throughout the eighteenth century the Montreal fur traders took the lion's share of the North American fur trade. The customs figures for fur imports at London, La Rochelle, and Rouen make this plain.[42] Moreover, the Albany merchants who dominated the Anglo-American fur trade admitted that they obtained the bulk of their furs clandestinely from the Canadians.[43] It could hardly have been otherwise, since they did not have access to the northwest, which produced the fine-quality furs. The minister of marine, Maurepas, and after 1749 his successor, Antoine-Louis Rouillé, comte de Jouy, continually demanded that the smuggling of Canadian furs to Albany be stopped, but to no avail.[44] They simplemindedly believed that if the English desired something, then France must strive to deny it them. The senior officials at Quebec well understood the complexity of the situation. They declared vociferously that they were doing everything possible to curb this clandestine trade, but the evidence indicates that their unenthusiastic efforts were less than efficacious. They tolerated the existence of an agent of the Albany traders at Montreal and frequent visits of the merchants themselves. Similarly, Montreal traders called at Albany from time to time, and credit arrangements between the merchants of the two centers were extensive.[45] One suspects that the governor-general and the intendant despaired of bringing first Maurepas, then Rouillé, ministers of marine, to grasp how closely intertwined were the economics and politics of the situation. Certainly they did not make a determined attempt to explain the subtleties of the issue.

The main agents of this clandestine trade were the Christian Indians of Sault St Louis and Lake of Two Mountains missions, both close by Montreal.[46] The Canadian officials claimed that they dared not forbid these Indians to trade at Albany whenever they pleased lest they become disaffected and remove from New France. Since their services were vital in time of war, and in peacetime as intelligence agents, they had to be indulged. Thus they quite openly transported Canadian furs to Albany, along with fine French cloth, wines, and spirits, for the accounts of Canadian merchants.[47] In fact, governor-general Beauharnois declared that the Mission Iroquois of Sault St Louis constituted virtually an independent republic over which he had no authority.[48]

Although the Canadian fur traders undoubtedly reaped considerable benefits from this clandestine trade, a far more significant consequence was that it removed any incentive the Albany merchants might have had to contest the hold of the French over the western nations.[49] This issue was of great concern to the crown officials of New York, who took an imperial view of the situation, but the Albany merchants were interested only in preserving their well-established Canadian trade. When furs were shipped to their doors by the Canadians at prices that afforded them a good profit, they saw no reason to incur the great risks, capital outlay, and trouble that would be involved in trying to compete with the Canadians on their ground, the Indian country of the northwest. Moreover, they lacked the birchbark canoes, the *voyageurs* to man them, and the prime requisite, the willingness to accept the Indians on their own terms – in short, all the special skills needed for this particular trade.[50] In November 1765, Sir William Johnson commented sadly on this phenomenon to the Lords of Trade:

> I have frequently observed to Your Lordships, that His Majesty's subjects in this Country seem very ill calculated to Cultivate a good understanding with the Indians; and this is a notorious proof of it, for notwithstanding the Expence of transporting Goods from New Orleans to the Illinois is greater than by the Lakes and Consequently French goods are in general Dearer than Ours, yet such is the Conduct of all persons under the Crown of France, whether Officers, Agents, Traders, that the Indians will go much farther to buy their Goods, and pay a much higher price for them. This all persons acquainted with the nature of the Commerce to the Westward can fully evidence.[51]

Nor was the trade all one way. The Iroquois made annual trips to Canada to confer with the French authorities. The crown officials of New York were deeply worried by the influence that the French gained over the Iroquois during these visits. The French entertained the Iroquois delegates lavishly, after a fashion that the British officials could not or would not match.[52] In October 1715, the Albany Indian commissioners stated: "Trade between Albany & Canada is of fatal Consequence to the Indian Interest of this Colony, that of our Indians who are employed in it many stay at Canada & others return so Attached to the French Interest & so Debauched from ours that it puzzels them how to preserve amongst them that Respect & Regard to this Gov't so necessary to the Public Good and Tranquillity."[53]

By 1720 the French had gained a secure hold on the Great Lakes basin by ringing it with garrisoned fur-trade posts. Although the mercantile interests of New York were not perturbed by this development, the crown officials were, and they sought to counter it. In 1719 the governor-general of New France, Vaudreuil, heard reports that New York intended to establish a fort at Niagara, which would have given the English access to the west, including the Mississippi Valley. Vaudreuil very adroitly forestalled them by obtaining the permission of the Senecas to establish a post on their land at the mouth of the Niagara River. Ostensibly, the post was to serve their needs; in reality, it barred the west to the English.[54] The following year another post was established at the Toronto portage, barring that route from Lake Ontario to Lake Huron.[55]

Although the Iroquois had given the French permission to establish the post at Niagara and bluntly told the protesting Albany authorities that they had "given the French liberty of free Passage thru Lake Ontario,"[56] they had no desire to see the French become overpowerful in the region. To balance their position they therefore granted New York permission to build a trading post at Oswego on the south shore of Lake Ontario across from Fort Frontenac. At the same time, deputies from the Iroquois Confederacy met with the Albany Indian commissioners, who reported that the Indians "exhort us to live in Peace and Quiet with the French and carry on our Trade without Molesting each other."[57] The Quebec authorities responded by claiming that the south shore of the Great Lakes belonged to France by right of prior discovery and conquest.[58] Governor-general Beauharnois began making preparations for a campaign to take and destroy Oswego, but he was restrained by the government in France, which at the time enjoyed good relations with Great Britain, this being the era of the *entente cordiale* established by Cardinal André-Hercule de Fleury and Robert Walpole.[59] Nevertheless, the Canadian authorities replaced the trading post at Niagara with a solid stone edifice that it would have required heavy cannon to demolish, greatly to the dismay of the Albany authorities.[60]

Events were to demonstrate that Oswego posed no serious threat to French control of the Great Lakes. The fear was that it would seduce the western nations out of the French alliance by undercutting the French prices for furs and, more particularly, by the unrestricted sale of liquor. But here again, as at Albany, the New York traders were their own worst enemies. They did indeed supply all the cheap liquor the Indians desired, but the latter, when under its influence, were unmercifully cheated and their womenfolk debauched.[61] This bred bitter resentment.

Oswego posed an additional problem for the authorities at Quebec. Some of the less scrupulous Canadian traders found it convenient to obtain large supplies of cheap rum there, as well as English woolens, which they traded at the distant Indian villages.[62] In an attempt to keep both the allied Indians and the renegade Canadians away from the English post, the French government retained the trade at forts Frontenac, Niagara, and Toronto as crown monopolies so that prices could be kept competitive with those at Oswego by selling at a reduced profit or even a loss if necessary. The commandants at these posts had to see to it that nothing transpired that could upset the Indians and endanger their alliance with the French.[63]

The French thus managed to maintain a tenuous hold over the interior of North America west of the Appalachians and in the vast region north and west of the Great Lakes as far as the Rocky Mountains. This tremendous feat was, moreover, accomplished at very little cost to the French Crown and by a mere handful of men. In 1754, when this military fur trade empire was nearing its greatest extent, the cost to the Crown for maintaining the garrisoned posts was but 183,427 *livres*.[64] The number of officers and enlisted men in these garrisons in 1750 was only 261,[65] but in addition there were the men engaged directly in the trade with the Indians – the *voyageurs*, traders, clerks, and merchants – whose number cannot be calculated with any great degree of accuracy. All that can be offered here is an educated guess that the number directly employed in the western fur trade for the period 1719–50 would range from about 200 for the earlier years to some 600 at most by mid-century.[66] This means that with fewer than 1,000 men France maintained its claim to more than half the continent.

Had the French been content to confine their activities to the fur trade, they might well have retained their control, in alliance with the Indian nations, over the northern half of the continent: that is, over the area that today forms the Dominion of Canada. However, the interests of the Canadian fur traders and French imperial policy began to diverge at mid-century, immediately after the War of the Austrian Succession. Fur traders from Pennsylvania and Virginia, serving as advance agents of land-speculation companies, had begun to penetrate the Ohio Valley by way of the Cumberland Gap with pack-horse trains.[67] To win the allegiance of the Indian nations, they flooded the region with cheap trade goods, liquor, and expensive presents for the chiefs. A Canadian officer later declared: "The presents that they receive are so considerable that one sees nothing but the most magnificent gold, silver, and scarlet braid."[68] The Canadian fur traders had no interest in the furs of that region, which were of poor quality.[69] They preferred to confine their activities to the northwest, where the furs were the best obtainable, river communications far easier than they were south of the Great Lakes, and the Cree tongue a *lingua franca* in the entire region.

Marquis Roland-Michel Barrin de la Gallissonière, governor-general of New France, in opposition to the prevailing and strongly held Canadian sentiment, advocated that the Ohio Valley be occupied by the French and that forts be built and garrisoned, merely to deny the region to the English. He freely admitted that it would be of no economic benefit to France in the foreseeable future, but he feared that were the English to succeed in occupying and settling the valley they would become extremely powerful and dangerous. They would even-tually sever communications along the Mississippi between Canada and Louisiana and then go on to conquer Mexico with its silver mines.[70]

The minister of marine, Rouillé, newly appointed to the post and without previous experience in colonial affairs, accepted this policy. Despite the strong opposition of the senior Canadian officials in the colonial administration,[71] and at immense cost in funds and Canadian lives,[72] the French drove the American traders out of the region. They established a chain of forts and supply depots from Lake Erie to the fork of the Ohio, thereby overawing the local tribes, who quickly abandoned their commercial alliance with the Anglo-Ameri-cans and pledged their support to the French.[73] This was accomplished by *force majeure* pure and simple, and the Indian nations remained in this uneasy alliance only as long as it appeared to them to suit their interests and, as events were to show, not a day longer.

Previously when the French had extended their fur-trade empire into new territory, they had always done so at the invitation, or at least with the tacit consent, of the Indians. In the Ohio Valley, however, Gallissonière's successor, Ange de Menneville, marquis Duquesne, made it plain to the Iroquois, who claimed sovereignty over the region, that he would brook no interference, that he regarded the valley as belonging to the French Crown, and that if they chose to oppose him he would crush them.[74] Some of his Canadian officers, long accustomed to dealing with the Iroquois, were more diplomatic. They pointed out that the French did not covet the land but merely wished to prevent the English from seizing it, and that the Indians could hunt right up to the walls of the French forts, whereas wherever the English went the forest was destroyed and the animals driven out, the Indians with them.[75]

Here also the Anglo-Americans were the agents of their own defeat. They had treated two nations on the frontiers of Pennsylvania and Virginia, the Shawnee and the Delaware, so ruthlessly, seizing their land by dint of fraudulent title deeds, debauching them with liquor, murdering them with impunity, that it did not require a great deal of persuasion by the French to bring these Indians into a close military alliance once hostilities broke out.[76] This rejection of the Anglo-Americans was immeasurably strengthened by the initial French victories, first over Major George Washington's motley provincial force at Fort Necessity, where Washington accepted humiliating terms and fled back over the mountains; then, a year later when Major-General Edward Braddock's army of 2,200 British regulars and American provincials was destroyed near Fort Duquesne by 250-odd Canadian regulars and militia and some 600 Indians.[77]

The French were now able to arm and send out Indian war parties, accompanied by a few Canadian regulars or militia, to ravage the frontiers of the English colonies from New York to Georgia, thereby retaining the initiative and tying down large British and provincial forces. Successful though it was, this strategy posed massive problems in logistics that the minister of marine, Jean-Baptiste de Machault d'Arnouville, and his staff at Versailles were never able to comprehend. Appalled by the Canadian accounts for 1753, he warned governor-general Duquesne that unless the excessive costs of the western posts were reduced, the king would abandon the colony.[78] He thereby blandly overlooked the fact that the expenditures had been incurred in consequence of his ministry's policy and direct orders. To implement this policy all the needs of the Indian allies had to be supplied.[79] This required the transport of vast amounts of goods from Montreal to forts Niagara and Duquesne by canoe, barque, horse, and pirogue. The wastage at the Niagara portage alone was appalling. In 1753 Duquesne complained to Captain Paul Marin de la Malgue, commander of the Ohio expedition, that he had learned that forty-eight canoe-loads of supplies had been stolen or spoiled by being left uncovered in the rain. He voiced the suspicion that the Canadians, who were bitterly opposed to the Ohio adventure, were destroying the supplies deliberately to force its abandonment.[80]

For many years the western Iroquois had demanded and received the right to carry all fur-trade and military supplies over the portage, which they regarded as their territory. This was a cost that the crown officials at Quebec had been quite willing to see imposed on the fur traders in order to maintain good relations with the Iroquois Confederacy. Governor-general Duquesne, however, considered excessive the 40,000 *livres* a year that it was now costing the Crown to have military supplies transported around Niagara Falls by the Senecas. At the grave risk of alienating them and the other Iroquois nations, he had horses shipped from Montreal and dispensed with the Senecas' services. Many of the horses then mysteriously vanished.[81]

For the Canadian officers charged with the implementation of these orders, the task at times seemed insuperable. A lack of rain meant low water in the shallow rivers that linked Lake Erie, with a 15-mile portage, to the Ohio. The supply boats and pirogues then had to be manhandled along the river beds, driving both officers and men to despair.[82] To make matters worse, the Indian allies were extremely demanding and wasteful. Their loyalty could be counted on only as long as their demands for goods and services were met, and frequently not even then. In 1756 Vaudreuil ruefully explained to the minister of marine:

I am not in the least surprised that expenses have risen so

230

high, the Indians are the cause of immense expenditures, forming the largest part of those charged to the Crown in the colony. One has to see to believe what they consume and how troublesome they are. I deny and reduce their demands as much as I can at Montreal, but despite it they succeed in having themselves equipped several times in the same campaign. They continually come and go between the army or the posts and Montreal, and one is forced to supply them with food for every trip, which they justify by claiming that they have been refused things by the army, or that having been on a raid they must now return home, or they dreamt that they ought to do so. Every time that one wants to send them to support the army one cannot avoid supplying them. When they go on a war party they are given 10, 12, or 15 days' rations . . . at the end of two days they return without food or equipment and say they have lost it all, so they have to be provided afresh. They consume an astonishing quantity of brandy and a commandant would be in grave difficulties were he to refuse them, and so it is with all their requests.[83]

One important factor, all too often overlooked, was that these Indian nations fought alongside the French purely to serve their own ends. They were allies, not mercenaries. In fact, they regarded the French as little more than an auxiliary force aiding them in their struggle to preserve their hunting-grounds from further encroachment by the Anglo-Americans and to oblige the latter to treat them with respect.[84] This was compellingly illustrated when, in May 1757, the American colonial authorities entered into negotiations with Iroquois, Shawnee, and Delaware tribes to end the fighting that had destroyed their frontier settlements to a depth of over 100 miles. For once, the Indian negotiators refused to be put off with vague promises; in the past, they had been hoodwinked all too often. Eventually a Moravian missionary, Frederick Post, who sympathized deeply with the Indians, went to the villages of the Shawnee and Delaware. There, within sight of Fort Duquesne, with frustrated French officers in attendance, the proposed terms of the Easton Treaty were promulgated.[85]

The Indian nations south of the Great Lakes then ceased

to support the French. When Brigadier-General John Forbes, marching on Fort Duquesne with an army of some 7,000 British regulars and American provincial troops, suffered heavy and humiliating losses at the hands of the Canadians and Indians in one brisk battle, he deliberately slowed his advance until he received word that the Indians had signed a separate peace, the Easton Treaty. That defection left the French no choice but to abandon Fort Duquesne and, with it, control of the Ohio Valley. Colonel Henry Bouquet commented: "After God the success of this Expedition is intirely due to the General, who by bringing about the Treaty of Easton, has struck the blow which has knocked the French in the head . . . in securing all his posts, and giving nothing to chance."[86]

The following year, 1759, Quebec and Niagara fell. Despite a valiant last attempt by the French and Canadians under François de Lévis to retake Quebec in the spring of 1760, 6 months later they were compelled to surrender to the armies of Major General Jeffery Amherst at Montreal. This spelled the end of French power on the mainland of North America.

The fate of that empire had been decided by the incompetence of its government at home and that of the headquarters staff – with the exception of the Chevalier de Lévis – of the army sent to defend Canada. During the course of the war there had been four controllers-general of finance, four of foreign affairs, four of war, and five of the marine.[87] In the fateful year, 1759, the minister of marine was Nicolas-René Berryer. Before his appointment to that post in November 1758 he had been *lieutenant de police* for Paris.[88] As for the army sent to Canada, its morale and efficiency steadily deteriorated under the command of the incompetent, defeatist Louis-Joseph, marquis de Montcalm. It was not a shortage of supplies or overwhelming enemy superiority or corruption that brought on the British conquest of Canada. The west was lost when the Indian allies defected. Louisbourg fell because it lacked a fleet to protect it. Canada fell after the loss of Quebec in a battle that should have been won crushingly by the French but was lost owing to the stupidity and panic of Montcalm.[89] Even then Quebec might well have been retaken by Lévis had the minister of marine dispatched in time the reinforcements that Lévis had requested.[90] Etienne-François, duc de Choiseul, who was given charge of the ministries of war, foreign affairs, and marine, then decided that it would serve the interests of France better were England to acquire Canada, since, with the menace of French power removed from mainland America, England's colonies could be counted on to strike for independence in the not-too-distant future. France's loss of Canada, Choiseul decided, would be as nothing compared to England's loss of her American colonies.[91]

If the Canadians had had control of French policy in North America, neither the decisive battle at Quebec nor, for that matter, the war itself would likely have taken place, for the Canadians had no real quarrel with the English colonies. In war the Anglo-Americans had demonstrated time and again that they were no match for the Canadians and their Indian allies. Their record in the Seven Years' War indicated clearly enough their lack of enthusiasm for the conflict.[92] The Canadians knew that they had little to fear from that quarter; nor did they have any illusions that they could conquer the English colonies. In commerce there was no real conflict between them. The fur trade was of vital economic importance to the Canadians but certainly not to France, and of little, and that declining, importance to the Anglo-Americans. Among the latter, a group of well-placed, rapacious land speculators and a barbarian horde of would-be settlers coveted the lands of the Indian nations on their frontier, a region that the Canadians had made plain was of no interest to them. The Albany merchants who dominated the Anglo-American fur trade chose not to compete with the Canadians; instead they entered into a cosy commercial partnership. They had not exhibited any eagerness to dispute the French hold on the west. As for the Hudson's Bay Company, its steadily declining returns indicated its inability to compete with the Canadians; moreover, it no longer had the same influence as it once had wielded in government circles. It was a monopoly, and all trade monopolies were then being looked at askance in Britain.[93] Only the shareholders would have wept had the Hudson's Bay Company been driven to the wall by the Canadians.

For over half a century the fur trade was used by France as an instrument of its foreign policy and, owing to the peculiar skills of the Canadians, with considerable success. By means of it, most of the Indian nations supported the French cause in the colonial wars, but they did so only as long as it appeared to them to serve their immediate interests. The French were acutely aware of the Indians' true feeling toward them. Governor-general Beauharnois remarked that they had their policies just as had the French. "In general," he stated, "they greatly fear us, they have no affection for us whatsoever, and the attitudes they manifest are never sincere."[94] A certain Monsieur Le Maire put the French position very succinctly, explaining that there was no middle course: one had to have the Indians either as friends or as foes, and whoever desired them as friends had to furnish them with their necessities, on terms they could afford.[95] The policy of the Indian nations was always to play the French off against the English, using the fur trade as an instrument of their own foreign policy.[96] Their tragedy was not to have foreseen the consequences were the French to be eliminated from the equation.

NOTES

This article was originally published in the *William and Mary Quarterly* (1983):341–62, and is reprinted by permission of the author.

1 On the Huron–Iroquois conflict see Bruce G. Trigger, *The Children of Aataentsic: A History of the Huron People to 1660*, 2 vols (Montreal, 1976), and John A. Dickinson, "Annaotaha et Dollard vus de l'autre côté de la palissade," *Revue d'histoire de l'Amérique française* 35 (1981):163–78.

2 The best study of this early period is Marcel Trudel, *The Beginnings of New France, 1524–1663*, trans. Patricia Claxton (Toronto, 1973). The period 1663–1701 is covered in W. J. Eccles, *Canada under Louis XIV, 1663–1701* (Toronto, 1964). The latter work is now somewhat dated.

3 In order of conquest or dispersal, these tribes were the Mahicans (1628); Hurons (1649); Neutrals (1651); Eries (1653–7); and Susquehannocs (1676).

4 Mémoire de Henri Tonty, Paris, Bibliothèque nationale, MS nouv. acq. 7485, f. 103; Duchesneau au ministre, 13 November 1680, Paris, Archives nationales, Colonies, C11A, vol. 5, ff. 39–40.

5 W. J. Eccles, *Frontenac: The Courtier Governor* (Toronto, 1959), 82–4, 107–10; François Vachon Belmont, *Histoire du Canada; D'après un manuscrit à la Bibliothèque du Roi à Paris* (Quebec, 1840), 14.

6 Belmont, *Histoire du Canada*, 15–16; Eccles, *Frontenac*, 167–71; Presens des Onontaguez à Onontio à la Famine le Cinq Septembre 1684, Le febvre de la barre, C11A, vol. 6, ff. 299–300.

7 Le roy au Sr. de Meules, 10 March 1685, B, vol. 11, f. 96.

8 Eccles, *Frontenac*, 157–97, 244–72.

9 Eccles, *Frontenac*, 328–33.

10 Eccles, *Frontenac*, 334–7; Marcel Giraud, *Histoire de la Louisiane française*. Vol. 1, *Le règne de Louis XIV* (1698–1715) (Paris, 1953), 13–23.

11 M. Tremblay à M. Gladelet, 28 May 1701, Quebec, Canada, Archives du Séminaire de Québec, Lettres, Carton O, no. 34.

12 Giraud, *Histoire de la Louisiane*, 1:39–43.

13 Yves F. Zoltvany, *Philippe de Rigaud de Vaudreuil: Governor of New France, 1703–1725* (Toronto, 1974), 39–41.

14 Zoltvany, *Philippe de Rigaud de Vaudreuil*, 40, 86–7; Champigny au ministre, 8 August 1688, C11A, vol. 10, ff. 123–4; Callières et Champigny au ministre, 5 October 1701, C11A, vol. 19, ff. 6–7. That this fear was soon to be realized is made clear in d'Iberville's journal for 1702, where he mentions his accepting furs from Canadian *coureurs de bois* for shipment to France: Richebourg Gaillard McWilliams, trans. and ed., *Iberville's Gulf Journals* (University, Ala., 1981), 165, 178.

15 Charles Edwards O'Neill, *Church and State in French Colonial Louisiana: Policy and Politics to 1732* (New Haven, Conn., 1966), *passim*.

16 Archives nationales du Québec, *Rapport de l'Archiviste de la Province de Québec* (Québec, 1921–), 1938–9, 69 (hereafter cited as *Rapport de l'Archiviste*).

17 Beauharnois et d'Aigremont au ministre, 1 October 1728, C11A, vol. 50, ff. 31–3; minister to La Jonquière and Bigot, 4 May 1749, State Historical Society of Wisconsin, *Collections*, (1908):25–6; Beauharnois to the minister, 18 October 1737, Michigan Pioneer and Historical Society, *Historical Collections* 34 (1905), 146–7.

18 For a revealing commentary on the working of a typical fur-trade company of the period, see Meuvret au Lt. Joseph Marin de la Malgue [Commandant, la Baie des Puants], 15 May 1752, Archs. Sém. Québec, Fonds Verreau, boite 5, no. 38 1/2. See also Acte de Société, 23 May 1726, Jean Le Mire Marsolet, de Lignery, Guillaume Cartier, Greffe J-B, Adhemar, Archives Nationales du Québec à Montréal, no. 1854.

19 Pierre-Jacques Chavoy de Noyan to the minister, 18 October 1738, Mich. Pioneer Hist. Soc., *Hist. Colls.*, 34 (1905):158–9; Le Conseil de Marine à MM de Vaudreuil et Bégon, 20 October 1717, C11A, vol. 37, ff. 378–9; Beauharnois et Hocquart au ministre, 5 October 1736, vol. 65, ff. 57–8. Greffe J., David, 28 April 1723, Archs. Québec, is but one of hundreds of permits that specify the obligations to the Crown of those allowed to trade in the west. See also ibid., Greffe J-B, Adhemar, no. 1257, 23 May 1724, and no. 1211, 8 May 1724; Beauharnois et d'Aigremont au ministre, 1 October 1728, C11A, vol. 50, ff. 31–3; Wilbur R. Jacobs, *Dispossessing the American Indian: Indians and Whites on the Colonial Frontier* (New York, 1972), 194 n. 38; and Zoltvany, *Vaudreuil*, 174–5.

20 Zoltvany, *Philippe de Rigaud de Vaudreuil*, 166–8, 196–209.

21 Canada. Conseil. MM de Vaudreuil et Bégon, 26 October 1720, C11A, vol. 41, ff. 390–1.

22 Parole de toute la Nation Abenaquise et de toutes les autres nations sauvages ses alliés au gouverneur de Baston au sujet de la Terre des Abenaquise dont les Anglois s'Emparent depuis la Paix . . . fait . . . au bas de la Rivière de Kenibeki Le 28 Juillet 1721, F3 Moreau de St Méry, Archives nationales, vol. 2, ff. 413–16.

23 Mémoire du Roy à MM de Beauharnois et Dupuy, 29 April 1727, *Nouvelle-France. Documents historiques. Correspondance échangée entre les authoritées française et les gouverneurs et intendants*, vol. 1 (Québec, 1893), 64.

24 E. E. Rich, *The History of the Hudson's Bay Company*, 1670–1870. Vol. 1, 1670–1763 (London, 1958), 423–5, 482–6; "Memorial of the Governor and Company of Adventurers of England Trading into Hudson's Bay to the Council of Trade and Plantations," in *Calendar of State Papers, Colonial Series, America and the West Indies*, ed. W. Noel Sainsbury et al. (London 1860–), 31: no. 360; Mr Delafaye to the Council of Trade and Plantations, 4 November 1719, ibid., no. 443; Observations et réflexions servant de réponses aux propositions de Messieurs les Commissaires anglais au sujet des limits a régler pour la Baie d'Hudson, *Rapport de l'Archiviste*, 1922–3, 95–6.

25 Rich, *Hudson's Bay Company*, 1:554, 434, 556, 575, and *The Fur Trade and the Northwest to 1857* (Toronto, 1967), 118.

26 Lawrence J. Burpee, ed., "The Journal of Anthony Hendry, 1754–55," Royal Society of Canada, *Proceedings and Transactions*, 2d ser., 8, pt. 2 (1907), 352–3.

27 Rich, *Hudson's Bay Company*, 1:482, 526, 429; Arthur J. Ray, "Indians as Consumers in the Eighteenth Century," in *Old Trails and New Directions: Papers of the Third North American Fur Trade Conference*, ed. Carol M. Judd and Arthur J. Ray (Toronto, 1980), 255–71; W. J. Eccles, "A Belated Review of Harold Adams Innis, *The Fur Trade in Canada*," *Canadian Historical Review* 60 (1979):427–34.

28 Mémoire ou Extrait du Journal Sommaire du Voyage de Jacques Legardeur Ecuyer Sr de St. Pierre . . . chargé de la Descouverte de la Mer de l'Ouest, Archs. Sém. Québec, Fonds Verreau, boîte 5, no. 54.

29 The population figures for these settlements are revealing: Detroit in 1750, 483; Illinois in 1752, 1,536; lower Louisiana in 1746, 4,100.

30 Denonville et Champigny au ministre, 6 November 1688, C11A, vol. 10, f. 8, and le ministre à Denonville, 8 January 1688, B, vol. 15, f. 20.

31 Similarly the Iroquois specifically rejected British claims that they were subjects of the British Crown: see Acte authentique des six nations iroquoises sur leur indépendance (2 November 1748), *Rapport de l'Archiviste*, 1921–2, unnum. plate following p. 108.

32 D'Iberville au ministre, 26 February 1700, C13A, vol. 1, f. 236; Pièces détachées judiciares 1720, Archs. Québec (Mtl.); Vaudreuil à Beauharnois, 9 November 1745, Henry E. Huntington Library,

San Marino, Calif., London Collection; Ordonnance de Beauharnois, 8 June 1743, Archs. Sém. Québec, Fonds Verreau, boîte 8, no. 96; Duquesne à Contrecoeur, 12 June 1753, boîte 1, no. 19; Duquesne à Contrecoeur, 24 June 1754, Fernand Grenier, ed., *Papiers Contrecoeur et autres documents concernant le conflit anglo-français sur l'Ohio de 1745 à 1756* (Québec, 1952), 193.

33 On this controversial issue, see Ray, "Indians as Consumers," in Judd and Ray, *Old Trails and New Directions*, 255–71, and Eccles, "Belated Review of Innis," 419–41.

34 Rich, *Hudson's Bay Company*, 1:545.

35 Calvin Martin, *Keepers of the Game: Indian-Animal Relationships and the Fur Trade* (Berkeley, Calif., 1978), 63–4; André Vachon, "L'eau de vie dans la société indienne," Canadian Historical Association, *Report* (1960) 22–32.

36 Ray, "Indians as Consumers," *Directions*, 255–71.

37 Arthur S. Morton, ed., *The Journal of Duncan M'Gillivray of the North West Company at Fort George on the Saskatchewan, 1794–5* (Toronto, 1929), 47.

38 Beauharnois et Hocquart au ministre, 12 October 1736, C11A, vol. 65, ff. 49–51; Observation de la Conseil de la Marine, 1 June 1718, C11A, vol. 39, ff. 242–6. See also Reuben Gold Thwaites, ed., *The Jesuit Relations and Allied Documents: Travels and Explorations of the Jesuit Missionaries in New France, 1610–1791* (Cleveland, Ohio, 1896–1901), *passim*.

39 Eccles, *Frontenac*, 66.

40 For a brief overview of this contentious issue, see Eccles, *Frontenac*, 61–8.

41 Peter Schuyler to Gov. Dongan, 2 September 1687, E. B. O'Callaghan et al., eds, *Documents relative to the Colonial History of the State of New-York* . . . (Albany, NY, 1856–87), 3:479, hereafter cited as *NY Col. Docs.*; Propositions made by four of the Chief Sachems of the 5 Nations to his Excell. Benjamin Fletcher . . . in Albany, 26 February 1692/3, *NY Col. Docs.* 4:24; 27 December 1698, Peter Wraxall, *An Abridgement of the Indian Affairs . . . Transacted in the Colony of New York, from the Year 1678 to the Year 1751*, ed. Charles Howard McIlwain (Cambridge, Mass., 1915), 31; Relation de ce qui s'est passé de plus remarquable en Canada . . . 1695, F3 Moreau de Saint-Méry, vol. 7, ff. 370–2, Archs. Nationales; Vaudreuil au ministre, 25 October 1710, *Rapport de l'Archiviste*, 1946–7, 385; Vaudreuil et Bégon au ministre, 20 September 1714, *Rapport de l'Archiviste*, 1947–8, 275–6; Beauharnois et Hocquart au ministre, 12 October 1736, C11A, vol. 65, ff. 44–6.

42 Eccles, "Belated Review of Innis," 434.

43 Thomas Eliot Norton, *The Fur Trade in Colonial New York, 1686–1776* (Madison, Wisc., 1974), 100–3, 122, 124.

44 Jean Lunn, "The Illegal Fur Trade out of New France, 1713–1760," Canadian Hist. Assn., *Report* (1939), 61–76; Wraxall, *New York Indian Records*, ed. McIlwain, *passim*.

45 Le Ch^{er} Dailleboust à Madame d'Argenteuil, 5 January 1715,

Université de Montréal, Montréal, Que., Collection Baby, g. 1/12; Ordonnance de Gilles Hocquart, 25 April 1738, C11A, vol. 69, ff. 180–3; Pierre-Georges Roy, ed., *Inventaire des Ordonnances des Intendants de la Nouvelle-France, conservées aux Archives provinciales de Québec* 1 (Beauceville, Que., 1919), 160–1, 222; J. W. De Peyster à Jean Lidius, 23 September 1729, Archs. Québec (Mtl.), NF 13–17, Procédures judiciares, III, ff. 389–93; Myndert Schuyler à Jean Lidius, 15 October 1729, NF 13–17, Procédures judiciares, III, ff. 389–93; Extrait des Registres du Conseil Supérieur de Québec, 28 September 1730, NF 13–17, Procédures judiciares, III, ff. 385–8.

46 Lunn, "Illegal Fur Trade," Canadian Hist. Assn., *Report* (1939), 61–76.

47 Vaudreuil et Bégon au ministre, 12 November 1712, *Rapport de l'Archiviste*, 1947–8, 183–4; Mémoire du Roy pour servir d'instructions au Sieur marquis de Beauharnois, gouverneur et lieutenant-genéral de la Nouvelle-France, 7 May 1726, *Nouvelle-France. Documents historiques*, 1:57; Report of Messrs. Schuyler and Dellius' Negotiations in Canada, 2 July 1698, *NY Col. Docs.*, 4:347; Bellomont to Council of Trade and Plantations, 24 August 1699, Sainsbury et al., *Calendar of State Papers*, 17:406.

48 Beauharnois to Maurepas, 21 September 1741, *NY Col. Docs.*, 9:1071.

49 Arthur H. Buffinton, "The Policy of Albany and English Westward Expansion," *Mississippi Valley Historical Review* 8 (1922):327–66.

50 For contemporary British comment on the superior skills of the Canadian traders, see *American Gazetteer . . .* (London, 1762), *s.v.* "Montreal": "The French have found some secret of conciliating the affections of the savages, which our traders seem stranger to, or at least take no care to put it in practice." See also Burpee, "Journal of Anthony Hendry," 307.

51 Johnson to the Lords of Trade, 16 November 1765, Public Record Office, CO 5/66, f. 296. I am indebted to Dr Francis P. Jennings for providing me with this piece of evidence.

52 For a specific instance of this, see David M. Hayne, ed., *Dictionary of Canadian Biography* (Toronto, 1969), *s.v.* "Teganissoreus."

53 Wraxall, *New York Indian Records*, ed. McIlwain, 111.

54 Zoltvany, *Philippe de Rigaud de Vaudreuil*, 169–9; Wraxall, *New York Indian Records*, ed. McIlwain, 132–5.

55 Percy J. Robinson, *Toronto during the French Régime: A History of the Toronto Region from Brulé to Simcoe, 1615–1793*, 2d edn (Toronto, 1965), 66.

56 Wraxall, *New York Indian Records*, ed. McIlwain, 161.

57 Wraxall, *New York Indian Records*, ed. McIlwain, 161.

58 Mémoire touchant le droit françois sur les Nations Iroquoises, 12 November 1712, C11A, vol. 33, f. 284. The Iroquois admitted to the Albany commissioners that the French had 5 posts on the south side of Lake Ontario, from Niagara to Cayouhage, east of Oswego. See 10 September 1720, Wraxall, *New York Indian Records*, ed. McIlwain, 130–1.

59 On Anglo-French relations at this time, see Paul Vaucher, *Robert Walpole et la politique de Fleury (1713–1742)* (Paris, 1924).

60 Zoltvany, *Philippe de Rigaud de Vaudreuil*, 199.

61 Wraxall, *New York Indian Records*, ed. McIlwain, 111, 113; Charles Thomson, *An Enquiry into the Causes of the Alienation of the Delaware and Shawanese Indians from the British Interest* . . . (London, 1759), 56, 76, 114, 118–22; Wilbur R. Jacobs, ed., *The Appalachian Indian Frontier: The Edmond Atkin Report and Plan of 1755* (Columbia, SC, 1954), *passim*.

62 Duquesne à Contrecoeur, 30 April 1753, Archs. Sém. Québec, 30 Fonds Verreau, boîte 1, no. 13.

63 14 March 1721, 25 April 1726, Roy, *Inventaire des Ordonnances des Intendants*, 1:196, 282; Hocquart au ministre, 25 October 1729, C11A, vol. 51, f. 264; Vaudreuil, Beauharnois, et Raudot au ministre, 19 October 1705, *Rapport de l'Archiviste*, 1938–9, 87–8.

64 Mémoire sur les postes de Canada . . . en 1754 . . . , *Rapport de l'Archiviste*, 1927–8, 353.

65 Extrait Général des Reveues des Compagnies Entretenues en la Nouvelle-France . . . 1750, Archs. Nationales, D2C, vol. 48, f. 130.

66 Many of the *voyageurs* hired to serve in the west had notarized contracts, a copy of which had to be preserved in an official register by the notary. Unfortunately, many *voyageurs* were instead hired *sous seing privé*, that is, with a written contract not drawn up by a notary. A few of the latter type of contract have survived by accident or because they were submitted as evidence in legal proceedings. Many men may well have been hired with a mere verbal understanding of the terms of service. Statistical studies based on the notarized contracts alone therefore cannot help but be misleading since there is no way of knowing what proportion of the total number of *voyageurs* employed in any given year the contracts represent: see Gratien Allaire, "Les engagements pour la traite des fourrures, évaluation de la documentation," *Revue d'histoire de l'Amérique française* 34 (1980):3–26.

67 W. J. Eccles, *France in America* (New York, 1972), 178–9.

68 La Chauvignery à [Contrecoeur], 10 February 1754, Archs. Sém. Québec, Fonds Verreau, boîte 1, no. 77.

69 As early as 1708 François Clairambault d'Aigremont, sent to investigate conditions in the west, stated in a momentous report to the minister that the French could not take enough precautions to conserve the trade north of Lake Superior, since the furs at Detroit and those of the region to the south were not worth much. The reluctance of the Canadian fur traders to engage in trade in the Ohio country is made plain in governor-general Duquesne's correspondence with Claude-Pierre Pécaudy de Contrecoeur, commandant at Fort Duquesne. Le Sr Daigremont au Ministre Pontchartrain, 14 November 1708, C11A, vol. 29, f. 175; Grenier, *Papiers Contrecoeur*, 126, 128, 209, 224, 248–9, 253.

70 Galissonière au ministre, 1 September 1748, C11A, vol. 91, ff. 116–22.

71 Donald H. Kent, *The French Invasion of Western Pennsylvania, 1753* (Harrisburg, Pa, 1954), 12; Sylvester K. Stevens and Donald H. Kent, eds, *Wilderness Chronicles of Northwestern Pennsylvania . . .* (Harrisburg, Pa, 1941), 56; Duquesne à Contrecoeur, 8 September 1754, Grenier, *Papiers Contrecoeur*, 250; Duquesne à Rouillé, 31 November (*sic*) 1753, C11A, vol. 99, ff. 139–43; Duquesne à Rouillé, 29 September 1754, C11A, vol. 99, ff. 242–3; Duquesne à Rouillé, C11A, vol. 99, f. 259.

72 By October 1753, of over 2,000 men who had left Montreal the previous spring and summer only 880 were fit for service: Duquesne à Marin, 16 November 1753, Grenier, *Papiers Contrecoeur*, 81; Ministre à Duquesne, 31 May 1754, B, vol. 99, f. 199; Kent, *French Invasion*, 64.

73 Duquesne à Contrecoeur, 1 July 1754, Grenier, *Papiers Contrecoeur*, 207–8.

74 In April 1754 Capitaine de Contrecoeur warned the Indians who were trading with the English at their post on the Ohio that he intended to drive the English out. If the Indians chose to support the enemy, they too would be crushed; it was up to them to decide whether or not they wished to be destroyed. Paroles de Contrecoeur aux Sauvages, Grenier, *Papiers Contrecoeur*, 116–17. See also Duquesne à Contrecoeur, 15 April 1754, Grenier, *Papiers Contrecoeur*, 113–16.

75 Duquesne à Contrecoeur, 14 August, Grenier, *Papiers Contrecoeur*, 248; Duquesne to the minister, 31 October 1754, *NY Col. Docs.*, 10:269; Thomas Pownall, cited in Louis De Vorsey, Jr, *The Indian Boundary in the Southern Colonies, 1763–1775* (Chapel Hill, NC, 1961), 56–7.

76 Thomson, *Enquiry into the Causes, passim*; Journal de Chaussegros de Léry, *Rapport de l'Archiviste*, 1927–8, 409–10.

77 For French and British casualties, see Grenier, *Papiers Contrecoeur*, 390–1.

78 Ministre à Duquesne, 31 May 1754, B, vol. 99, f. 199.

79 Vaudreuil au ministre, 13 October 1756, C11A, vol. 101, ff. 117–19.

80 Duquesne à Marin, 20 June, 10 July 1753, Archs. Sém. Québec, Fonds Verreau, boîte 5, nos. 62, 66:6; Duquesne à Contrecoeur, 22 July, 6 August 1753, boîte 1, nos. 27, 28; Varin à Contrecoeur, 18 August 1753, boîte 5, no. 311.

81 Mémoire sur les sauvages du Canada jusqu'à la Rivière de Mississippi . . . Donné par M. de Sabrevois en 1718, C11A, vol. 39, f. 354; Varin à Contrecoeur, 17 May, 1 June, 26 July 1753, Archs. Sém. Québec, Fonds Verreau, boîte 4, nos. 501, 502, 307; Varin à de la Perrière, 21 October 1754, boîte 8, no. 78; Contrecoeur à Douville, 14 April 1755, Grenier, *Papiers Contrecoeur*, 310–11.

82 Duplessis Faber à Lavalterie, 16 April 1756, BABY, no. 137; Péan à Contrecoeur, 15 June 1754, Archs. Sém. Québec, Fonds Verreau, boîte 1, no. 80; Varin à Contrecoeur, 4 February 1753, boîte 1, no. 294; Varin à (?), 10 May 1753, boîte 1, no. 300; Contrecoeur à Douville, 14 April 1755, Grenier, *Papiers Contrecoeur*, 310; La

Perrière à Contrecoeur, 20 April 1755, Grenier, *Papiers Contrecoeur*, 321; Benoist à Contrecoeur, 30 June 1755, Grenier, *Papiers Contrecoeur*, 370–3; Saint-Blin à Contrecoeur, au for [sic] de la riviere au beouf [sic] le 3 juilietts [sic] 1755, Grenier, *Papiers Contrecoeur*, 374–5; Journal de Joseph-Gaspard Chaussegros de Léry, 1754–5, *Rapport de l'Archiviste*, 1927–8, 385.

83 Vaudreuil au ministre, 13 October 1756, C11A, vol. 101, ff. 117–19.

84 Thomson, *Enquiry into the Causes*, 108–14.

85 Thomson, *Enquiry into the Causes*, 138–60.

86 Niles Anderson, "The General Chooses a Road," *Western Pennsylvania Historical Magazine* 42 (1959), 138, 249, quotation on p. 396.

87 Lee Kennett, *The French Armies in the Seven Years' War: A Study in Military Organization and Administration* (Durham, NC, 1967), 3–13.

88 H. Carré acidly remarked, in describing the chaos that reigned in the Ministry of Marine, "enfin le lieutenant de police Berryer, sous l'administration duquel s'effondra la marine. A la fin, il suspendit les travaux des ports et vendit à des particuliers le matériel des arsenaux. Choiseul, son successeur, relèvera la marine, mais trop tard pour le succés de la guerre engagée" (*La Règne de Louis XV (1715–1774)*, in Ernest Lavisse, ed., *Histoire de France . . .* 8, pt. 2 (Paris, 1909), 272).

89 W. J. Eccles, *The Battle of Quebec: A Reappraisal*, French Colonial Historical Society, Proceedings of the Third Annual Meeting (Athens, Ga, 1978), 70–81.

90 28 December 1758, C11A, vol. 103, ff. 453–5; Guy Frégault, *La Guerre de la conquête* (Montreal, 1955), 365–72.

91 Mémoire du duc de Choiseul, December 1759, Paris, Bibliothèque Nationale, MS nouv. acq. 1041, ff. 44–63.

92 One interesting aspect of this attitude, as manifested in New England, is discussed in F. W. Anderson, "Why Did Colonial New Englanders Make Bad Soldiers? Contractual Principles and Military Conduct during the Seven Years' War," *William and Mary Quarterly*, 3d ser., 38 (1981):395–417.

93 Rich, *Fur Trade and the Northwest*, 115, and *Hudson's Bay Company*, 1:554, 572, 575–86.

94 Beauharnois au ministre, 17 October 1736, C11A, vol. 65, f. 143.

95 Public Archives of Canada, MG7, 1, A–Z fonds français, MS 12105, Mémoire de La Maire 1717, f. 83.

96 Conférence avec les Onondagués et Onneiouts, 28 July 1756, and Conférence, 21 December 1756, C11A, vol. 101, ff. 55–61, 263.

Part III

TRANSITIONS
*c.*1770–1888

9

THE END OF THE OLD ATLANTIC WORLD: AMERICA, AFRICA, EUROPE, 1770–1888

J. R. McNeill

A series of dramatic events and sweeping changes created the Atlantic world in the sixteenth century. That world slowly unraveled between 1770 and 1888, as the constituent societies reorganized themselves with different linkages. Connections that had mattered greatly in the seventeenth or eighteenth century dwindled into insignificance by the end of the nineteenth.

From 1492 to 1770 Atlantic America and much of Atlantic Africa and Atlantic Europe participated in economic systems based upon seaborne trade and, to a very large extent, slave labor. By 1888 all this had changed: the rise of the United States of America had altered the patterns of Atlantic commerce; land-based trade and transport reduced the relative importance of sea links; and slavery and the slave trade were abolished, almost severing the links between Africa and America. In 1770 the old colonial systems of the Atlantic world remained intact; by 1888 European formal empires had all but disappeared from the Americas, while newer versions were soon to establish themselves in Africa. Only the century after Columbus saw shifts in the Atlantic world as great as those in the century after 1770.

The end of the Atlantic world proceeded from many causes. Some were slow social movements, comprehensible only in retrospect; others were events as dramatic as those of the age of the conquistadors. Here the causes will be presented in 3 main categories: (1) demographic and ecological changes; (2) economic and geographic changes; and (3) sociopolitical and geopolitical changes. As in the sixteenth-century opening of the Atlantic world, many of these transitions fed upon, deepened, and extended one another, to the point where their cumulative effect may fairly be called revolutionary. In examining these intertwined currents, one theme will rise to the surface time and again: the increasing importance of land transport in defining (social, economic, political) communities of people, and the decreasing role of sea links. The Portuguese caravel opened the Atlantic world, and the railroad closed it.

I

The demographic and ecological changes that contributed to the closing of the Atlantic world look small and slow compared to the upheavals of the sixteenth century that Crosby described. Certainly they are less conspicuous. Taking the anthropocentric point of view rather than a fully ecological one, the key trends to observe are population growth through natural increase, and currents of migration.

Around the Atlantic basin, as around most of the globe, population grew steadily after 1770. The basic reasons were much the same everywhere. Epidemic disease took a smaller and smaller toll, in the Atlantic as elsewhere, because the speed and volume of human interaction had grown to the point where few populations entirely lacked the portfolio of immunities necessary for survival in the face of infection. Henceforth, individuals who moved from one disease environment to another did so at great risk, as had always been the case, but those who stayed put, if they survived childhood, stood a much better chance of living a long (and reproductive) life than did people in the sixteenth century. Thus mortality remained high, for example, among strangers visiting tropical America, as they were entering a new disease environment, one of the most lethal on the planet. But lifespans lengthened among the settled peoples of Atlantic Europe, Atlantic America (with some exceptions), and, probably – there are no data – Atlantic Africa, contributing strongly to rapid population growth.

The second basic reason for the Atlantic world's rapid population growth was the effects of the Columbian exchange of food crops. This exchange, of course, began in the fifteenth century, but in many cases, especially in Europe and Africa, it took generations for new crops to catch on. The potato and maize, for example, acquired demographic importance only long after their introduction to Europe. Eventually (by the late eighteenth century) the potato had begun to support growing numbers of people in Northern Europe, while maize did the same in Southern Europe. Together these crops permitted greater population densities than ever before from Ireland to Portugal, and many places in between.[1] In Atlantic Africa, maize, peanuts, and cassava boosted yields and agricultural production, and presumably population, in the savanna and forest zones from Senegal to Angola.[2] The reduction of the slave trade (after 1850) may also have contributed to population growth in Atlantic Africa, although great controversy surrounds the question of the demographic impact on Africa of the slave trade.[3] In the Americas too a broader distribution of native and imported crops (and animals) allowed a better fit between environment and agriculture, improving the food supply to people from Argentina to Newfoundland – except perhaps, in those sugar monoculture zones of tropical America, where food production was restricted in order to maximize the harvests of sugar cane.

In North America population growth came fastest among those of European or African descent; the Amerindian populations continued to suffer from alien diseases and from the continued loss of the lands by which they had garnered their livelihoods. Whereas in Atlantic Europe and Africa the Columbian exchange supplemented existing agricultural systems, with effects that told very strongly afer 1770, in North America one set of systems of human ecology, and a set of human populations, by and large replaced another. Agriculture was Europeanized and, in cases such as South Carolina rice, Africanized. This process was by no means a full substitution: native American crops (particularly maize) and methods (particularly shifting cultivation) were widely adopted by Europeans upon arrival in the Americas. In any case, whatever the proportions between indigenous and imported crops and practices, agriculture in the Americas grew increasingly efficient over ever-greater spaces after 1770, permitting denser settlement and greater population.

Such transformations in human ecology, with their demographic consequences, spread very unevenly in the Americas. The process leapt the Appalachians in the eighteenth century, and by 1880 had reached the Rockies and (by sea) California and British Columbia. In Central and South America the same pattern of ecological replacement tempered by agricultural borrowing existed in some places (notably Argentina and southern Brazil), but not, by 1888, on anything like the scale of North America. Hence, in part, the slower pace of natural increase among people of European and African descent in South than in North America. Instead, population growth derived in much larger part from the demographic resurgence of Amerindians – and the emergence and expansion of mestizos and other groups of mixed descent. In highland regions such as Central Mexico and much of Central America, Amerindian populations had survived the repeated onslaughts of Old World diseases. Numbers ceased to decline somewhere about 1650, and then slowly began to grow, as populations painfully acquired disease immunities. By 1770, Amerindian numbers were growing everywhere in tropical America; by 1888 the population of Mexico and Central America approached the levels of 1519.

The natural increase in population around the Atlantic basin represents a fundamentally new ecological situation established after the disruptions of the sixteenth century. New synergies developed among crops, animals, microbes, and human beings, permitting more efficient human domination of local environments and food chains. This situation has endured to the present, allowing more or less steady demographic growth around the Atlantic – although other circumstances soon led to even faster growth elsewhere.

Population growth came fastest in the temperate zones of North America. This had to do partly with the less hostile disease environment (colder weather permits fewer microorganisms), and partly with the slave regime of the tropics, where many factors converged to suppress birth rates and raise death rates. It had to do as well with the easy availability of land, which promoted earlier marriage and larger families in temperate America than in more crowded Atlantic Europe. It also had to do with currents of migration after 1770.

Three streams of migration fed population growth in the Americas after 1770. Two large ones, the first voluntary and the second forced, came from Europe and Africa; the third, much smaller, came from Asia. To some degree, these currents contributed to population growth in the Atlantic basin as a whole, because although only the smaller one brought people in from well outside the Atlantic, the largest, that from Europe, put people in circumstances where they preferred large families to small ones. The African current put people in circumstances where family life was difficult and children few. Cumulatively, the transatlantic migrations from Europe and Africa probably accelerated natural increase in the Atlantic world as a whole, but not by much.

The Atlantic slave trade reached its height shortly after 1770. Its peak decade was the 1780s, but it flourished from 1720 to 1850, and constituted one of the sinews of the Atlantic world. The slave trade to the British and French Caribbean declined sharply with its legal abolition in the British Empire in 1807 and in the French in 1815; only a small, clandestine trade remained. But new destinations took the place of the French and British Caribbean. More and more slaves went to the mining districts and coffee plantations of southern Brazil and the sugar plantations of Cuba. Similarly, traditional sources of the supply of slaves sometimes closed down because of local depopulation or the interventions of African states or the British Royal Navy, but slavers opened up new frontiers, especially in Angola. By the 1820s slaving expanded quickly into Madagascar and Mozambique (outside of Atlantic Africa), an indication of the inability of Atlantic African supply to match Atlantic American demand. Many of the old slave sources on the West African coast remained in business, if considerably diminished, until the 1880s. Perhaps one-half of the roughly 10–11 million slaves transported from Africa to the Americas made the voyage after 1770.[4]

The second major current came from Atlantic Europe. Portugal, Spain, and France provided rather few migrants, although after 1840 parts of Portugal and Spain began to send more sons (fewer daughters) to South America and the Spanish Caribbean. The majority of migrants came from Britain, Ireland, and Germany, where population pressure and inheritance patterns generated a large contingent of people with poor prospects in life and acute vulnerability to any economic disruption. North America was the answer for many. Migrant numbers, while growing, remained small until the 1840s, when the potato crop failed in Ireland, leading to mass starvation and the emigration of millions to Britain, to British colonies (chiefly Canada), and to the United States. Almost simultaneously, German emigration surged, as depression in agriculture and handicrafts provoked a torrent, and failed revolutions (1848) produced an additional trickle of refugees. These were the first great pulses of modern European migration to America. Later, after 1880, a Caucasian tidal wave of more than 50 million people would transform the size and composition of North American population. This wave broke over Argentina and southern Brazil as well, where Italian immigrants replaced slave labor on coffee plantations. But all this was still to come: only the first ripples had reached the Americas in 1888.

The smaller current of migration to Atlantic America brought people from afar. In a sense it was a renewal of an ancient migration, the one that had peopled the Americas in the first place: it came from Asia. It added to the total population of the Atlantic world directly, albeit modestly, unlike the larger currents from Africa and Europe. Hundreds of thousands of East and South Asians were transported to the American tropics in the nineteenth century, generally as replacements for the reduced numbers of imported African slaves. They worked in mines and on plantations (and in canal and railroad construction) in Cuba, Trinidad, Guyana, Panama, and many parts of Pacific America, from Chile to British Columbia. As immigrants to a sharply different disease environment from that which they had known in China or India, they suffered greatly from disease in the Americas, as well as from labor conditions that did not differ too greatly from slavery. This current of migration, like that from Europe, grew notably after 1880, and came to include Filipinos, Japanese, and others, in addition to Chinese and Indians.

These three migration currents strongly affected the racial and ethnic composition of the population of Atlantic America. Until 1820 the cumulative volume of African migration exceeded that from Europe by about four or five to one. Only in the 1880s did the sum of European migrants since 1492 equal and then overtake the total number of Africans introduced into the Americas.[5] Europeans dominated demographically in Atlantic America because their rates of natural increase were much higher, a function of their concentration in favored zones and the forced concentration of Africans in zones where natural decrease prevailed.[6] Taking Atlantic America as a whole, at the moment of abolition (1834–88) Blacks acquired their freedom just as the Caucasian tidal wave was about to hit, and Blacks would become, increasingly, a minority population in the hemisphere. This irony was invisible to most freed slaves, however, as in much of Atlantic America – northeast Brazil and most of the Caribbean islands, for example – local black majorities remained through slavery and abolition.

In addition to its effect on the composition of American populations, the growth and migration of the century after 1770 fueled the westward surge of Atlantic America. From Canada to Brazil, populations began to spill over natural boundaries into the broad interiors of the North and South American continents, displacing the remaining Amerindians. Eventually this process would create large countries, help to create national markets, and bring about many other circumstances that remain in place today. In this sense, demographic and ecological change underlay the economic and political transitions of 1770–1888.

II

The economic and geographic shifts of the century after 1770 were huge. They consisted of economic growth, at considerably faster rates even than the demographic expansion, and a clear reorientation away from the Atlantic and toward the continental interiors.

With population growth came a corresponding expansion in nearly every economic activity in the Atlantic world. The extractive industries – mining, timber, fishing, whaling, fur – all spread territorially and most (not the fur trade) intensified as well. In some cases, resource depletion propelled extractive frontiers inland: the fur trade is perhaps the best example. New technologies, especially in mining, led to the exploitation of new resources. Coal, for instance, became more useful after the advent of steam engines, and consequently was mined far and wide in Atlantic Europe and America. The quest for more precious metals and useful ores helped to push Atlantic economies inward toward richer deposits: westward in North America, and eastward in Europe. The timber industry also pushed inland in North America, as good tall timber near the coast grew scarce. By the 1880s the great north woods of

Michigan, Wisconsin, and Minnesota (and Ontario) were the center of the lumber business. Whaling and fishing remained anchored in Atlantic ports, although the sphere of operations by the 1840s extended from the Arctic to the Pacific South Seas.

Part of the impetus for the intensification of extractive economies came from industrialization. It amounted to a basic transformation of parts of the Atlantic world, and contributed to the ending of it. Industrialization, the application of machine power to production, began in Britain. It spread in fits and starts to favored locations in Europe and North America. Its success depended on certain geographic and sociopolitical circumstances. Its first requirements were accessible sources of energy (first water power, then coal) and, for heavy industry, appropriate metals. But industrialization also needed accessible funds for capital investment and a ready supply of labor. Only in a few places could all these (and some other) conditions be met. Where they could, fast and fundamental changes took place, building up a local or regional productive economy that often had worldwide reach in marketing. The basic ingredients of production for European or North American factories normally did not come from the perimeters of the Atlantic world, but from nearby: coal and ore were too bulky, and thus too costly, to ship long distances before the 1880s. (Cotton, essential for light industry, was the great exception. But after 1861, Britain came to depend much less on American cotton.) Labor also generally came from nearby villages. Capital, to be sure, was more mobile, and British capital did migrate across the Atlantic throughout the nineteenth century. But with industrialization, the importance of the Americas to Europe declined.

The goods the factories made were sold far and wide. In Britain especially, they spearheaded a strong export economy in the nineteenth century, one which extended to continental Europe, Asia, Africa, and the Americas. In marketing, the transatlantic connection was only one of many links between the factories and consumers. Thus the economic and social transformation that we call industrialization contributed to the geographic reorientation away from the Atlantic. The key economic linkages for industrial centers became at once more local and more global, and the intermediate economic community of the Atlantic world faded.

The largest expansion in the economies of Atlantic lands came in agriculture. Here the Americas greatly outstripped Atlantic Europe, where agriculture entered a long depression in the 1840s, chiefly on account of effective competition from North America. Europeanized agriculture (using some indigenous American crops) reached into the US and Canadian prairies by the mid-nineteenth century. These lands had been exploited mainly as hunting-grounds by the Amerindians of the plains, and now began to support larger populations of settlers. Similar expansions of agriculture took place in the Argentine Pampas and the backlands of Brazil, accompanied, as in North America, by campaigns to drive out (or exterminate) the remaining Amerindians. In many cases population growth (partly from immigration) drove these agricultural expansions. But often the construction of canals and then railroads made commercial agriculture practical in the deep interiors of the American continents. Indeed some of this tilt toward the continental interiors involved the most thoroughly commercial agriculture in existence: the plantation. Brazilian coffee and US cotton forged westward, linked to the coasts and the Atlantic economy by rails. Argentine wheat, late in the century, while not a plantation crop, was also grown primarily for Atlantic markets, and not for local subsistence. The same is true of the wheat frontier in Minnesota and the Dakotas. Without the new transport links (canals, rails, and steamships), agricultural expansion in the Americas would have proceeded at a pace dictated by subsistence needs rather than market opportunities, which is to say, much more slowly. Coffee and cotton would scarcely have expanded at all without the impetus of distant markets. Sugar played no role in this westward push, as for ecological and economic reasons it was confined to coastal lowlands.[7]

The surge in American agriculture lasted throughout the nineteenth century. It led to hard times in rural Europe, because American producers of wheat enjoyed many advantages (better soils, larger scale of operations) which allowed their grain to sell for less in European cities once rails and steamships lowered transport times and costs. Cheaper grain benefited European city-dwellers but hurt peasants (and some landlords). Millions of peasants in Germany, Scandinavia, and the British Isles gave up at home and moved to the American plains and prairies, accelerating the wheat expansion that would deepen the crisis that beset their cousins who stayed behind.[8]

It is hard to discern any clear trend in agriculture in Atlantic Africa between 1770 and 1888. Africa did not produce food crops for transoceanic export on any scale, nor did imports from the Americas have any strong impact. The spread of American crops, with their higher yields, probably mitigated any need to expand agriculture territorially into continental interiors. And the slower pace of development in transport and market networks meant that food production was tied much more closely to the rate of population growth in Africa – and that rate, while unknown, was probably modest. Other crops with industrial applications, such as palm oil in the Niger delta, did expand after the mid-nineteenth century. But such crops were few in number, export volumes remained small, and their total effect upon African agriculture appears minuscule. In the absence of clear evidence, it is probably best to conclude that before 1880 the tumultuous and intertwined agricultural history of Europe and the Americas had no parallel, and very little impact, in Atlantic Africa.

The new transport networks, while pushing centers of production toward the continental interiors in Europe and the Americas, helped boost transatlantic trade. Gradually greater and greater traffic, cheaper and cheaper transport, and more and better economic information circulated around the Atlantic, so that large parts of the basin functioned as a more efficient economic unit than ever before. This worked to the advantage of the best-informed and most flexible traders and producers, who could adjust prices and products in light of information about distant markets. Initially, Atlantic Europeans profited most from this integration of the Atlantic economy, while Atlantic Africans probably profited least. But as early as the 1770s merchant groups in the Americas, especially in New England and Philadelphia, but also in Bahia and Havana, could compete successfully with their rivals in Europe. As they did so, they began to develop inter-American trade, which was illegal in the days of the European empires, but nonetheless widespread. With the independence of the United States and subsequently most of Spanish America, this trade became (in most cases) legal and grew conspicuously. As the United States developed in size and sophistication, its traders began to supplant those of Europe in their connections with the Caribbean, Central America, and Canada.

At the same time some West African traders managed to amass considerable fortunes, first through the slave trade, but later, as that dwindled, through so-called legitimate trade in palm oil, fibers, and a welter of other goods (many of which, ironically, were produced by slave labor). The success of West African traders is partially obscured to us because they generally did not leave behind archives detailing their achievements, or monumental buildings of the sort that attest to the prosperity of merchants, many of them slave traders, in Liverpool, Nantes, Boston, or Vera Cruz. Rich Africans preferred to express their wealth in terms of people – retainers, dependants, slaves, large extended families – rather than in terms of fixed property. With the decline of the slave trade and the rise of legitimate trade, West Africa did business more and more with Europe and less and less with the Americas.

The general quickening of trade in the Atlantic world produced a range of economic repercussions. It put far larger market areas in touch with the most efficient producers, including those of industrializing Britain. Initially this led to much hardship, as less efficient producers were undercut. This happened to European farmers, to African ironsmiths, and to spinners and weavers everywhere outside the British factory system. Consumers soon came to enjoy cheaper goods and sometimes broader choice – the usual advantages of specialization and trade. At the same time they became vulnerable to interruptions of trade, as they came to depend increasingly on distant production.

More fundamentally, this quickening of trade helped to develop national markets in the large countries of the Americas, especially the United States. The early political independence of American countries helped in this regard: national markets never develop in colonies. A big and fast-growing national market in the United States encouraged larger and larger production runs and permitted ever greater economies of scale. By 1890 the United States was the largest agricultural producer in the Atlantic world and the foremost industrial country in the entire world.[9]

The key to the rise of the United States was the economic integration of large spaces, made possible by improvements in transport infrastructure and in the organization of markets. To an extent parallel processes had begun in other large countries of the Americas, chiefly Canada (a set of colonies until 1867) and Argentina. This integration of larger economic spaces involved a tilt toward the interior in every case: inland population grew faster than did that of the coasts throughout the nineteenth century, and centers of wealth also sprang up wherever a rich hinterland could be linked to national (and transatlantic) markets. The construction of canals and railroads gave rise to Chicago, Cleveland, Córdoba (Argentina), and many other fast-growing cities that, together with the coastal ports (New York, Baltimore, Buenos Aires) organized the integration of the continental interiors into national (and international) economies.

This tilt toward the interior took place to a lesser degree in Europe and Africa. Canals and railroads improved the efficiency of inland transport in Atlantic Europe, and assisted in the conspicuous rise of regions such as the Ruhr and Alsace-Lorraine, or the British Midlands. Industry developed wherever coal and iron ore could be brought together. In France the effects are easy to see: the great buildings of the Atlantic ports (Bordeaux, Nantes, Saint Malo) date from the eighteenth century; those of eastern France (Nancy, Metz) from the nineteenth. The economic center of gravity of all Europe moved to the eastward, with the rise of Germany and the (relative) decline of the Atlantic countries.

In Africa canals and railroads came by and large only after 1888, although some were built in French Algeria and British South Africa well before that. Nowhere in Africa did railroads promote the economic integration of African regions: instead they were built to assist in the export of African commodities to Europe. Their effect, therefore, was sharply different from the impact of railroads in the United States. In Africa too, however, the economic center of gravity began to shift inland as the nineteenth century wore on. Coastal peoples, in their interaction with the wider world, had acquired skills and technologies that their neighbors often lacked. They did not hesitate to use their increased economic and military formidability against their inland neighbors, extending, for example, the slave trade and other extractive pursuits several hundred kilometers inland. Eventually Africans set up plantations in places where a rich hinterland could be linked to large markets, just as in the Americas at the same time. With the decline of the transatlantic slave trade, more and more African slaves worked mines and plantations in Africa instead of those in the Americas. Whereas unfortunate European peasants now crossed the Atlantic in unprecedented numbers, unfortunate African slaves increasingly stayed in Africa as slavery there extended its domain. At the time of slavery's abolition in the Sokoto Caliphate (northern Nigeria), a quarter of the population of about 10 million was enslaved. This makes Sokoto one of the major slaveholding societies in the Atlantic world, along with the United States (4 million slaves at abolition) and Brazil (1.5 million). Altogether there were many million slaves in West Africa by the end of the nineteenth century; some societies, such as Dahomey and Ashanti in the forest zone, and Sokoto in the Sudanic belt, developed plantation agriculture.[10] (It should be understood that African slavery is a loose category including many different shades of dependence and obligation, and many different labor regimes. African slavery was sufficiently distinct from the so-called "chattel slavery" of the Americas that many historians prefer other terms, such as "servile persons" or "conscripted dependants" instead of "slaves.")[11]

In the nineteenth century Africans also created new empires in the interior reaches of the continent. Africans (especially West Africans), like many peoples of the world, had built and destroyed empires for centuries and millennia. Those built in the nineteenth century often used military and other skills and technologies acquired through outside contacts, and for this reason are sometimes known as "secondary empires." Samori Touré built a sprawling West African empire (c.1880–98) pushing inward from Guinea to what is now northern Ivory Coast and Ghana; in Ethiopia (not Atlantic Africa of course), Menelik built an empire largely through canny use of imported military technique, as did the Boers in the South African Transvaal. This inland surge wrought great havoc in Africa, often weakening existing states (and obliterating some), and helping to prepare the way for the European conquest that came between 1880 and 1914.

Both in the Americas and in Africa the zone of Atlantic influence stretched inland after 1770, bringing economic change and often political disruption with it. As a rule, less complex (sociologically) and more isolated societies were transformed into, or replaced by, more complex and stratified societies more closely linked to international trade. Initially, this was simply an expansion of the Atlantic world. In Africa that remained the case, but in the Americas the stretch into the interior led to political, social, and economic units that were more and more continental and less and less Atlantic. And eventually, in the Americas, at least in Mexico, Central America, the Caribbean and Canada, the Atlantic link led more and more often to the United States rather than to Europe.

III

Sociopolitical and geopolitical structures normally must adjust to economic and geographic changes of great magnitude. This was certainly true in the Atlantic world of 1770–1888. The social, political, and geopolitical transitions flowed directly from the economic changes and geographic tilts; indeed, to a considerable degree they followed the same rhythm.

The vast expansion of commerce and then, in places, industry, subverted what had often been fairly stable social structures in Europe, Africa, and the Americas. In the Americas, and even more so in Europe and Atlantic Africa, the rising wealth and influence of mercantile and entrepreneurial classes created a political rival to old elites, whose power was often based on the control of land in Europe and the control of labor in Africa (in each case the scarcer factor of production being the more valuable). The rising classes accelerated the economic changes – agricultural expansion, industrialization, market integration – that helped to undermine the economic unity of the Atlantic world. At the same time, they helped to reorganize some Atlantic societies into new class configurations. Here and there lords and peasants, masters and slaves gradually converted themselves (or found themselves converted) into employers and laborers, with money more overtly defining their relationships. After abolition, a revised caste system developed in American lands with substantial black population. In the United States, all those of African descent, however partial, were (and are) considered as a group, within which social gradations were primarily those of class and gender. But in the Caribbean and Brazil, the system of social rank incorporated fine distinctions based on ancestry and skin color. Race and class together formed a complex matrix that defined social rank.

Social changes always benefit some and hurt others, and the injured parties rarely acquiesce easily. In the Atlantic world, these shifts in the social framework translated readily into political action. Many power struggles resulted. The ones in which new elites proved successful (Congo, France, Haiti) we call social revolutions. In some settings these revolutions generated, and in turn were furthered by, new ways of thinking about social relations, new freedoms, and new taboos.

One of these, probably the most important, was the idea that slavery was unjustifiable, an idea that had been distinctly a minority opinion (except among slaves) in Africa and the Americas before 1770 (or indeed 1800). But slavery was logically incompatible with the ideologies of the American (meaning the US) and French revolutions, with their emphasis upon the rights of man, from which only the most tortured logic could exclude Africans and African Americans. The United States managed to live with this tortured logic for another 3 generations; in the British and French Empires slavery came to an end in 1834 and 1848 respectively. Slavery disappeared quickly from those parts of Spanish America which acquired independence between 1810 and 1826. Abolition came to the Dutch West Indies in 1862, a year before Abraham Lincoln's Emancipation Proclamation (and a year after the abolition of serfdom in Russia). Slavery endured longest in Cuba and Brazil, where it disappeared at last in 1888. In Haiti, where slaves and others revolted in 1791, and the United States, where planters revolted in 1861, abolition came amid great violence; elsewhere it proceeded more or less peacefully. In Africa, slavery remained a viable institution into the early twentieth century. Its legal abolition generally followed the imposition of colonial rule, and came without great struggle, despite the fears of both African elites and colonial administrators. Indeed abolition in Atlantic Africa did rather little to change social relations there.[12]

The abolition of slavery in the Americas came at a time when population growth reduced the economic logic of slavery: with more and more people around, many slaveholders increasingly saw that they could do business on the basis of wage labor and dispense with slavery altogether. It is a matter of debate among historians as to whether economic change lay behind abolition or not.[13] In any case, abolition of the slave trade preceded abolition of slavery in the Americas. As slave populations began to reproduce themselves biologically, the need diminished for constant influxes from Africa; this happened in the United States in the eighteenth century, but not in Brazil and the Caribbean until well into the nineteenth. It is for this reason that while the United States became the largest slave society in the Americas, it imported only about 5 per cent of the total of slaves transported across the Atlantic.

From the Haitian revolution to the final abolition of slavery in Brazil (1804–88), American slavery and the Atlantic slave trade disappeared in a great age of liberation. The results varied from place to place. In the more densely populated islands of the Caribbean, Barbados, or Antigua, for example, slavery gave way to wage labor, as ex-slaves found few alternatives to their former labor. In Jamaica, however, many ex-slaves fled to the mountains, eventually forming a free peasantry. Sugar production declined sharply in the British and French Caribbean upon abolition. In every case, the abolition of slavery led to new social structures, usually ones more complex than the sharply stratified but relatively simple hierarchy of slave society.[14] Abolition was part and parcel of the general social reorganization of the Atlantic world in the nineteenth century.

While the economic and geographic changes of 1770–1888 created new social alignments that eventually required political upheavals, they also led to political changes that did not involve much shuffling of the social order. In the United States, for example, the Revolution of 1776–83 created a new country, but rather little in the way of social realignment. The Revolution was driven by the ambitions of New England commercial elites in alliance with southern planters, and to some extent by the logic of expansion into the transappalachian interior (although this was but little advanced in the 1770s). Those elites remained in place until 1865 at least; in social terms the Civil War was more revolutionary than the American Revolution.

In the rest of the Americas, political independence rarely disturbed the social order fundamentally. In Canada the creation of a new nation proceeded by slow degrees, through constitutional negotiations culminating in the Confederation of 1867. This too reflected the wishes of Canadian elites, and marked no significant change in the social order. In Latin America new nations were born through violent revolution (Mexico, Colombia, Venezuela, Uruguay) as well as through almost peaceful transfer of power (Brazil). Most of these new nations were created between 1808 and 1826, when Napoleon invaded Spain and installed his brother on the throne, which the colonies (and Spain) rejected. The colonies rebelled, and Napoleonic Spain could do nothing to stop them. When Napoleon was ejected from Iberia, the Spanish tried and failed by force of arms to reconstitute their empire, and were left only with Cuba and lesser sugar islands of the Caribbean. Again, these political changes reflected the ambitions of indigenous elites, usually locally born people of Iberian descent (called Creoles). In Cuba, where independence from Spain came late (1898), sugar planters wanted to retain the colonial tie so as to have a guaranteed market for sugar. In smaller Caribbean islands independence generally came only well into the twentieth century – if then. Elsewhere in Latin America, the rising commercial classes fought for independence so as to escape the restrictions of empire. As in North America, this did not imply any considerable change in the social order – to the dismay and disillusionment of many, from Boston to Buenos Aires, who had joined these revolutions.

In Atlantic Europe and Africa disruptive social change preceded what was often violent political change, ushering in new eras. Revolutions and rebellions punctuated the history of Spain (1807, 1812, 1820, 1836–7, 1840–2, 1854, 1868) and France (1789–94, 1830, 1848, 1870–1), while in England social unrest simmered without boiling over. In European history the period from 1770 to 1850, or 1870, is often termed the Age of Revolutions; the title applies equally well to Atlantic Africa.[15] In both settings, old elites and rulers often found themselves entirely displaced by new men with new sources of wealth and power at their disposal. Thus the rise of new states and rulers followed upon the rise of new social classes – or at least the retooling of old ones. This was most conspicuous where the connections to the Atlantic world of burgeoning commerce were strongest: on the West African slave coasts, in the Congo/Angola region, and in Britain and France.

As a broad generalization, it is fair to say that the economic and geographic shifts of 1770–1888 led to political change everywhere, but to conspicuous social change more in Atlantic Africa and Europe than in the Americas. This is because the old social and political elites in Europe derived their positions from ownership of land; those in Africa derived theirs chiefly from control over people; while those in the Americas, especially North America, derived theirs chiefly from control of commerce. Therefore the great intensification of Atlantic trade proved more socially disruptive in Africa and Europe than in America. Naturally this sweeping formula does not account neatly for everything. In the southern United States and northern Brazil, for instance, political power rested with planters as much as merchants. This proposition can be no more than a rough generalization, because social and political changes, in the Atlantic world as everywhere, proceed from many causes, not merely the expansion of commerce. Urbanization and industrialization in Europe and North America, for instance, promoted fundamental changes in social and political structures, especially after 1850. Further, the degree to which Atlantic societies were tied into the commercial world of the seas varied greatly, so what took place within that world had impacts of highly variable magnitude around the Atlantic. Trade meant everything to a sugar island like Cuba, but rather little to the subsistence cultivators of Spanish Galicia. No pat formula can do justice to the nuances of sociopolitical change over a broad range of societies, but as a first approximation, the above characterization of the differences among Africa, America, and Europe seems helpful.

The century after 1770 saw major geopolitical shifts as well as sociopolitical ones in the Atlantic world. The critical changes were the rise of the United States; the decolonization of most of Latin America, and the translation of parts of it into the economic orbit of the United States; and the rise of European imperial activity in Atlantic Africa. All of these are interrelated; all have been touched upon above. A brief summary here should suffice.

The rise of the United States – economically, politically, and eventually militarily – derived from its successful inland expansion and its integration of giant spaces, many of them naturally rich. By the end of the 1880s, the United States led the world in steel production, in total railroad track, in total industrial output, in agricultural productivity per worker, and possibly in standard of living. In 1865 it had (temporarily) the largest army in the world and would soon build one of the largest navies. Thus equipped, the United States late in the century would begin to construct its own empire and spheres of influence, in keeping with the practices of the European states and Japan. By land this was a straightforward process, paralleled by the simultaneous overland extension of the Russian empire. It required only the power to undo the Amerindian peoples of North America, which the United States did with no visible strain and few pangs of conscience.

By sea it was a much more complicated (and smaller) affair, requiring the fulfilment of several conditions. The first was the demise of Spain as an imperial power (largely completed by 1826) and the failure of Britain to gobble up the freed Spanish colonies (an opportunity definitively forsaken by 1840). Next was the failure of the dream of Simón Bolívar, the great liberator in South American history, who hoped for a United States of South America (a chance lost by 1830). Finally, it required the failure of Argentina to emerge as a hemispheric rival to the United States (which may appear implausible now but was by no means impossible in 1888 – or even 1910). History, as this example illustrates, is not merely what happened, but what happened in the context of what might have happened. With no effective resistance from Amerindians, Europeans, or Latin Americans, the United States acquired a few territories in the Atlantic, such as Puerto Rico, the Virgin Islands, and briefly Cuba, as well as Alaska (where the Russian empire ended) and Hawaii in the Pacific. These acquisitions contributed comparatively little to the wealth and power of the emergent United States; its informal empire, meaning its spheres of political and economic influence in Mexico, Central America, the Caribbean, and eventually Canada contributed somewhat more. But all told the overseas empire, formal and informal, meant little next to the land empire within North America.

The rise of the United States did not undermine the European empires in the Americas. Rather, decolonization helped to accelerate that rise. The Monroe Doctrine, which attempted to proclaim the Americas a sphere of influence of the United States, was scarcely plausible when announced in 1823. Only Britain's developing interest in US cotton ensured British acquiescence in this presumption. But by 1888 the premises of the Monroe Doctrine would soon be realized.

Decolonization in the Americas began with the United States itself in 1776. Next came Haiti (1791–1804), then most of Spanish America (1810–26), and Brazil (1822–3), where the Portuguese court fled and then established the only durable monarchy in the history of the Americas. By 1830 the only European colonies in the Americas were the Canadian ones, already embarked upon their slow evolution toward independence, British Honduras in Central America, and most of the Caribbean islands. Of these only Cuba and Jamaica counted for much, and even these became progressively less important as the nineteenth century wore on and the great wealth of the continental interiors entered the Atlantic economy. Indeed, sugar from the American tropics fell into sharp depression with the rise of sugar beet in Central and Eastern Europe (after 1815) and the development of cane production in the Indian Ocean islands of Réunion and Mauritius, in Pacific islands such as Fiji and Hawaii, in Peru, Natal (South Africa), and Queensland (Australia). By 1850 Europe could satisfy its sweet tooth without depending on the Caribbean (or Brazil). Increasingly, Caribbean sugar went to the United States, and not across the Atlantic.

In effect, Europe reduced its dependence on the Americas between 1770 and 1850. While most of the Americas depended on Europe for markets and manufactures, Europe in the eighteenth century had grown dependent on the Americas for cheap sugar, coffee, cotton, and other "colonial" products. With the long Napoleonic Wars (1791–1815) continental Europe was cut off from the Americas by the British Royal Navy – it was this that provoked the rise of sugar beet. Napoleon sought to isolate Britain from the continental economy with his so-called "Continental System," making a virtue of a necessity.

With peace in 1815, continental Europe, especially France, developed stronger links with the Ottoman lands of southwest Asia and North Africa (for cotton), with the Indian Ocean world (for sugar), and with Russia (for timber). Thus continental Europeans successfully found the products formerly derived from tropical and temperate America from other sources. So they never reestablished the old bonds with the Americas.

By 1888 the position of the United States in the Americas was strong and quickly growing stronger. European empires (including the British) had changed their focus to Africa and Asia. Europeans had been active in these lands for centuries, of course, but now turned to empire building with renewed vigor. Cotton from India and Egypt, and eventually coffee from Kenya (and, of course, sugar beet), helped to wean Europe from its dependence on products from the Americas, although tobacco and grains continued to fill transatlantic hulls through the nineteenth century. None of this required empire, of course, but industrial might, combined with medical advances that rendered the diseases of the tropics almost negligible, made this new burst of colonialism cheap and easy, whatever its motives. Within the confines of the Atlantic world, colonialism had begun to take on a north–south profile more than an east–west one: Europeans had lost most of their empires in America and were creating new ones in Africa; meanwhile, the United States was, more informally than formally, building its own hemispheric empire. A fundamental geopolitical shift had taken place, whereby transatlantic connections now mattered much less. It was as if geopolitics now recognized the tectonic plates that underlie the continents, separating the Old World from the New.

IV

The Atlantic world in European terms – and Europeans created and controlled it – was a component of the Old Regime. The Old Order derived a certain stability from durable structures, such as its demographic regime of slow growth, its agrarian basis of wealth, its monarchical polities. These structures, while never truly immobile, shifted and in cases dissolved after 1770, and the unity, integrity, and coherence of the Atlantic world went with it.

In American terms the Atlantic world represented an attachment and a dependent relationship, one characteristic of both newly implanted and mature colonies. But with population growth, geographic expansion, and railroads providing large-scale continental economic integration, the necessity and utility of transatlantic connections diminished, except in the small island colonies of the Caribbean.

In African terms the Atlantic world meant connections to an oceanic world in which the ships, and thus the mobility, knowledge, and power, belonged to others. At first it meant a geographic shift of trade away from the trans-Saharan routes that helped to sustain the great empires of the Sahel and Sudan – Mali and Songhai, for example – to the coast and seaborne routes. For centuries after this sixteenth-century shift the African states that developed their power most rapidly were the winners in the desperate struggles to use new technologies and skills imported from the Atlantic world. By the nineteenth century those struggles extended well inland, and with American abolition some of the features of slave plantation society were transplanted to Africa. Then, at the end of the century, the imperial rivalries of the European powers came to Africa in a sudden deluge. Thus Africa did not withdraw gradually from the Atlantic world; rather, the influence of the Atlantic connections extended ever more broadly over Africa, and some of the features of the Atlantic political economy (plantations, European empire) were relocated to African soil after their demise elsewhere. Despite the end of the slave trade, the most conspicuous link between African and other Atlantic societies, closure of the Atlantic world remained incomplete in Africa.

NOTES

1 By 1850 their importance extended well beyond Atlantic Europe, as far east as Russia and the Balkans.
2 Cassava, also known as manioc, is a root crop native to the American tropics. It grows well even in poor soils, in conditions of variable rainfall, and provides more food per acre (or hectare) than any other tropical plant: see Alfred W. Crosby, *The Columbian Exchange* (Westport, Conn.: Greenwood Press, 1972), 173–4.
3 See Patrick Manning, *Slavery in African Life* (Cambridge: Cambridge University Press, 1990), for a recent summary of scholarly opinion.

4 Philip D. Curtin, "Migration in the Tropical World," in *Immigration Reconsidered: History, Sociology, Politics*, ed. Virginia Yans-McLaughlin (New York, 1990), 21.
5 See David Eltis, "Free and Coerced Transatlantic Migration: Some Comparisons," *American Historical Review* 88 (1983):255.
6 Slave populations in the United States grew from natural increase; in the Caribbean and Brazil they did not. This strongly suggests that it was the epidemiological position, more than the social position, of slaves that governed their rates of natural increase – unless one takes the view (I do not) that US slavery was more benign than Caribbean or Brazilian.
7 Both coffee and cotton, like wheat and sugar, were introductions to the Americas in the Columbian exchange. Coffee, originally from Ethiopia, came as late as the 1760s. Wheat originated in southwest Asia, sugar cane in New Guinea, and cotton probably in India.
8 Incidentally, in moving across the Atlantic, European peasants apparently found themselves able to eat much better than in Europe. They were taller, which suggests that as children they got more protein. In the eighteenth and nineteenth centuries those of European descent in the United States were 4–8 centimeters taller than their brethren in Europe. The same was true of Africans: even as slaves their nutrition in the Americas was generally superior to levels obtaining in West Africa. In the Caribbean, locally born slaves were 2–6 centimeters taller than those born in Africa: John Komlos, "Anthropometric History: What Is It?" *Journal of Social and Biological Structures* 14, no. 3 (1991):353–6; Eltis, "Free and Coerced Transatlantic Migrations," 280; Kenneth Kiple, *The Caribbean Slave: A Biological History* (Cambridge: Cambridge University Press, 1984), 23–31, 76–88.
9 Rondo Cameron, *A Concise Economic History of the World* (Oxford: Oxford University Press, 1989), 229.
10 Paul Lovejoy, "The Impact of the Atlantic Slave Trade on Africa: A Review of the Literature," *Journal of African History* 30 (1989):392.
11 A recent review of these distinctions is Igor Kopytoff, "The Cultural Context of African Abolition," in *The End of Slavery in Africa*, ed. Suzanne Miers and Richard Roberts (Madison: University of Wisconsin Press, 1988), 485–503.
12 See Miers and Roberts, *The End of Slavery in Africa*.
13 See, among recent works, Robin Blackburn, *The Overthrow of Colonial Slavery, 1776–1848* (London: Verso, 1988); David Eltis, *Economic Growth and the Ending of the Transatlantic Slave Trade* (Oxford: Oxford University Press, 1987); Seymour Drescher, *Econocide: British Slavery in the Era of Abolition* (Pittsburgh, Pa: University of Pittsburgh Press, 1977); Roger Anstey, *The Atlantic Slave Trade and British Abolition, 1760–1810*, Cambridge Commonwealth Series (London: Macmillan, 1975).
14 Sidney W. Mintz, "Slavery and the Rise of Peasantries," *Historical Reflections* 6 (1979):213–43. See also Manuel Moreno Fraginals,

Frank Moya Pons and Stanley Engerman, eds, *Between Slavery and Free Labor: The Spanish-Speaking Caribbean in the Nineteenth Century* (Baltimore, Md: Johns Hopkins University Press, 1985).

15 E. J. Hobsbawm, *The Age of Revolution* (London: Weidenfeld & Nicolson, 1962); Mayer disputes this notion, claiming that the old regimes in Europe often survived until 1914: Arno Mayer, *The Persistence of the Old Regime* (New York: Pantheon, 1981). See also Jerome Blum, *The End of the Old Order in Rural Europe* (Princeton, NJ: Princeton University Press, 1978).

GLOSSARY

batab	hereditary ruler of a town (Maya)
bourgeois *gentilhomme*	middle-class gentleman
carreira do Brasil	the Portuguese Brazil trade
carreira da India	the Portuguese– (East) India–southeast Asia trade
casse-tête	club
casta	Mexican racial category denoting mixed ancestry
cofradía	brotherhood; here a parish confraternity dedicated to cult of one or more saints
conquistadores	Spanish conquerors in the Americas
coureurs de bois	Canadian middlemen in the fur trade
cruzob	a Maya group devoted to the Speaking Cross
donativo real	Brazilian captaincy
fex maris	literally, feces of the sea
guaxima	Brazilian plants which yield a jute-like fiber
huipil	long, blouse-like woman's garment (Maya)
ladeiras	slopes or steep streets
macehual	Indian commoner (Maya)
maestros cantores	Maya officials in charge of liturgy and catechism
mal do bicho	a form of dysentery, common among Africans arriving in Brazil
marinheiros	mariners
milpa	clearing in forest for planting maize; Mesoamerican slash and burn (swidden) agriculture
parcialidades	Mexican wards or subdivisions of towns
pardo	mulatto; person of mixed race
ponta do curral	literally, corral point; here, place of quarantine
prêto	Black; a black person
razzia	a raid; here, a slave raid
reconquista	Christian reconquest of Iberia from Muslims
regateiras	fishwives
Senado da Câmara	Brazilian governmental body; town council
sertão	Brazilian backlands; savanna

SELECT BIBLIOGRAPHY
Recent books of interest available in English

AMERINDIANS

Axtell, James, *The Invasion Within: The Contest of Cultures in Colonial North America* (New York, 1985)
_____ *The European and the Indian: Essays in the Ethnohistory of Colonial North America* (New York, 1981)
Clendinnen, Inga, *The Aztecs: An Interpretation* (New York, 1991)
Crosby, Alfred, *The Columbian Exchange* (Westport, Conn., 1972)
Denevan, William M., ed., *The Native Population of the Americas in 1492* (Madison, Wis., 1976)
Dobyns, Henry, *Their Number Become Thinned: Native American Population Dynamics in Eastern North America* (Knoxville, Tenn., 1983)
Gibson, Charles, *The Aztecs under Spanish Rule: A History of the Indians of the Valley of Mexico, 1519–1810* (Stanford, Calif., 1964)
Hemming, John, *Red Gold: The Conquest of the Brazilian Indians* (Cambridge, Mass., 1978)
Jennings, Francis, *Empire of Fortune: Crowns, Colonies, and Tribes in the Seven Years War* (New York, 1988)
Merrell, James, *The Indians' New World: Catawbas and their Neighbors from European Contact through the Era of Removal* (Chapel Hill, NC, 1990)
Morner, Magnus, *Race Mixture in the History of Latin America* (Boston, Mass., 1967)
Richter, Daniel, and James H. Merrell, *Beyond the Covenant Chain: The Iroquois and their Neighbors in Indian North America, 1600–1800* (Syracuse, NY, 1987)
Trigger, Bruce, *Natives and Newcomers: Canada's Heroic Age Reconsidered* (Kingston and Montreal, 1985)
Wallace, Anthony, *The Death and Rebirth of the Seneca* (New York, 1970)

RACE RELATIONS, THE SLAVE TRADE, AND SLAVERY

Anstey, Roger, *The Atlantic Slave Trade and British Abolition, 1760–1810* (New York, 1975)

Beckles, Hilary, *Natural Rebels: A Social History of Enslaved Black Women in Barbados* (New Brunswick, NJ, 1989)

Blackburn, Robin, *The Overthrow of Colonial Slavery, 1776–1848* (London, 1988)

Conrad, Robert, *Children of God's Fire* (Princeton, NJ, 1983)

Craton, Michael, *Testing the Chains: Resistance to Slavery in the British West Indies* (Ithaca, NY, 1980)

Curtin, Philip, *The Atlantic Slave Trade: A Census* (Madison, Wis., 1969)

Davis, David Brion, *Slavery and Human Progress* (New York, 1984)

Drescher, Seymour, *Capitalism and Antislavery: British Mobilization in Comparative Perspective* (New York, 1987)

Eltis, David, *Economic Growth and the Ending of the Transatlantic Slave Trade* (New York, 1987)

Gemery, Henry A., and Jan S. Hogendorn, *The Uncommon Market: Essays in the Economic History of the Atlantic Slave Trade* (New York, 1979)

Genovese, Eugene, *Roll, Jordan, Roll: The World the Slaves Made* (New York, 1974)

Higman, Barry, *Slave Populations of the British Caribbean, 1807–1834* (Baltimore, Md, 1984)

Inikori, J. E., ed. *Forced Migration* (London, 1982)

Jordan, Winthrop, *White Over Black: American Attitudes Towards the Negro, 1550–1812* (Chapel Hill, NC, 1968)

Kiple, Kenneth, *The Caribbean Slave: A Biological History* (New York, 1985)

Klein, Herbert, *African Slavery in Africa and the Caribbean* (New York, 1986)

Kulikoff, Allan, *Tobacco and Slaves: The Development of Southern Cultures in the Chesapeake, 1680–1800* (Chapel Hill, NC, 1986)

Lovejoy, Paul, *Transformations in Slavery: A History of Slavery in Africa* (Cambridge, 1983)

Mattoso, Katia M. de Quieiros, *To Be A Slave in Brazil, 1550–1888* (New Brunswick, NJ, 1986)

Miers, Suzanne, and Igor Kopytoff, eds, *Slavery in Africa: Historical and Anthropological Perspectives* (Madison, Wis., 1977)

Miers, Suzanne, and Richard Roberts, eds, *The End of Slavery in Africa* (Madison, Wis., 1988)

Miller, Joseph, *Way of Death: Merchant Capitalism and the Angolan Slave Trade, 1730–1830* (Madison, Wis., 1989)

Palmer, Colin, *Human Cargoes: The British Slave Trade to Spanish America, 1700–1739* (Urbana, Ill., 1981)

—— *Slaves of the White God: Blacks in Mexico, 1570–1650* (Cambridge, Mass., 1976)

Patterson, Orlando, *Slavery and Social Death: A Comparative Study* (Cambridge, Mass., 1982)

Phillips, William D., *Slavery from Roman Times to the Early Transatlantic Trade* (Minneapolis, Minn., 1985)

Postma, Johnannes, *The Dutch in the Atlantic Slave Trade, 1600–1815* (New York, 1985)

Rawley, James, *The Transatlantic Slave Trade: A History* (New York, 1981)

Robertson, Claire, and Martin Klein, eds, *Women and Slavery in Africa* (Madison, Wis., 1983)

Sheridan, Richard B., *Doctors and Slaves: A Medical and Demographic History of Slavery in the British West Indies, 1680–1834* (New York, 1985)

Solow, Barbara, ed., *Slavery and the Rise of the Atlantic System* (New York, 1991)

Stein, Robert Louis, *The French Slave Trade in the Eighteenth Century: An Old Regime Business* (Madison, Wis., 1979)

SETTLEMENT AND SOCIAL DEVELOPMENT

Andrews, Kenneth R., *Trade, Plunder, and Settlement: Maritime Enterprise and the Genesis of the British Empire, 1480–1630* (Cambridge, 1984)

—— *Spanish Caribbean: Trade and Plunder, 1530–1630* (New Haven, Conn., 1978)

Bailyn, Bernard, *Voyagers to the West: A Passage on the Peopling of America on the Eve of the Revolution* (New York, 1986)

Bethell, Leslie, ed., *Cambridge History of Latin America*, 3 vols (Cambridge, 1984–5)

Breen, T. H., *Tobacco Culture: The Mentality of the Great Tidewater Planters on the Eve of the Revolution* (Princeton, NJ, 1985)

Canny, Nicholas, *Kingdom and Colony: Ireland in the Atlantic World, 1560–1800* (Baltimore, Md, 1988)

Cronon, William, *Changes in the Land: Indians, Colonists, and the Ecology of New England* (New York, 1983)

Demos, John Putnam, *Entertaining Satan: Witchcraft and the Culture of Early New England* (New York, 1982)

Dunn, Richard S., *Sugar and Slaves: The Rise of the Planter Class in the English West Indies, 1624–1713* (New York, 1972)

Eccles, W. J., *Essays on New France* (Toronto, 1987)

Goslinga, Cornelis, *The Dutch in the Caribbean and in the Guianas 1680–1791* (Dover, NH, 1985)

Greene, Jack P., *Pursuits of Happiness: The Social Development of Early Modern British Colonies and the Formation of American Culture* (Chapel Hill, NC, 1988)

Greene, Jack P., and J. R. Pole, eds, *Colonial British America: Essays in the New History of the Early Modern Era* (Baltimore, Md, 1984)

Greer, Allan, *Peasant, Lord, and Merchant: Rural Society in Three Quebec Societies, 1740–1840* (Toronto, 1985)

Isaac, Rhys, *The Transformation of Virginia, 1740–1790* (Chapel Hill, NC, 1983)

Karras, Alan L., *Sojourners in the Sun: Scottish Migration to Jamaica and the Chesapeake, 1740–1820* (Ithaca, NY, 1992)

Kim, Sung Bok, *Landlord and Tenant in Colonial New York: Manorial Society, 1664–1775* (Chapel Hill, NC, 1978)

Landsman, Ned, *Scotland and its First American Colony, 1683–1765* (Princeton, NJ, 1985)

Lockridge, Kenneth, *A New England Town, the First Hundred Years: Dedham, Massachusetts, 1636–1736* (New York, 1970)

Lynch, John, *The Spanish-American Revolutions, 1808–1826* (New York, 1973)

Meinig, D. W., *Atlantic America, 1492–1800* (New Haven, Conn., 1986)

Morgan, Edmund, *American Slavery, American Freedom: The Ordeal of Colonial Virginia* (New York, 1975)

Nash, Gary, *The Urban Crucible: Social Change, Political Consciousness, and the Origins of the American Revolution* (Cambridge, Mass., 1979)

Reid, John C., *Acadia, Maine, and New Scotland: Marginal Colonies in the Seventeenth Century* (Toronto, 1981)

Sanchez Albornoz, Nicolas, *The Population History of Latin America* (Berkeley, Calif., 1974)

Schwartz, Stuart, *Sugar Plantation in the Formation of Brazilian Society: Bahia, 1550–1835* (New York, 1985)

Socolow, Susan, *The Merchants of Buenos Aires, 1778–1810: Family and Commerce* (Cambridge, 1978)

TRANSATLANTIC EMPIRES

Boxer, C. R., *The Portuguese Seaborne Empire, 1415–1825* (London, 1969)
—— *The Dutch Seaborne Empire, 1600–1800* (New York, 1965)

Canny, Nicholas and Anthony Pagden, eds, *Colonial Identity in the Atlantic World, 1500–1800* (Princeton, NJ, 1987)

Curtin, Philip, *The Rise and Fall of the Plantation Complex* (New York, 1990)

Davies, K. G., *The North Atlantic World in the Seventeenth Century* (Minneapolis, Minn., 1974)

Davis, Ralph, *The Rise of the Atlantic Economies* (Ithaca, NY, 1973)

Elliott, J. H., *The Old World and the New, 1492–1650* (Cambridge, 1970)

Geggus, David, *Slavery, War, and Revolution: The British Occupation of Saint-Domingue, 1793–1798* (Oxford, 1982)

Graham, Gerald, *The Tides of Empire* (Montreal and London, 1972)

Lang, James, *Conquest and Commerce: Spain and England in the Americas* (New York, 1975)

McAlister, Lyle N., *Spain and Portugal in the New World, 1492–1700* (Minneapolis, Minn., 1984)

McNeill, John, *Atlantic Empires of France and Spain: Louisbourg and Havana, 1700–1763* (Chapel Hill, NC, 1985)

Marcus, G. J., *The Conquest of the North Atlantic* (New York, 1981)

Mintz, Sydney, *Sweetness and Power: The Place of Sugar in Modern History* (New York, 1986)

Parry, J. H., *The Spanish Seaborne Empire* (London, 1966)

———— *Trade and Dominion* (London, 1971)

Pocock, J. G. A., *The Machiavellian Moment: Florentine Political Thought and the Atlantic Republican Tradition* (Princeton, NJ, 1975)

Steele, Ian, *The English Atlantic 1676–1740: An Exploration of Communication and Community* (New York, 1986)

Walker, Geoffrey, *Spanish Politics and Imperial Trade, 1700–1789* (Bloomington, Ind., 1979)

Watts, David, *The West Indies: Patterns of Development, Culture, and Environmental Change since 1492* (Cambridge, 1987)

Wallerstein, Immanuel, *The Modern World-System.* Vol. 2, *Mercantilism and the Consolidation of the European World Economy, 1600–1750* (New York, 1980)